SO-ANX-376

WITHDRAWN

THE MODERN ARAB WOMAN
A Bibliography

by

MICHELLE RACCAGNI

The Scarecrow Press, Inc.
Metuchen, N.J. & London
1978

Library of Congress Cataloging in Publication Data

Raccagni, Michelle, 1939-
    The modern Arab woman.

    Includes indexes.
    1.   Women--Arab countries--Bibliography.   I.   Title.
Z 7964. A7R32   [HQ1784]   016. 30141'2'09174927   78-15528
ISBN 0-8108-1165-0

TABLE OF CONTENTS

iii

Table of Contents iv

v   Table of Contents

Table of Contents   vi

INTRODUCTION

This bibliography was originally intended as a source from which information on Egyptian and Tunisian women could be drawn. It soon became evident that there existed considerable data on the modern Arab woman in general whose compilation was necessary before a more specific project could be undertaken. It was also noted that although English and French items appeared in most bibliographical sources, Arabic sources were often omitted, and thus some important data were often ignored. An attempt has been made to establish a thorough list of all books, articles, reports and dissertations in Western languages, principally English and French, as well as Arabic. Although modern times in the Middle East are conventionally considered as starting in 1798 with the French invasion of Egypt, only a few entries cover the first half of the 19th century. Since matters pertaining to the Arab woman enjoy ever-growing interest, I have attempted to list all items including dissertations in progress up to 1976. When additional information was known, it has been briefly given.

This bibliography was started in Tunis in 1971 with the compilation of the relevant titles from the Bibliothèque Nationale and the Institut des Belles Lettres Arabes. The catalogues of the New York Public Library, Columbia University, New York University and Princeton University were consulted upon my return to the United States. A research fellowship from the American Research Center in Egypt during the year 1975 enabled me to collect additional information in Cairo.

Although I have tried my best to give the dates of publication and names of publishers, this type of information is at times among the best guarded secrets of the mysterious East and any supplementary information or correction will be gratefully accepted.

I would like to express my gratitude to the American Research Center in Egypt whose generous support enabled me to conduct research in Cairo. Among the many persons I would like to thank for their help and contributions are Mesdames Inji Efflatoun and Fatma Nimet Rashid, who kindly allowed me to consult documents in their possession; Dr. Ahmad Khalifah, director of the Center for Social Studies, Cairo; Mr. Isma'il Mahir 'Ali al-Arna'uti, librarian of the Center for Social Studies, Cairo; Mr. Richard Dewey, associate university librarian, the American University in Cairo, who put his own unpublished manuscript at my disposal and provided me with constant advice and encouragement during my stay in Cairo; Messrs. Jean Fontaine and Michel Lelong from IBLA, Tunis; Père de Sa from Institut Dominicain, Cairo; Messrs. 'Abd al-Rahim Nasrallah and 'Adil Shahin who devoted much of their time to help me translate news articles; Mrs. Fawziyah Sidqi, Messrs. Chris Eccel, Michel Heine, and Peter McKay; and finally Mr. Phil Pritchard, whose help in proofreading the manuscript went beyond the call of ordinary friendship.

The transliteration system used is the National Standards Institute system [American National Standard System for the Romanization of Arabic, New York, 1972] except for proper names of North African authors who, writing often in French, have adopted their own transliteration of their family name. The use of accents has been simplified, notably in the removal of the macron over vowels and the dot beneath h's, s's and t's. Alphabetization has been without regard to initial "al-" or "el-."

For the sake of simplification, titles of Arabic articles have been translated into English and dates of periodical articles have been given in English.

A list of generally useful bibliographies and indexes follows:

Abstracta Islamica, 1965-1972.

Allman, James; Cherifa Ben Achour; and Toby Stone. A Bibliography of Recent Social Science Research on the Family in the Arab States. Beirut: UNESCO, 1974.

Annuaire de l'Afrique du Nord, 1962-1973.

Center for the Study of the Modern Arab World. St Joseph's
University. Beirut. Arab Culture and Society in Change:
A Bibliography. Beirut: Dar el-Mashreq, 1973.

Conference on the State of the Social Sciences in the Middle East.
Alexandria, July 1-10, 1974. Country Reports.

Coult, Lyman H., Jr. An Annotated Bibliography of the Egyptian
Fellah. Coral Gables: University of Miami Press, 1958.

Dewey, Richard H. "An Annotated Bibliography on Social Relations in the Arab States of the Middle East, 1955-1964."
Unpublished ms.

Dissertation Abstracts, 1960-1976.

Gulick, John, and Margaret Gulick. An Annotated Bibliography
of Resources Concerned with Women in the Modern Muslim
Middle East. Princeton, N.J.: Princeton University Program in Near Eastern Studies, 1973.

Hansen, Henny Harald. The Kurdish Woman's Life, 1961 (see
entry 1865).

Kashaf al-Ahram, 1974-1976.

Library of Congress. Catalog. Books: Subjects, 1950-1975.

Mansur, Ahmad Muhammad. Halil al-matbu'at al-misriyah,
1940-1956. Cairo: American University in Cairo Press,
1975.

Maunier, René. Bibliographie économique, juridique et sociale
de l'Egypte moderne (1798-1916). Cairo: Imprimerie de
l'Institut Français d'Archéologie Orientale, 1918.

Nasir, 'Aidah Ibrahim. al-Kutub al-'arabiyah allati nashrat fi
al-jumhuriyah al-'arabiyah al-muttahidah (Misr) bayn 'ami
1940-1962. Cairo: American University in Cairo Press, 1969.

Nelson, Cynthia. "Public and Private Politics: Women in the
Middle Eastern World." American Ethnologist, 3 (Aug. 1974),
551-563 [contains mentions of many useful sources, including
manuscripts].

Pearson, J. D. Index Islamicus, 1956-1975. Cambridge: W.
Heffer & Sons.

Prothro, Edwin Terry, and Lutfy Najb Diab. Changing Family
Patterns in the Arab East. Beirut: American University
in Beirut Press, 1974 [contains mentions of many useful

sources].

al-Qazzar, Ayad. Women in the Arab World: An Annotated Bibliography. (AAUG Bibliography Series, no. 2.) Detroit: Arab-American University Graduates; reprinted, Austin: Center for Middle Eastern Studies, University of Texas, 1977 (Middle East Monograph, no. 2) [an annotated bibliography of over 200 works in English].

Revue des Etudes Islamiques, 1926-1964.

University of Michigan. Library. Women in the Near East. 1974.

I

GENERAL

(1) GENERAL

1   "A quoi rêvent les jeunes filles?" Contact, 14 (Nov. 25-Dec.
    10, 1973), 16-17.

2   'Abd al-Razzâq, Mustafa.   "Woman Builds" (in Arabic).   al-
    Hilal, 1934, 36.

3   Abhath muqarinah fi huquq wa-wajibat al-mar'ah fi Afriqiya wa-
    Asiya wa-khassatan fi Misr.   Cairo: Permanent Organiza-
    tion for Afro-Asian Peoples Solidarity, 1972.   Comparative
    research on the rights and duties of women in Asia and
    Africa, with special reference to Egypt.

4   Abudabbeh, Nuha.   "Arab Women in the Migratory Process:
    A Pilot Study."   Paper presented at the Conference on De-
    velopment in the Arab World, New York, Oct. 1-3, 1976.

5   Abu al-Su'ud, Ahmad Fu'ad.   al-Mar'ah al-sharqiyah, n. p.
    n. d.

6   Abu Rizq.   al-Mar'ah hiya al-asl.   Nablus: al-Matba'ah al-
    'asriyah, 1957.   Against the superficial imitation of
    Western women by Arab women.

7   'Ali, 'Ali Muhammad.   Isti'bad al-mar'ah.   Cairo: Dar al-
    qawmiyah lil-tiba'ah wa-al-nashr, n. d.

8   Aluf, Nadarah Nikulah.   Dahaya al-bashariyah.   Zahlal: al-
    Matba'ah al-sharqiyah, 1910.   A collection of short essays
    dealing with modern problems.   The author describes the
    condition of women, the neglect of their education and pre-
    vailing double standards.

9   al-'Amri, Muhammad al-Hadi.   "Motherhood in Law and Lit-
    erature" (in Arabic).   al-Fikr, 1 (Oct. 1970), 52-55.

10 Ansari, Ghaus.   Status of Woman in Different Societies (A
    Comparative Study).   Kuwait: Kuwait University, 1971.
    A very short and sketchy study.

1

11   al-'Aqqad, 'Abbas Mahmud. Hadhihi al-shajarah wa-al-insan
     al-thani. Cairo: Maktabat gharib, 1968.

12   _____. "Is Woman the Origin of Inspiration?" (in Arabic).
     al-Hilal, 1934, 2-4.

13   _____. al-Mar'ah dhalika al-lughz. Beirut: Dar al-kitab
     al 'arabi, 1970.

14   _____. "The Place of Woman in the Modern Age" (in
     Arabic). Kitab, July 1951, 664-668.

15   Arnaud, Gabriel. "L'homme et la femme, la femme et
     l'homme." Terre Entière, Nov.-Dec. 1965, 42-65.

16   Attanoux, B. d'. "Situation et rôle de la femme musulmane."
     Revue Franco-Saharienne, 3 (July-Aug. 1902).

17   Badran, Hoda. "Deliberations of the International Women's
     Year Conference and Its Relationship to the Arab Region."
     Paper delivered at the Seminar on the Status of Woman in
     the Islamic Family. Cairo: Dec. 20-22, 1975. Hoda
     Badran is the regional advisor on services for women,
     UNICEF Office for the Eastern Mediterranean Region.

18   Berger, Morroe. "The Arab Danse du Ventre." Dance Per-
     spectives, 10. An intelligent article about belly dancing
     which refutes common prejudices.

19   Bolen, Carl van. Erotik des Orients. Das Liebesleben der
     orientalischen Hochkulturen: Indien, Persien, die arabis-
     chen Völker, China und Japan. Liebesmagie und Geheim-
     Lehren. Munich: Heyne, 1967.

20   Burghardt, Friedrich. Die Orientalin. Düsseldorf: Hellas-
     Verlag, 1958. A German journalist describes the ways of
     life of women from Morocco to the Far East.

21   Charnay, J. P. "Condition féminine et rapports sociaux,"
     Cahiers de l'Orient Contemporain, 26:77 (Oct. 1969), 4-6;
     26:78 (Dec. 1969), 4-7.

22   Chebat, Fouad. "La Femme du diplomate arabe." Annales
     de la Faculté de Droit de Beyrouth, 55 (1968), 55-58.

23   Churchill, Charles W. "The Arab World." In Raphael Patai,
     ed., Women in the Modern World, New York: Free Press,
     1967; 106-28.

24   Cohen, A. "The Politics of Marriage in Changing Middle
     Eastern Stratification Systems." In L. Plotnicov, and
     Arthur Tuden, eds., Essays in Comparative Social Strati-
     fication, Pittsburgh: University of Pittsburgh Press, 1970;
     195-209.

25 al-Daghshi, Kamil Mahmud. Kayfa tajdhib qalb al-mar'ah.
    Cairo: al-Matba'ah al-fakhriyah, 1940.

26 Damaschino, N. "Etude historique sur la condition des femmes
    en Orient." Revue de l'Orient, de l'Algérie et des Colo-
    nies, 1858, 41-87.

27 Deonna, Laurence. Moyen-Orient: femmes du combat, de la
    terre et du sable. Geneva: Labor & Fides, 1970.

28 "Les Droits de la femme arabe." Sada al-ahali, March 25,
    1951.

29 Eloui, Ali. Die moderne Frau im Morgen und Abendland. Ber-
    lin: Morgen und Abendland Verlag, 1921.

30 "Une Expérience sur le travail de la femme." Nouvelles Eco-
    nomiques. 60 (Jan. 15, 1970), 2; 61 (Jan. 30, 1970), 2.

31 Fahmi, Murqus. al-Mar'ah fi al-sharq. 1894. A Christian
    lawyer pleads for the suppression of the veil and polygamy,
    and for women to obtain the right to divorce or contract
    mixed marriages.

32 Farid, Mahmud Kamil. al-Mar'ah fi al-'ahd al-qadim wa al-
    hadith. Cairo: Matba'at al-Taraqi, n.d.

33 Faris, Bashir. "Woman and the Arts" (in Arabic). al-Hilal,
    1934, 78-80.

34 "La Femme en évidence," Ici l'Afrique, 2 (Oct. 21, 1968), 40-
    43.

35 "La Femme orientale est-elle tenue en servitude?" Jeune
    Afrique, 290 (July 17, 1966), 42-43.

36 "Femmes--elles s'en mêlent." Jeune Afrique, 660 (Sept. 1,
    1973), 52.

37 Fergany, Nader. "Arab Women and National Development: A
    Demographic Background." Seminar on Arab Women and
    National Development, co-sponsored by UNICEF and the
    Arab League, Cairo, Sept. 1972.

38 Fernea, Elizabeth Warnock, and Basima Qattan Bezirgan. Mid-
    dle Eastern Muslim Women Speak. Austin: University of
    Texas Press, 1976. A collection of biographical statements
    by and about Middle Eastern women.

39 Filesi, Teobaldo. L'istituto della famiglia e le costituzioni
    degli stati africani. Roma: Istituto Italiano per l'Africa,
    1964.

40 "Focus on Population in the Middle East and North Africa. "
    Mid East, 8:5 (Sept. -Oct. 1968), 2-40. Deals more spe-
    cifically with Turkey, Algeria, Morocco, Egypt and Iran.

41 "Friendship between One Sex and the Other" (in Arabic). al-
    Ahram, Aug. 2, 1975, 9.

42 Gamil, Muhammad. al-Mar´ah fi al-tamaddun al hadith. Bei-
    rut: Matba'at al-salam, 1927. The national development
    of feminism from the Middle Ages until the present day.

43 al-Ghazali, Muhammad. Min huna na'lamu. Cairo: Dar al-
    kutub al-hadithah, n. d. A very popular and often reprinted
    book by a conservative sheikh; includes a section on women
    pp. 171-212, and an appeal to increase population, 235-
    241.

44 _____. Our Beginning in Wisdom. Washington, D. C. :
    American Council of Learned Societies, 1953. A transla-
    tion of the previous work.

45 Ghemrred, Dalila. "La Femme. " al-Nasr, March 8, 11, 13,
    15, 18, 1969.

46 Ghudban, Muhammad. "Social reflections" (in Arabic). al-
    Mar´ah, 10 (Oct. 5, 1966).

47 Graziani, Joseph. "The Momentum of the Feminist Movement
    in the Arab World. " Middle East Review, winter 1974-75,
    26-33.

48 _____. "The Status of Women in the Contemporary Muslim
    Arab Family. " Middle East Review, winter 1976/77, 41-51.

49 Hasan, I'tidal. "Woman Is No Less Capable Than Man" (in
    Arabic). al-Mar´ah al-jadidah, 3 (April 1970), 15.

50 Holler, Joanne E. Population Growth and Social Change in the
    Middle East. Washington, D. C. : Population Research
    Project, George Washington University, 1964.

51 Houghton, Ross C. Women of the Orient. Cincinnati: Hitch-
    cock & Walden, 1877; New York: Nelson & Phillips, 1877.
    Includes chapters on Egyptian and Syrian women.

52 Hourani, Furugh. "Uncertain Equality. " London Times,
    March 8, 1968, p. ii (of the Special Report on the Arab
    World). Change should come through education, not legis-
    lation.

53 Hughes-Hallett, F. Awakening Womanhood. London: Church
    Missionary Society, 1927.

54 Husayn, 'Abd Allah. al-Mar'ah al-hadithah wa kayfa nasusah.
     Cairo: al-matba'ah al-'asriyah, 1927.

55 Ibrahim, Zakariah. Sikulujiyat al-mar'ah. Cairo: Maktabat
     Misr, 1956.

56 Jansen, Michael Elin. "Nursing in the Arab East." Aramco
     World Magazine, March-April 1974, 14-23.

57 Kaddoura, Ibtihaj. "Le Rôle majeur de la femme." al-Afkar,
     June 1961, 68-69.

58 Khaki, Ahmad. al-Mar'ah fi muhtalaf al-'usur. Cairo: Dar
     al-ma'arif, 1946.

59 Khalil, 'Abd al-Salam Muhammad. "A Good Family Is the
     Basis of a Good Society" (in Arabic). al-Mujtama' al-
     jadid, 1 (July 1970), 38-39.

60 al-Khammash, Salwa. al-Mar'ah al-'arabiyah wa-al-mujtama'
     al-taqlidi al-mutakhallif. Beirut: Dar al-haqiqah, 1973.
     The Arab woman in a traditional, backward society.

61 Khayrat, Mahmud. al-Mar'ah bayna al-madi wa al-hadir.
     Cairo: Idarat majallat al-ikha, 1928.

62 Kol'tsova-Masal'skaya, Elena Mikhailovna (Gihka), Knyaginya.
     Les femmes en Orient, by Mme la Comtesse Dora d'Istria
     [pseud]. Zürich: Meyer & Zeller, 1860.

63 Laidlaw, R. G. B. "Some Reflections on Nursing in the
     Middle East," Middle East Forum, 37 (Oct. 1958), 23-24.
     Nursing is looked down upon as a menial job.

64 Lebanese Women's Council. Women in Arab Laws. Beirut,
     1975. Includes the papers and recommendations of the
     delegates of 13 Arab states to the LWC panel held in May
     1974.

65 al-Madani, Hashim Daftardar. al-Mar'ah fi al-siyasah wa-al-
     ijtima'. Beirut: Dar al-insaf, 1950.

66 al-Majdhub, Muhammad. Ta'ammulat fi al-mar'ah wa-al
     mujtama'. Beirut: Dar al-'arabiyah lil-tiba'ah wa-al-
     nashr wa-al tawzi', 1970.

67 Mathews, B. "Women in the Near East." Moslem World, 9
     (1919), 240-246.

68 Mazhar, Isma'il. al-Mar'ah fi 'usur al-dimuqratiyah. Cairo:
     Maktabat al-nahdah al-misriyah, 1949.

69 Midfa'i, S. "Women in the Middle East." Islamic Review,

11 (Nov. 1952), 34-36.

70 al-Misri, Ibrahim. Qalb al-mar´ah. Cairo: Dar al-hilal, 1970.

71 Musa, Salamah. al-Mar´ah laysat lu'bat al-rajul. Cairo: Salamah Musa lil-nashr wa-al-tawzi, n. d.

72 _____. Fann al-hubb wa-al-hayah. Beirut: Maktabat al-ma'arif, 1960.

73 Nelson, Cynthia. "Public and Private Politics: Women in the Middle Eastern World." American Ethnologist, 3 (August 1974), 551-64.

74 Ouali, Khelifa. "La Femme au travail. Surmonter les ambiguités psychologiques." Révolution Africaine, 264, (March 7, 1968), 22-23.

75 Peristiany, Jean G., ed. Honour and Shame: The Values of Mediterranean Society. London: Weidenfeld and Nelson, 1965.

76 Pitt-Rivers, J. "Women and Sanctuary in the Mediterranean." Echanges et Communications--Mélanges C. Levi-Strauss, 2 (1970), 862-875.

77 Polk, William. "Social Modernization: The New Man." In Georgiana G. Stevens, ed., United States and the Middle East, New York: Prentice-Hall, 1964; 30-52. About the modernization of social groups, women being one of the groups considered.

78 Pruvost, L. "Condition juridique, politique et sociale de la femme: le 9ème Congrès de l'I.D.E.F." IBLA, 134 (1974), 349-64.

79 al-Qalamawi, Suhayr. "Women win their way to higher public posts." London Times, July 24, 1969, p. ii. The law is in favor of women's rights and education is changing customs. Includes figures on progress in education and different jobs held by women.

80 Rushdi, Inji, et al. "The History and Struggle of the Afro-Asian Women is a Solid Basis for the Unity of Their Peoples and Countries" (in Arabic). al-Ahram, May 19, 1974, p. 3, col. 1.

81 al-Sa'dawi, Nawal. al-Mar´ah wa-al-sihhah wa-al-hubb. Cairo: Majallat al-sihhah, n.d. A sexual hygiene guide for women written by a woman doctor whose books have raised many controversies.

7 General

82 Salim, Mahmud Muhammad. "Woman in Positive Law," (in Arabic), al-Mar'ah, 9 (May 1, 1969), 49.

83 al-Sarraf, I'tisam Ahmad. al-Mar'ah fi rakb al-iman, ed. and rev. by Yusuf 'Abd al-Hadi al-Shal. 2nd ed. Cairo: Matba'at al salafiyah wa maktabatuha, 1974.

84 Schneider, Jane. "Of Vigilance and Virgins: Honor, Shame and Access to Resources in Mediterranean Societies." Ethnology, 10 (1971), 1-24.

85 Seklani, M. "Demography and Socio-Cultural Environment in the Arab Countries." Beirut: UNICEF, Eastern Region, 1970.

86 al-Shal, 'Abd al-Ghani al-Nabawi. 'Arusat al-mawlid. Cairo: Dar al-Katib al-'Arabi, 1967.

87 al-Shalabi, Mahmud. Sirr al-mar'ah. Cairo: Maktabat nahdat Misr, 1965.

88 Sha'rawi, Huda. Dur al-mar'ah fi al-nahdah al-sharqiyah. Cairo: Matba'at Misr, 1935. The leading Egyptian feminist of the time examines the role of women in the Eastern awakening.

89 al-Shintinawi, Ahmad. Tatawwur al-'ilaqat al-jinsiyah. Cairo: al-maktabah al-anjlu-al-misriyah, 1969.

90 Sidqi, Ni'mat. al-Tabarruj, 4th ed. Cairo: Matba'at al-'Asimah, 1971. A code of proper behavior by a very conservative lady.

91 al-Siman, Jadat. "Sexual Revolution and Leftist Revolution." (in Arabic). Mawaqif, 11-12 (Dec. 1970), 67-73.

92 Smith, Margaret. "The Women's Movement in the Near and Middle East." Asiatic Review, April 1928, 188-204.

93 Spitler, James. "Sex Differentials in the Labor Force of the Middle East." Paper presented at the Conference on Development in the Arab World, New York, Oct. 1-3, 1976.

94 Sweet, Louise E. Peoples and Cultures of the Middle East. 2 vols. Garden City, N.J.: National History Press, 1970.

95 Tadrus, Khalil Hana. Imra'ah tantazir al-hubb. Cairo: Matba'at dar al-misriyah, 1971.

96 Tahir, Ahmad. al-Mar'ah, kifahha wa-'amalha. Cairo: Dar al-Jamahir, 1964.

General   8

"Tant qu'elles auront peur nous n'avancerons pas." <u>Jeune</u>
    <u>Afrique</u>, 340 (July 16, 1967), 442-43.

98 al-Torki, Soraya. "Men-Women Relationship in Arab Socie-
    ties: A Study of the Economic and Political Conditions
    of the Status of Women. " Unpublished research pro-
    posal, 1973.

99 Ungör, Beraët Zeki. "Women in the Middle East and North
    Africa and Universal Suffrage. " <u>Annals of the American</u>
    <u>Academy of Political and Social Science</u>, 375 (January
    1968), 72-81.

100 Van Dusen, Roxann A. "The Study of Women in the Middle East:
    Some Thoughts. " <u>Middle East Studies Association Bulletin</u>,
    May 1, 1976, 1-19. A "state of the art" article which in-
    cludes a short bibliography.

101 Vénard, Maurice. "La Femme en Orient. " <u>Bulletin de la</u>
    <u>Société de Géographie d'Alger et de l'Afrique du Nord</u>,
    26 (1921), 234-54.

102 Waheed, K. A. "Woman's Place in National Life. " <u>Islamic</u>
    <u>Literature</u>, Dec. 1951, 15-37.

103 Wajdi, Muhammad Farid. "Woman Destroys" (in Arabic).
    <u>al-Hilal</u>, 1934, 37-44.

104 Wakin, Edward. "Veiled Revolution. " <u>Midstream</u>, 4 (1959),
    79-85. The author considers that the creation of Israel
    has had a modernizing impact on the Arab world.

105 Watson, H. "The Role of Women in a Developing Society. "
    <u>Arab World</u>, 13:2 (Feb. 1967), 3-6.

106 "Woman in 1967" (in Arabic). <u>al-Mar'ah</u>, 8 (Aug. 1967), 20-
    21.

107 Woodsmall, Ruth F. <u>Women and the Near East</u>. Washing-
    ton, D. C. : Middle East Institute, 1960. A survey of
    the condition of women from Turkey to Indonesia, includ-
    ing many statistics and data on Arab women.

108 Wyon, Olive. <u>The Dawn Wind: A Picture of Changing Con-</u>
    <u>ditions Among Women in Africa and the East</u>. London:
    Christian Student Movement Press, 1931.

109 Youssef, N. "Cultural Ideals, Feminine Behavior and Kin-
    ship Control. " <u>Comparative Studies in Society and His-</u>
    <u>tory</u>, 15 (1973), 326-347.

110 Zerkime, Mounira. "Journée internationale de la femme. "
    <u>Révolution Africaine</u>, 264 (March 7, 1968), 24-25.

9 Islam

111 Zinih, Khalil. Taqwim al-mar'ah. Alexandria: Matba'at
jaridat al-basir, 1927.

(2) ISLAM

General

112 al-Abbani, Muhammad Nasir al-Din. Hijab al-mar'ah al-
muslimah. Beirut: Manshurat al-maktab al-islami,
1965/66. A compilation of religious laws concerning
women and the hadith on which they are based.

113 Abbasi, A. de Zayas. "Woman in Islam." Islamic Literature, 5 (Feb. 1953), 119-25; 6 (Jan. 1954), 55-61.

114 Abbott, Nabia. "Woman." In Ruth N. Anshen, ed., Mid
East: World Center, Yesterday, Today and Tomorrow,
New York: Harper and Bros., 1956; 196-212. Women's
status in Christianity and Islam and in the present
Middle East.

115 'Abd al-Rahman, 'A'ishah (Bint al-Shati'). "Islam and
Woman" (in Arabic). Da'wat al-Haqq, 9-10 (Aug. 1968),
7-9.

116 _____. al-Mafhum al-islami li-tahrir al-mar'ah. Cairo:
Jami'at Omdurman al-Islamiyah, 1967.

117 _____. "The Personality of Woman in the Holy Qur'an"
(in Arabic). Paper delivered at the Seminar on the
Status of Woman in the Islamic Family, Cairo, Dec. 20-
22, 1975. The author thinks that Islam granted considerable rights to women that only political decadence
prevented them from enjoying.

118 'Abd al-Wahid, Mustafa. al Islam wa al-mushkilah al-
jinsiyah. Cairo: Maktabat al-Mutanabbi, 1972. Islam
and sexual ethics.

119 Abu al-'Uyun, Mahmud. "Woman at al-Azhar" (in Arabic).
al-Hilal, 1934, 97-100.

120 al-Afghani, Sa'id. al-Islam wa-al-mar'ah. Damascus: Dar
al-Fikr, 1964.

121 Afza, N. "Woman in Islam." Islamic Literature, 13:10
(1967), 5-24.

122 Ahmad, M. A. D. "The Status of Woman in Islam." The
Islamic Review, 1933, 49-58.

123 Alihé Hanoun. Les Musulmanes contemporaines. Paris:

n.p., 1894.

124 Amir 'Ali. "The Influence of Women in Islam. " Nineteenth
     Century, May 1899, 755-74. The author thinks that Is-
     lam never hampered the intellectual development of wo-
     men and that only political decline brought about a de-
     terioration of their status.

125 Amiruddin, Begum Sultan Mir. "The Status of Woman in Is-
     lam. " Islamic Review, 26 (1938), 103-110, 130-135.

126 _____. "Woman's Status in Islam: A Moslem View. "
     The Moslem World, 28 (1938), 153-163. An apology for
     the condition of Muslim women.

127 al-'Amri, Muhammad al-Hadi. "Woman and Her Cultural Ac-
     complishment in Islamic Civilization" (in Arabic). al-
     Fikr, 10 (July 1970), 71-73.

128 Ansari, Makram. "Islam and Woman" (in Arabic). al-Jaza'-
     iriyah, 4 (May 1970), 42-43; 8 (Aug. 1970), 10-11.

129 Antonini, Paul. "La Condition de la femme dans les pays
     musulmans. " La Réforme Sociale, Série 2, 5 (1888),
     619-625.

130 al-'Aqqad, 'Abbas Mahmud. al-Mar'ah fi al-Qur'an. Cairo:
     Kitab al-Hilal, 1962.

131 Arnaldez, R. "Le Coran et l'émancipation de la femme. "
     In La Femme à la recherche d'elle-même: Semaine de
     la pensée Marxiste, Paris: La Palatine, 1965; 38-54.

132 al-Asafi, Muhammad Mahdi. al-'Alaqah al-jinsiyah fi al-
     Qur'an al-Karim; dirasah li-qadaya al-mar'ah al-
     mu'asirah 'ala daw' al-Qur'an al-Karim. al-Najaf:
     Maktabat al-Tarbiyah, 1968.

133 Attanoux, B. d'. "Condition sociale de la femme musulmane
     en Afrique. " Revue de l'Islam, Jan. 1897, 4-6, 21-23.

134 Awad, B. A. "The Status of Women in Islam. " Islamic
     Quarterly, 8 (1967), 17-24. An apology for the status
     of women in Islam without any examples or quotations.

135 Ben Mostepha. Respect aux droits de la femme dans l'Is-
     lamisme. Algiers: Imprimerie P. Fontana, 1895.

136 Benabed, H. "La Condition de la femme musulmane:
     l'Islam et l'Occident. " Cahiers du Sud, 1947, 211-20.

137 Bousquet, G. H. L'Ethique sexuelle de l'Islam. Paris:
     Maisonneuve et Larose, 1966. A scholarly and lively

book by a long time resident of the Maghreb, a revised edition of his La Morale de l'Islam et son éthique sexuelle, published in 1953.

138 Bullough, Vern L., and Honnie Bullough. "Women in Islam." In Bullough and Bullough, The Subordinate Sex, Urbana: University of Illinois Press, 1973; 134-52.

139 Cadi. "De la religion mahométane: sur la femme musulmane." Société de Géographie et d'Archéologie d'Oran. Bulletin Trimestriel, 43 (1923), 53-70.

140 Charnay, Jean-Paul. "La Musulmane dans la ville moderne." Politique Etrangère, 34 (1971), 141-146.

141 _____. "Social Relationship and the Condition of Women." In Islamic Culture and Socio-Economic Change. Leiden: E. J. Brill, 1971; 52-70.

142 Chemli, Mongi. "The Problem of Woman in the Commentary of al-Manar" (in Arabic). Hawliyyat al-jami'ah al-tunisiyah, 3 (1966), 5-27.

143 Chouiter, Ali. "Woman in Islam" (in Arabic). Majallat al-mar'ah, 5 (May 10, 1965), 14-15.

144 Cobbold, Z. E. "La Femme dans l'Islam." Jeune Islam, 1 (1949), 18.

145 Daffa', Muhammad Khalifah. "Woman in Islam" (in Arabic). al Mar'ah, 2 (Feb. 1967), 32-33.

146 Darwazah, Muhammad 'Izzat. al-Mar'ah fi al-Qur'an wa-al-Sunnah. Sidon: al-Maktabah al-'asriyah, 1968.

147 Debèche, Djamila. "La Femme musulmane dans la société." In Contacts en Terre d'Afrique, Meknès: Créer, 1946; 141-61.

148 Decroux, Paul. "La Femme dans l'Islam moderne." Gazette des Tribunaux du Maroc, 994 (Feb. 11, 1947).

149 Deprez, Jean. "Mariage mixte, Islam et Nation." Revue Algérienne, 1 (1975).

150 Djebar, Assia. Women of Islam. London: André Deutsch, 1961. Mostly an illustrated book, including an interview with President Bourguiba, 41-76.

151 Ehrenfels, U. R. "Ambivalent Attitudes to Womanhood in Islamic Society." Islamic Culture, 25 (1951), 73-88.

152 _____. "History of Womanhood in Islamic Society."

Islamic Review, 12 (1949), 31-36.

153 _____. "Traces of Islam." Islamic Culture, 9 (1935), 603-609.

154 Faizi, Tarikh. "La Situation de la femme en Islam." La Pensée, 1 (1952), 11-17.

155 Fath-Allah, Hamzah. Bakurat al-kalam 'ala huquq al-mar'ah fi al-islam. Bulaq: al-Maktabah al-kubra al-amiriyah, 1308 (i.e. 1891/92).

156 "La Femme musulmane au Moyen-Orient." El-Djeich, 25 (May 1965).

157 Fernea, Robert A., and Elizabeth W. Fernea. "Variations in religious observances among Islamic women." In Nikki R. Keddie, ed., Scholars, Saints and Sufis: Muslim Religious Institutions in the Middle East Since 1500. Berkeley: University of California Press, 1972; 385-401.

158 Fu'ad, Ni'mat Ahmad. "Woman in Islam" (in Arabic). al-Mar'ah, 1 (January 2, 1969), 30-31.

159 Gardet, Louis. "Les Communautés musulmanes devant les problèmes politiques et économiques," Economic et Humanisme, 2 (1943), 523-547.

160 Gaudio, Attilio. La Révolution des femmes en Islam. Paris: R. Julliard, 1957. A sympathetic plea in favor of Muslim women. Includes the text of resolutions of the Third Congress of the Arab Feminist Union (Beirut, 1954), text of the 1956 fatwa of al-Azhar against the holding of public functions by women and their right to vote and the sections of the Tunisian code related to marriage and divorce.

161 al-Ghumari, Ahmad ibn Muhammad. al-Afdal wa-al-minnah fi ru'yat al-nisa' li-Allah ta'ala fi al-jannah. Cairo: Matba'at al-sa'adah, 1963.

162 al-Hajjaji, Ahmad Anas. Ma'a al-mar'ah al-muslimah. Cairo: Qism al-akhwat al-muslimat, 1947.

163 al-Hajrasi, Amjad. "Woman in Muslim and European Societies" (in Arabic). al-Mar'ah al-jadidah, 7 (March 1970), 10-11.

164 Hartmann, M. "La Femme dans l'Islam." Le Lotus, 1 (Sept. 1901), 306-07.

165 Hashimi, Tijani. "al-Mar'ah al-muslimah" (in Arabic). al-Tahdit al-islami, April-May 1966, 82-119.

166 Hassum, H. C. "Social Rights of Muslim Women." Asian
Review, 52 (April 1956), 158-160.

167 "How Islam Honored Woman" (in Arabic). al-Ahram, Oct.
10, 1974, p. 10, col. 1.

168 Hussein, Aziza (Shukri). Women in the Moslem World.
Washington, D. C.: Egyptian Embassy, 1954. Based
upon a lecture given at the University of Chicago.

169 Ibn Ou Alfourat. "Quelques Réflexions sur la femme musulmane à travers les âges." L'Afrique et l'Asie, 51
(1960), 46-50. Islam does not oppress women. There
were many illustrious Muslim women. The Muslim woman has many rights she ignores and should ask for.

170 al-Ibrashi, Muhammad 'Atiyah. Makanat al-mar'ah fi al-
Islam. Cairo: Dar al-sha'b, 1971.

171 "L'Islam et la femme." La République (Oran), Nov. 29,
1968.

172 al-Jamazi, 'Abd al-Amir Mansur. al-Mar'ah fi zill al-Islam.
Beirut: Matba'at Bahus wa-Shartuni, 1973.

173 Kemal, Ali. "La Condition de la femme musulmane," Revue
de l'Islam, 1902, 97.

174 Khattab, 'Abd al-Mu'izz. Rawabit al-usrah fi al-Qur'an al-
Karim. Cairo: Matba'at al-Ma'rifah, 1970.

175 al-Khayyat, 'Abd al-'Aziz. "An Islamic Viewpoint on the
Concept of Association of Both Sexes and Its Rules."
Paper delivered at the Seminar on the Status of Woman
in the Islamic Family. Cairo: Dec. 20-22, 1975. The
author is Jordan's Minister of Awqaf, Islamic Affairs
and Holy Places.

176 al-Khuli, al-Bahi. al-Islam wa-qadaya al-mar'ah al-
mu'asirah. Kuwait: Dar al-qalam, 1970. Written by
an Egyptian author, a former Muslim brother.

177 Kidwai, M. H. "Woman under Islam." Islamic Review, 6
(1918), 171-172.

178 Lahbabi, Muhammad 'Aziz. "The Person in Islam: The
Condition of Woman" (in Arabic). Da'wat al-haqq, 6-7
(May 1968), 13-16; 9-10 (Aug. 1968), 15-16; 1 (Nov.
1968), 35-38.

179 Laizi, Faruk. "La Situation de la femme en Islam." La
Pensée, Nov. 1962, 11-17.

180 La Motte Capron, A. Maîtrot de. "La Femme dans le
     Qoran." Bulletin de la Société de Géographie d'Alger et
     de l'Afrique du Nord, 1938, 93-119.

181 Lebon, Gustave. "Woman in Islam" (in Arabic). al-Usbu'
     al-thaqafi, 54 (June 22, 1973), 6-7.

182 Loreau, A. "La Condition de la femme en Islam et son
     évolution." Le Droit des Femmes, May 1954, 14.

183 Matwi, Ahmad al Harrani. al-Mar'ah fi-nazar al-Islam.
     Tunis: Arts Graphiques, n.d.

184 Meissa, M. S. La femme musulmane. Casablanca: Imp.
     Réunies, 1928. The author believes enthusiastically in
     the beneficient influence of French colonization in up-
     grading the status of Muslim women.

185 "Modernisme en Islam." En Terre d'Islam, 43 (Jan. 1931),
     2-11.

186 Muhammad, 'Abd al-Hamid Ibrahim. al-Mar'ah fi al-Islam.
     Cairo: al-Dar al-qawmiyah lil-tiba'ah wa-lil-nashr,
     1963.

187 Nabhani, Kouriba. "La Femme en Islam." Documentation
     Nord-Africaine, 157 (Nov. 3, 1954).

188 Nançon, Alfred. "La Condition des femmes dans l'Islam."
     Revue de l'Islam, 4 (1899), 97-99, 113-117.

189 al-Naqdi, Ja'far ibn Muhammad. Kitab al-Islam wa-al-
     mar'ah. Baghdad: n.p., 1929-30.

190 al-Nawawi, 'Abd Allah. al-Mar'ah al-muslimah fi al-mujtama'
     al-muslimah. Cairo: Matba'at al-sa'adah, 1970.

191 al-Nawawi, 'Abd al-Rahman Husayn. al-Din wa al-mar'ah.
     Cairo: Matba'at Amin 'Abd al-Rahman, 1966.

192 Nejjari, Fathi. "Dans quelle mesure existe-t-il une égalité
     entre hommes et femmes en Islam." La Pensée, 1
     (Nov. 1962), 35-40.

193 Nyland, P. "Woman in Judaism and Islam." Moslem World,
     6 (1916), 291-295.

194 "The Position of Woman in Islam." Islamic Review, 12
     (Dec. 1919), 439-445.

195 Raineau, Michel. "Les Deux Types de la femme musulmane
     d'aujourd'hui." Le Monde Colonial Illustré, 65 (Jan.
     1929), 18.

15   Islam

196 Rashid, Zaynab. "Social Responsibility of Woman in Islam."
     Paper presented at the Seminar on the Status of Woman
     in the Islamic Family, Cairo, Dec. 20-22, 1975. The
     author is dean of the Girls Faculty at al-Azhar Univer-
     sity.

197 Raynaud, E. La Femme dans l'Islam. Paris: n. p., 1912.

198 Rondot, Pierre. "Bref Aperçu des problèmes modernes de
     la famille musulmane." L'Afrique et l'Asie, 1 (1961),
     20-24.

199 Rouhani, Dr. "Personnalité de la femme en Islam." Pensée
     chiite, (1960), no. 1, 27-36; no. 2, 21-30; no. 3, 31-36.

200 Sabri, Mustafa. Qawli fi al-mar'ah wa-muqaranatuhu bi-
     aqwal muqallidat al-gharb. Cairo: al-Matba'ah al-
     salafiyah, 1354. The author was a former Sheikh al-
     Islam of the Ottoman Empire.

201 Saleh, Saneya. "Women in Islam: Their Status in Religious
     and Traditional Culture." International Journal of Sociol-
     ogy of the Family, 2 (March 1972), 35-42.

202 Salman, A. M. M. "Polygamy and the Status of Women in
     Islamic Society" (in Arabic). Majallat al-Azhar, 33
     (1961), 17-24.

203 Sami, Husayn. Huquq al-mar'ah wa-wajibatuha fi al-Islam.
     Cairo: al-Matba'at al-salafiyah, 1934.

204 Shaltut, Mahmud. "The Position of Women in Islam" (in
     Arabic). Majallat al-Azhar, 7 (1960-61), 6-23.

205 _____. The Quran and Woman. (Annotated English ver-
     sion with Arabic text.) Cairo: International Islamic
     Centre for Population Studies and Research, al-Azhar,
     1975. The most recent and best translation of a stan-
     dard religious book on women.

206 Shanan, Naadirah. "The Muslim Woman and Imaamate."
     Islamic Review, 5 (May 1965), 23-28.

207 al-Sharbasi. "Mission of the Muslim Woman" (in Arabic).
     al-Mar'ah al-jadidah, 8 (Oct. 15, 1970), 48-70.

208 al-Sharqawi, Muhammad. "Islam Protects Woman Against
     the Suspicion of Man" (in Arabic). al-Mar'ah al Jadidah,
     March 1970, 23.

209 al-Shayyal, Ahmad Muhammad. al-Mar'ah fi al-Islam.
     Cairo: al-Matba'ah al-salafiyah, 1346 (1927-1928).

210 Sokolnicki, Michel de. Mahomet, législateur des femmes; Ses opinions sur le Christ et les chrétiens. Paris: Comon & Cie, 1846. The author, a feminist in favor of female education, is of the opinion that Islam is much more liberal than Judaism, Christianity and oriental religions.

211 "Sokolnicki, de. Mahomet, législateur des femmes." Revue des Deux Mondes, March 1, 1847, 964-969. Review of de Sokolnicki's book, by Gérard de Nerval who does not see a tremendous difference in the legal positions of the Catholic and the Muslim woman.

212 Sultan, Jamil. Hujjat al-Muslim fi al-radd al-mufhim. Beirut: Dar al-anwar, 1972. Studies on the position of the Muslim woman in answer to some vicious propaganda.

213 al-Talib, N. "Status of Women in Islam." Islamic Literature, 15 (1969), 57-64.

214 Tomiche, Nada. "La Femme en Islam." In Histoire Mondiale de la Femme. Paris: Nouvelle Librairie de France, 1967. Vol. 3, 97-156.

215 Van Sommer, Annie, ed. Our Moslem Sisters: A Cry of Need from Lands of Darkness by Those Who Heard It. New York: Fleming-Revell, 1907.

216 Wafi, 'Ali 'Abd al-Wahid. al-Mar'ah fi al-Islam. Cairo: Maktabat Gharib, 1971.

217 Wanner, Léo. "L'Evolution de la femme dans l'Islam moderne." L'Egyptienne, 154 (April 1939), 21-25. Mrs. Wanner, general secretary of a Franco-Muslim association, sees equal rights between sexes as the worst illusion. She advises girls to learn home economics.

218 Woodsmall, Ruth Frances. Moslem Women Enter a New World. New York: Round Table Press, 1936. A valuable survey of the condition of Muslim women between the two World Wars.

219 Youssef, Nadia Haggag. "Social Structure and Female Labor Force Participation in Developing Countries: A Comparison of Latin America and Middle Eastern Countries." Unpublished Ph.D. dissertation, University of California at Berkeley, 1970.

220 _____. Women and Work in Developing Societies. (Population Monograph Series No. 15.) Berkeley: University of California Press, 1974.

Law

221 Amir, 'Ali. The Legal Position of Women in Islam. Lon-
    don: University of London Press, 1912.

222 Anderson, J. N. D. "Developments in Shari'a law, II."
    Muslim World, 41 (1951), 34-48. About Muslim law
    courts.

223 Bahim, Muhammad Jamil. al-Mar'ah fi al-ta'rikh wa-al-
    Shar'ah. Beirut: n.p., 1921.

224 al-Bardisi, Muhammad Zakariya. al-Ahwal al-shakhsiyah.
    Cairo: Matba'at Dar al-ta'lif, 1965.

225 Ben Muhammad, Ali. "Woman in Muslim Legislation" (in
    Arabic). al-Dabas, 3 (Aug. 1967), 30-36; 4 (Oct. 1967),
    12-18; 5-6 (Nov. -Dec. 1967), 55-58.

226 Debèche, Djamila. "La Femme et la condition juridique en
    pays d'Islam." Dialogue, 7 (Jan. 1964), 20-23.

227 Emilia, Antonio d'. "Intorno alla moderna attivita legislativa
    di alcuni paesi musulmani nel campo del diritto privato."
    Oriente Moderno, 33 (1953), 301-21.

228 Esposito, John L. "Women's Rights in Islam." Islamic
    Studies, 2 (1975), 99-114. How strong social customs
    wrongly attributed to Islam lowered women's status.

229 al-Faruqi, Lamia L. "Women's Rights and the Muslim Wo-
    men." Islam and the Modern Age, 3:2 (1972), 76-99.

230 Fattal, A. "Evolution et tradition dans l'Islam actuel: à
    propos des droits de la femme." La Bourse Egyptienne,
    June 14, 1952.

231 Feroze, Muhammad Rashid. "The Reform in Family Laws
    in the Muslim World." Islamic Studies, 1 (1962), 107-
    130.

232 Gibb, H. A. R. "Women and Law." In Colloque sur la So-
    ciologie Musulmane. Brussels. Actes. 11-14 Septem-
    ber 1961. Brussels: Centre National pour l'Etude des
    Problèmes du Monde Musulman Contemporain, 1962.

233 Habibi, Syed Ahmad Moinuddin. "A Critique of the Legal
    Reforms in the Muslim World." World Muslim League
    Magazine, Aug. 1965, 35-46.

234 Hayes, H. E. E. "Woman's Place in Islam and British
    Law." Moslem World, 7 (1917), 127-130.

235 Helou, Rahmin. Etude sur la condition juridique des femmes musulmanes. Paris: V. Giard et E. Brière, 1896.

236 Ibn Muhammad, 'Ali. "Woman in Muslim Law" (in Arabic). al-Qabas, 7 (Feb. 1968), 37-42.

237 al-'Idawi, 'Abd al-'Aziz. "The Position of Women in the View of the Islamic Legislation and Modernity." Qada wa-tashri', 9 (Nov. 1959), 614-621.

238 al-Kattani, Muhammad al-Muntasir. Fityat tariq wa-al-ghafiqi. Beirut: Dar Idris lil-ta'lif wa-al-tarjamah wa-al-nashr, 1972. Articles on the status of women in Islam and the right of land ownership.

239 Layish, Aharon. Women and Islamic Law in a Non-Muslim State. New York: Halsted Press, and Jerusalem: Israel University Press, 1975.

240 Linant de Bellefonds, Y. Traité de droit musulman comparé. 3 vols. Paris: Mouton & Co., 1965-1973. Vol. 2 is devoted entirely to marriage.

241 Maghniyah, Muhammad Jawad. al-Zawaj wa-al-talaq 'ala al-madhab al-hamsah. Beirut: Dar al-'ilm lil-malayin, 1960.

242 Makhluf, Hasanan. "Islam and the Rights of Women" (in Arabic). al-Misri, May 1, 1952.

243 Pesle, Octave. La Femme musulmane dans le droit, la religion et les moeurs. Rabat: La Porte, 1946.

244 Rafi-ud-Din Ahmad. "Are English Women Legally Inferior to Their Mohamedan Sisters?" Imperial and Asiatic Quarterly Review, 2nd series, 1 (1891), 410-429.

245 al-Sharqawi, Muhammad. "Islam is Just Toward Woman and Gives Her Her Inheritance Share" (in Arabic). al-Mar'ah, 7 (April 3, 1969), 28-29.

246 al-Siba'i, Mustafa. al-Mar'ah bayna al fiqh wa-al-qanun. Aleppo: al-Maktabah al-'arabiyah, 1967.

247 Soorma, C. A. "Proprietary & Personal Rights of Women in Islam." Islamic Review, 37 (June 1949), 16-17.

248 Wafa'i, Ibtihaj. Khasa'is al-mar'ah fi al-fiqh al-Islami (qism al-ibadat). Beirut: Maktabat al-Risalah, 1973.

249 El Yafi, Abdallah. "Condition privée de la femme dans le droit de l'Islam" (thesis). Paris: n.p., 1926.

Veiling of Women

250   al-Albani, Muhammad Nasir al Din. Hijab al-mar'ah al-
      muslimah fi al-Kitab wa-al-Sunnah. Beirut: al-Maktab
      al-islami, 1965.

251   al-Gawish, Ahmad Muhammad Sa'id. Awjab al-wajibat fi
      lizum al-hijab lil-mar'ah bi-al-din wa-al-fatrah. Cairo:
      Matba'at al-i'timad, 1920.

252   Hamdan, Salim. al-Madaniyah wa-al-hijab. Beirut:
      Matabi' quzma, 1928.

253   Hume-Grifith, Mrs. M. E. Behind the Veil in Persia and
      Turkish Arabia. London: Seele & Co., 1909. Account
      of an eight-year residence in the Middle East.

254   Keddie, Nikki, and Lois Beck, eds. Women in the Muslim
      World. Cambridge, Mass.: Harvard University Press
      [in press, mid-1978].

255   L. M. "La Question du Voile (mas'alat oul hijab). Revue du
      Monde Musulman, 12 (1910), 463-478. The campaigns of
      the Egyptian Muhammad Tawfiq and the Iraqi Jamil
      Zahawi against the veil and the bitter reactions of their
      detractors.

256   Maudoodi, Syed Abul 'Ala. al-Hijab. Beirut: Dar al-Fakr,
      1967.

257   Mazza, G. "La Donna musulmana strippera il velo mille-
      nario?" Missioni Consolata, 3 (March 1965), 14-17.

258   Murphy, Robert. "Social distance and the veil." American
      Anthropologist, 66 (1964), 1257-1274.

259   al-Sanusi, Mustafa Zaghlul. al-Mar'ah bayn al-hijab wa-al-
      sufur. Beirut: Dar maktabat al-hayah, 1967. Deals
      with the religious duties of women.

260   Tillion, Germaine. "Les Femmes et le voile dans la civili-
      sation méditerranéenne." In Etudes Maghrébines: Mé-
      langes Charles-André Julien, Paris: Presses Univer-
      sitaires de France, 1964; 25-38.

261   Yusuf of Najaf and Gilan. "In Defense of the Veil." The
      Moslem World, 3 (July 1943), 203-212. This article is
      a translation by Charles Pittman of extracts from a book
      entitled The Means of the Chastity of Women: A Volume
      on Chastity, by Hajji Shaykh Yusuf of Najaf and Gilan
      (Resht, Iran, ca.1926), pp. 294 ff.

(3) THE ARAB WOMAN IN GENERAL

262 'Abd al-Hamid, Fawziyah. "Woman in the Evolving Arab
          Society" (in Arabic). al-Mar´ah, 5 (May 1967), 30-31,
          47.

263 'Afifi, 'Abd Allah. al-Mar´ah al-'arabiyah fi jahilitiha wa-
          Islamiha. Cairo: Matba'at al-ma'arif, 1932.

264 _____. al-Mar´ah al-'arabiyah fi zilal al-Islam. Beirut:
          Dar al-katib al-'arabi, 197-.

265 'Amir, Ibrahim. "A Social View of the Arab Woman" (in
          Arabic). al-Hilal, April 1971, 24-33.

266 "The Arab Woman: An Untypical View. " Aramco World
          Magazine, 2 (March-April 1971), 1-40.

267 "The Arab Woman: Her Militant and Social Role" (in Arabic).
          al-Idha'ah wa-al-talfazah, 271 (May 15, 1971), 10.

268 al-Ashur, Shakir. "The Arab Woman and the Socialist Trans-
          formation" (in Arabic). Adab, 18 (March 1970), 34-37.

269 Berque, Jacques. Les Arabes d'hier à demain. Paris:
          Editions du Seuil, 1969. See Chapter IX, "Intercession
          de la femme, " 193-212.

270 Charles, Nick. "Women in the Arab World. " Middle East
          Sketch, 1 (March 1975), 28-30.

271 Daylami, Nazihah Jawdat. "Some Problems of Arab Women"
          (in Arabic). Kitab al-ba'th, 29 (June 1958).

272 Dearden, Ann, ed. Arab Women. London: Minority Rights
          Group, 1975. A concise report on the status of women
          in every Arab country. Very informative.

273/4 "[Dearden's] 'Arab Women'. " The Egyptian Gazette, Dec.
          15, 1975, 2. A violent criticism of the preceding work,
          judged from a Reuter report. The author insists that
          Muslim women are not discriminated in the least and
          even have rights that some Western women are still
          fighting for.

275 Dodd, Peter C. "Women's Honor in Contemporary Arab So-
          ciety, " Paper delivered at the Seventh World Congress
          International Sociological Association, Varna, Bulgaria,
          Sept. 1970. Section on Family Research. Abstracted
          in Sociological Abstracts, 18 (1970), 785-786.

276 al-Dukakni, 'Abd al-Hamid. "The Changing Role of Women

in the Arab Experience" (in Arabic). Adwa, Dec. 1966.

277 "La Femme arabe au travail. " Ferida, 1 (May 1975), 24-25.
Concerning a congress held in Tunis, Dec. 14-17, 1974.

278 "La Femme et la législation des pays arabes à la lumière
des accords internationaux. " Travaux et Jours, 52
(July-Sept. 1974), 71-76.

279 Garaudy, Annie. L'amore tra gli arabi. Bologna: Capitol,
1968.

280 Hanna, Jurj. Ahadith ma'a al-mar'ah al-'arabiyah. Beirut:
Dar Bairut lil-tiba'ah wa-al-nashr, 1958.

281 Hashim, Husayn. "Past and Present for the Arab Woman"
(in Arabic). Risalat al-Jam'iyah, 1968. Moral advice to
women.

282 "The Heart is the Symbol of the African and Arab Women
Community" (in Arabic). al-Ahram, Jan. 11, 1974,
p. 12, col. 7.

283 Henein, Georges. "Ni poids ni mesure--cessez de vous
penchez. " Jeune Afrique, 288 (July 3, 1966), 31. The
author does not think the Maghrebine woman needs any
improvement of her rights.

284 Hilal, Jamil M. "Father's Brother's Daughter Marriage in
Arab Communities: A Problem for Sociological Explanation. " Middle East Forum, 4 (1970), 73-84.

285 _____. "The Management of Male Dominance in Traditional Arab Culture: A Tentative Model. " Civilisations,
21 (1971), 85-95. Describes the "exploitative" and "pro-
tective" attitudes of men towards women.

286 Hubaysh, H. "The Role of Woman in Arab Armies" (in
Arabic). al-Jundi al-Lubnani, 36:1 (July 1972), 20-25.

287 'Ilmi, 'Adwiyya. "The Arab Woman in the Modern Age" (in
Arabic). Afkar, April 11, 1967, 4-20.

288 Iskander, M. "Can We Plan for the Future? The Prospects
and Problems of Arab Children and Youth. " Mid East
Forum, 2-3 (1970), 5-18.

289 Jessup, Henry Harris. The Women of the Arabs. New
York: Dodd & Mead, 1873. The first half-century of
the Mission Work for Syrian Woman among Syrian,
Lebanese and Druze women.

290 Kesler, Suad Wakim. "Values of Women College Students in

the Arab Middle East. " Unpublished Ph. D. dissertation,
Cornell University, 1956.

291 al-Khalidi 'Anbara, Salam. "Women's Role in Arab Society. "
     Islamic Review, 37:1 (Nov. 1949), 19-24. An apology
     for woman's condition in past and present Islam.

292 al-Khammash, Salwa. al-Mar´ah al-'arabiyah wa-al-mujtama'
     al taqlidi al-mutakhallif. Beirut: Dar al-adab, 1973.
     The Arab woman and the traditional underdeveloped so-
     ciety.

293 al-Mala´ikah, Nazik. "Social Centers in the Life of the Arab
     Woman" (in Arabic). Adab, 4 (April 1970), 11-13.

294 Matraji-Idris 'Aidah. "Feminine Literature and Arab Socie-
     ty" (in Arabic). al-Adab, 18 (Oct. 1969), 11-13.

295 Melconian, Marlene. "Arab Women: In Hot Pursuit of a
     Feminist-Oriented Economy. " The Arab Economist,
     Aug. 1975, 18-26. Information about how Arab women
     spend their money and their importance in the labor
     force.

296 Muhyi, Ibrahim 'Abd Allah. Mushkilat al-mar´ah fi al-bilad
     al-'arabiyah. Baghdad: Matba'at al-rabitah, 1958.

297 Muhyi, Ibrahim Abdulla. "Women in the Arab Middle East. "
     Journal of Social Issues, 15 (1959), 45-57. Reprinted
     in Richard H. Nolte, ed. , The Modern Middle East (New
     York: Atherton Press, 1963), 124-40.

298 Mukhtar, Bahirah. "On Arab and African Women" (in Arabic).
     al-Ahram, Jan. 12, 1974, 8.

299 Najmun Nisa, Begum. "Arab Attitude Towards Women. "
     Proceedings All-Pakistan Historical Conference, 1 (1951),
     44-59.

300 Naser, Abdallah Omar. "The Educational Philosophy of Cer-
     tain Prospective American and Arab Women Teachers. "
     Unpublished Ph. D. dissertation, University of Florida,
     1966.

301 Nelson, Cynthia. "Public and Private Politics: Women in
     the Middle Eastern World. " American Ethnologist, 3
     (Aug. 1974), 551-64. The author underlines the unsus-
     pected power of women as "information brokers, reputa-
     tion builders and maintainers, as 'power' of their own. "

302 Paret, Rudi. Zur Frauenfrage in der arabisch-islamischen
     Welt. Stuttgart: Kohlhammer, 1934. Analyzes the
     works of Nazirah Zayn al-Din, al-Tahir al-Haddad and

Muhammad Rashid Rida.

303   Perron, Dr. Femmes arabes avant et depuis l'islamisme.
      Paris: Librairie Nouvelle, 1858.

304/5 Piesse, Louis. La Femme arabe: d'après les notes re-
       cueillies et classées par M. Louis Piesse. Paris, 1887.
       Offprint from Revue de l'Afrique Française.

306   al-Sa'id, Aminah. "The Arab Woman: Where To?" (in Ara-
      bic). Hawwa', Jan. 26, 1976. The Arab woman has no
      choice. She must either admit defeat or speed the pro-
      cess of her liberation.

307   Sa'id, B. "The Arab Woman in the Pre-Islamic Period and
      in Islam" (in Arabic). al-Aqlam, 7 (March 1968), 32-
      46.

308   Sa'id, Khalidah. "The Arab Woman: A Human Being Ac-
      cording to Others, Not on Her Own" (in Arabic).
      Mawaqif, 11/12 (Dec. 1970), 81-90, 91-100.

309   Samaan, N. J. "La Femme arabe au seuil de la liberté."
      Croissance des Jeunes Nations, 23 (June-July 1963), 29-
      31.

310   Sayigh, Rosemary. "The Changing Life of Arab Women."
      Mid East, 6 (1968), 19-23.

311   al-Sharif, Munir. Mustaqbal al-mar'ah al-'arabiyah fi al-
      mujtama' wa-al-bayt. Damascus: al-Matba'ah al-
      'ummumiyah, 1953.

312   "Should the Arab League Have a Permanent Women's Com-
      mittee?" (in Arabic). al-Ahram, Nov. 8, 1974, p. 12,
      col. 1.

313   Shukri, Ghali. 'Azmat al-jins fi al-qissah al-'arabiyah.
      Cairo: al-Hai'ah al-misriyah al-'ammah lil-ta'lif wa-
      al-nashr, 1971.

314   Shwidi, Muhammad. "Woman in the Arab Society" (in Ara-
      bic). al-Mar'ah, 12 (Dec. 5, 1966), 23-25.

315   Shwidi, Salim. "Woman in Arab Society" (in Arabic). al-
      Mar'ah, 2 (Feb. 1967), 26-29; 3 (March 1967), 20-21,
      61; 4 (April 1967), 31, 55; 5 (May 1967), 23-42.

316   al-Tanahi, Tahir. "Women from the Arab East" (in Arabic).
      al-Hilal, 1934, 112-117.

317   Thabit, Munirah. "The Political Rights of Women in the
      Arab East" (in Arabic). al-Mustami' al-'arabi, 7 (1946),

7, 27. A demand for political equality as per the
United Nations Charter.

318 Tibi, B. "The Problem of the Emancipation of Women in
Modern Arab Society" (in Arabic). al-Tali'ah 4:11 (1968),
68-79.

319 "Today's Arab Women." Arab World, 4 (May-June 1958), 1-
18.

320 Tomiche, Nada. La Condition de la femme dans le Moyen-
Orient arabe: Notes et études documentaires. Paris:
La Documentation Française, 1955.

321 van Ess, Dorothy. Fatima and Her Sisters. New York:
John Day Co., 1961.

322 Viguera Franco, E. de. "La condición de la mujer en el
derecho árabe e islámico." Cuadernos de Estudios Africanos, 4 (1948), 77-91.

323 "Voices [raised] to Have the Arab Women Employed in Administrative Positions" (in Arabic). al-Ahram, Nov. 4,
1974, p. 8, col. 1.

324 "Women in the Arab World." Arab World, 3 (May-June
1957), 8-10.

325 Youssef, Nadia H. "Social Structure and Female Labor
Force: The Case of Women Workers in Muslim Middle
Eastern Countries." Demography, 8:4 (Nov. 1971), 427-39.

(4) BEDOUIN WOMEN

326 Bujra, Abdullah. "The Relationship Between the Sexes
Amongst the Bedouin in a Town." Paper presented at
the Mediterranean Social Science Conference, Athens,
1966.

327 Célarié, Henriette. Nos Soeurs musulmanes; scènes de vie
du désert. Paris: Hachette, 1925. Célarié describes
her travels in the Sahara oases.

328 [Père] Anastase Marie de St. Elie (O. Carm.). "La Femme
du désert autrefois et aujourd'hui." Anthropos, 3 (1908),
53-67, 181-192.

329 Lewando-Hundt, G. A. "The Status of Women Among No-
madic and Settled Bedouin." Ph.D. dissertation, Dept.
of Social Anthropology, Edinburgh University (in progress).

330 Muhsam, H. V. "Fertility and Reproduction of the Bedouins."
     Population Studies, 4 (March 1951), 354-63.

331 _____ . "Some Notes on Bedu Marriage Habits. " In Cor-
     rado Gini, ed. , XIV International Congress of Sociology,
     Rome: Società Italiana di Sociologia; 1950.

332 Randolph, R. , and A. Coult. "A Computer Analysis of Be-
     douin Marriage. " South Western Journal of Anthropology,
     24 (1968), 83-99.

(5) VILLAGE WOMEN

333 Abu-Zahra, N. "On the Modesty of Women in Arab Muslim
     Villages: A Reply. " American Anthropologist, 72 (1970),
     1079-1087. A rebuttal to the 1968 article of Richard
     Antoun (see no. 335).

334 Antoun, Richard T. "Antoun's Reply to Abu-Zahra. " Ameri-
     can Anthropologist, 72 (1970), 1088-1092. Antoun's de-
     fense against Abu-Zahra's objections (see no. 333).

335 _____ . "On the Modesty of Women in Arab Muslim Vil-
     lages: A Study of the Accommodation of Traditions. "
     American Anthropologist, 70 (1968), 671-697. Field work
     in Kufr al-Ma´ village, northeast Jordan, but author
     makes many references to other Arab communities.

335a Letts, S. and J. Letts. "Women in Rural Arab Society: Old
     Roles and New in the Sultanate of Oman" (in Arabic). Jour-
     nal of the Gulf and Arabian Peninsula Studies, 10 (April
     1977), 101-111.

(6) MARRIAGE AND THE FAMILY

General

336 "A propos du mariage. " Jeune Afrique, 116 (Jan. 7-13, 1963), 2.

337 'Abd al 'Aziz, Muhammad. Fann al-zawaj. Cairo: Matba'at
     al-shabab, 1924. Unoriginal book on the secrets of mar-
     ried bliss.

338 'Abd al-'Aziz, Salih. al-Sihhah al-nafsiyah lil-hayah al-zawjiyah.
     Cairo: al-hay´ah al-misriyah al-'ammah lil-kitab, 1972.

339 Abu-Lughod, Ibrahim. "The Arab Family in Flux. " Near
     East, Nov. 1955, 8-12.

340 el-Akel, Abderrazak. "Derecho conyugal o derechos de la
     mujer en el-Islam" (résumé of a doctoral thesis).

Cuadernos de la Biblioteca Española de Tetuan, 8 (1973), 87-103.

341/2   al-Albani, Muhammad Nasir al-Din.   Adab al-zawaj fi al-Sunnah al-mutahharah.   Damascus: al-Maktab al-Islami, 1968.

343   al-'Alwaji, 'Abd al-Hamid; al-Zawj al-marbut, mawqif al-'aqidah al-sha'biyah min ma'sat al-'aris al-makhdul fi lailat al-kukhlah.   Baghdad: Matba'ah as'ad, 1964.

344   Aouissi, Mechri.   "Les Causes classiques de l'instabilité du mariage."   Revue Algérienne des Sciences Juridiques, Economiques et Politiques, 4 (1968), 1051-1064.   Written by a sheikh.

345   As'ad, Yusuf Mikha'il.   al-Jins wa-al-usrah.   Cairo: Maktab al-dumyati lil tiba'ah wa-al-nashr, 1969.

346   al-Atiqi, A.   "The Family in an Urban Society" (in Arabic).   al Majal, 46 (1973), 11-5.

347   'Awwa, Bashir.   al-Usrah bayn al-Jahiliyah wa-al-Islam wa-awda'ah al-rahinah.   Damascus: Dar al-fikr al-islami, 196-?   The family from the Jahiliyah and Islam to the present day.

348   al-Azniqi, Muhammad ibn Qutb al-Din.   Murshid al-muta'ahhil.   Beirut: al-Matba'ah al-anisiyah, 1895/1896.   Guide to married life.

349   al-Bana, 'Abd al-Jawad.   Woman and Family in the Sunnah of the Prophet (Selected texts).   Cairo: International Islamic Centre for Population Studies and Research, Al-Azhar, 1975?   A compilation of hadiths to show how women are honored and taken care of in Islam.   The Arabic text is given along with its English translation.

350   Barbet, C.   "Le Mariage chez les musulmans."   Nouvelle Revue Pratique de Droit International Privé, 1910, 229 ff.

351   Beck, Dorothy Fahs.   "The Changing Moslem Family of the Middle East."   Marriage and Family Living, 19 (1957), 340-47.

352   Ben Naceur, Mahmoud.   "Notes sur le mariage musulman."   IBLA, 3 (1939), 168-174.

353   Berque, Jacques.   Le Système de parenté dans les sociétés musulmanes.   Paris: Ecole Pratique des Hautes Etudes, 1959.

354   Chamberlayne, J. H.   "The Family in Islam."   Numen, 15 (1968), 119-141.

355 Chelhod, Joseph. "Le Mariage avec la cousine parallèle dans le système arabe." L'Homme, 3-4 (1965), 113-73.

356 Clavel, E. "De l'étude des institutions musulmanes; Du rôle de la femme dans la famille." Revue Internationale de Legislation et de Jurisprudence Musulmanes, 1895, 191-92, 219-24, 249-56.

357 Cuisenier, J. "Endogamie et exogamie dans le mariage arabe." L'Homme, 2 (1962), 80-105.

358 el-Daghestani, Kazem. "The Evolution of the Muslim Family in the Middle Eastern Countries." International Science Bulletin, 5 (1953), 681-91.

359 Dicaprio, J. M. "The Family in Islam." Islamic Culture, 12:10 (Oct. 1966), 37-48.

360 El-Din-Ali, B. "Planning for Development of the Arab Family." Arab Journal, 4 (1966), 33-37.

361 Dirks, Sabine. La Famille musulmane: son évolution au 20ème siècle. Paris: Mouton, 1969.

362 Dodd, Peter C. "Family Honor and the Force of Change in Arab Society." International Journal of Middle East Studies, 4 (1973), 40-54.

363 Farida. "La Famille bourgeoise tunisienne: l'autorité paternelle vue par une jeune fille." IBLA, 3 (1939), 65-73.

364 _____. "L'Autorité paternelle vue par une jeune fille." Etudes Sociales Nord Africaines, 7-8 (1950), 24-27.

365 Fathi, Muhammad. al-Zawaj al-sa'id. Cairo: Maktabat al-Nahdah, 1956.

366 Foudil, Abdel Kader. "De quelques causes modernes d'instabilité du mariage." Revue Algérienne de Sciences Juridiques, Economiques et Politiques, 4 (Dec. 1968), 1101-1109.

367 Goode, William. "Changing Family Patterns in Arabic Islam." In William J. Goode, World Revolution and Family Patterns, New York: The Free Press, 1963; 87-163.

368 Halil, Jamil. "Father's Brother's Daughter Marriage in Arab Communities: A Problem for Sociological Explanation." Middle East Forum, 4, 73-84.

369 al-Hamdany, M. , and B. Abu-Laban. "Game Involvement and Sex-Role Socialization in Arab Children." International Journal of Comparative Sociology, 3 (1971), 182-91.

General   28

370 Harfouche, Jamal. "The Family Structure in the Changing
     Middle East and the Pre-School Child. " Beirut:
     UNICEF, PSWG/PSC 14.

371 Hashim, Abul. "Muslim View of the Family and the Place
     of Women in Islamic Society. " Islamic Review, 50
     (April 1962), 20-22.

372 al-Hifni, Mahmud Ahmad.   Thalatha a'ras awdat bi-al-
     khizana ila al-iflas.   Cairo: Dar al-katib al-'arabi,
     1968.

373 Jacob, J. A. "Maximes et proverbes populaires arabes: la
     famille. " Mélanges de l'Institut Dominicain d'Etudes
     Orientales du Caire, 7 (1962), 35-80.

374 Jammes, R. "Amour, mariage et vie conjugale dans la so-
     ciété musulmane. " Liens, 9 (1959), 3-12.

375 Jamous, Raymond. "Réflexions sur la segmentarité et le
     mariage arabe. " Annales Marocaines de Sociologie,
     1969, 21-26.

376 Karmi, H. S. "The Family as a Developing Social Group in
     Islam. " Asian Affairs, Feb. 1975, 61-68. Outline of
     the history of the family in the Arab world.

377 Keyser, James M. B. "The Middle Eastern Case: Is There
     a Marriage Rule?" Ethnology, 13 (July 1974), 293-309.

378 Khuri, Fuad I. "Parallel Cousin Marriage Reconsidered: A
     Middle-Eastern Practice that Nullifies the Effects of
     Marriage on the Intensity of Family Relationships. "
     Man, 5 (1970), 597-618.

379 Kirru, Abu al-Qasim Muhammad. "Marriage: Rights and
     Duties" (in Arabic). al-Sha'b, 77 (March 16, 1967), 38,
     43.

380 Lashhar, Muhammad. "Family and Its Role in Society" (in
     Arabic). al-Mar'ah, 8 (Aug. 1967), 22.

381 Lecerf, J. "Note sur la famille dans le monde arabe et
     islamique. " Arabica, 3 (1956), 31-60.

382 al-Madani, Muhammad Muhammad. Ra'y jadid fi ta'addud
     al-zawaj. Cairo: Matba'at Ahmad Makhimar, 1958.

383 Madkur, Muhammad Sallam. Ahkam al-usrah fi al-Islam.
     Cairo: Dar al-nahdah al-'arabiyah, 1969/70.

384 _____. al-Islam wa-al-usrah wa al-mujtama'. Cairo:
     Dar al-Nahdah al-arabiyah, 1968.

385 Mahdi, Kamil. Min al-khutubah ila al-zifaf. Cairo: Makta-
     bat al-Khankī, n. d.

386 Maktab al-Buhuth al-Ijtima'iyah. Dirasah ijtima'iyah lil-
     usrah. Cairo: 1970.

387 Melikian, Levon H. "The Dethronement of the Father."
     Middle East Forum, 36 (Jan. 1960), 23-25. How the au-
     thority of the father has declined in the Middle East.

388 Muradpuri, M. "Problems of Marriage." Islamic Litera-
     ture, 16 (1970), 281-285.

389 Murphy, Robert F., and Leonard Kasden. "The Structure of
     Parallel Cousin Marriage." American Anthropologist,
     61 (Feb. 1959), 17-29. Description of Bedouin social
     structure.

390 Mus'ad, Luwis. Kaifa tabni al 'a'ilah. Cairo: Maktab al-
     anjlu-al-misriyah, 1948.

391 Mustafa, 'Abd al-Latif. Hayyat al-zawjin. Cairo: n. p.,
     1324 A. H. (1906/1907).

392 N. L. "La Dot, un symbole dénaturé." Révolution Africaine,
     104 (Jan. 23, 1965), 9.

393 Nahas, M. Kamel. "The Family in the Arab World." Mar-
     riage and Family Living, 16 (1954), 293-300. Reprinted
     in Ailon Shiloh, ed., People and Culture of the Middle
     East (New York: Random House, 1969).

394 Najarian, Pergrouzhi. "Adjustments of the Family and Pat-
     terns of Family Living." In Actes du XVIIe Congrès In-
     ternational de Sociologie. Beirut: Institut International
     de Sociologie, 1958; 425-448. Also in Journal of Social
     Issues, 3 (1959), 28-44.

395 _____. "Changing Patterns of Arab Family Life." Middle
     East Forum, 1 (Jan. 1960), 11-17.

396 Patai, Raphael. "Cousin-Right in Middle Eastern Marriages."
     South Western Journal of Anthropology, Winter, 1955,
     371-390.

397 _____. "Cousin-Right in Middle Eastern Marriages." In
     Abdulla A. M. Lutfiyya and Charles W. Churchill, eds.
     Readings in Middle Eastern Societies and Cultures. The
     Hague: Mouton, 1970.

398 _____. Sex and Family in the Bible and the Middle East.
     New York: Doubleday and Co., 1959. The continuity of
     customs and laws in the Middle East.

399 Prémare, L. de. "Ethique musulmane et relations sociales
     dans la famille maghrébine. " Unpublished master's thesis
     (psychology), Aix-en-Provence University, 1973.

400 Prothro, Edwin Terry, and Lutfy Najib Diab. Changing Fam-
     ily Patterns in the Arab East. Beirut: American Uni-
     versity of Beirut, 1974.

401 Qaddura, Zahia. "The Concept of the Islamic Family. " Pa-
     per delivered at the Seminar on the Status of Woman in
     the Islamic Family, Cairo, Dec. 20-22, 1975.

402 al-Qasir, Malihah 'Awni. Asl al-'a´ilah. Baghdad: n.p. ,
     1964.

403 al-Qattan, Manna' Khalil. Nizam al-usrah fi al-islam.
     Riyadh: Dar al-thaqafah al-islamiyah, 1951.

404 Ripinsky, M. "Middle Eastern Kinship as an Expression of
     a Culture Environment System. " Muslim World, 3 (July
     1968), 225-241.

405 Rizq Allah, Iskandar. "The Place of Marriage in Society" (in
     Arabic). al-Muqtataf, Dec. 1886, 141-44.

406 al-Sadat, Sakinah, ed. al-Mar´ah wa al-bayt, dalil al-mar´ah
     ila al-jamal, al-anaqah, al-bayt al-hadith. Cairo: Dar
     al-'arabiyah lil tiba'ah wa-al-nashr wa-al-a'lam, 1972.
     A book of advice to women: they should not try to be
     beautiful dolls but use their brains and administer their
     home soundly.

407 al-Sadr, Husayn al-Sayyid Muhammad Hadi. Fi qadaya al-
     zawaj wa-al-usrah. al-Najaf: Matba'at al-adab, 1970.
     Deals with legal, matrimonial, and familial issues.

408 al-Sa'i, Ibrahim Zaki. Al-Hayah al-jinsiyah bayna al-rajul
     wa-al-mar´ah. Alexandria: Dar al-sharq al-awsat lil-
     tiba'ah wa-al-nashr, 1967.

409 Sa'id, Muhammad Mazhar. al-Usrah wa al-mujtama'. Cairo:
     n.p. , 1964.

410 Salhim, 'Azizah. "The Necessity of an Agreement Between
     the Behaviors and Tempers of the Spouses" (in Arabic).
     al-Mar´ah, 2 (Feb. 1961), 21.

411 al-Sharqawi, 'Uthman al-Sayyid. al-Islam wa-al-hayah al-
     zawjiyah. Cairo: Dar al-Katib al-'arabi, 1967.

412 al-Shintinawi, Ahmad. 'Adat al-zawaj wa-sha'a´iruhu. Cairo:
     Dar al-ma'arif, 1957.

413 al-Siba'i, Muhammad. Qanun al-zawaj al-hadith. Cairo:
     Matba'at al-sa'adah, 1919. A thick book concerned with
     all aspects of marriage, pregnancy and the education of
     children.

414 Veli, H. Il fidanzamento e le nozze nell'Islam. Rome:
     Casa Ed. Italia, 1914.

415 Wafi, 'Ali 'Abd al-Wahid. al-Usrah wa-al-mujtama'. Cairo:
     Maktabat nahdah Misr, 1966.

416 Wajjaj, al-Husayn. "Marriage in Islam" (in Arabic). al-
     Iman, Aug.-Sept. 1966, 17-21.

417 Wood, L. A. "An Inquiry Into the Preference for Parallel
     Cousin Marriage Among the Contemporary Arabs." Un-
     published Ph.D. dissertation, Columbia University, 1959.

418 Yaljin, Miqdad. al-Bayt al-islami kama yanbaghi an yakun.
     Cairo: Dar al-Hilal, 1972.

419 Youssef, N. "Differential Labor Force Participation of Wo-
     men in Latin America and Middle Eastern Countries:
     The Influence of Family Characteristics." Social Forces,
     2 (Dec. 1972), 135-153. Why Middle Eastern women
     work proportionally less than Latin American women.
     Includes statistical data.

420 Zanati, Mahmud Sallam. Ikhtilat al-jinsayn 'inda al-'arab.
     Alexandria: Dar al-Jami'ah al-misriyah, 1959.

421 _____. Ta'addud al-zawjat lada al-shu'ub al-Ifriqiyah.
     Cairo: Dar al-ma'arif, 1963.

                              Family Law

422 'Abd al-Wahid, Mustafa. al-Usrah fi al-islam, 'ard 'amm
     li-nizam al-usrah fi daw'al-Kitab wa-al-Sunnah. Cairo:
     Maktabat al-mutanabbi, 1972. The family in Islam: a
     general presentation of family law in the light of the
     Qur'an and the Tradition.

423 Abu al-Nur, Muhammad al-Ahmadi. Manhhaj al-Sunnah fi al-
     zawaj. Cairo: Dar al-turath al-'arabi, 1972.

424 Abu Zahrah, Muhammad. Muhadarat fi 'aqd al-zawaj wa-
     atharuhu. Cairo: Jami'at al-duwal al-'arabiyah, Ma'had
     al-dirasat al-'arabiyah al-'ulyah, 1971. Lectures on
     marriage contracts and their effects.

425 'Amir, 'Abd al-'Aziz. Khawatir hawla qanun al-usrah fi al-
     Islam. Beirut: Jami'at Bairut al-'arabiyah, 1962.

Thoughts about family law in Islam.

426 Anderson, James N. D. Changing Law in Developing Coun-
     tries. New York: Frederick Praeger, 1963. Three of
     these essays deal with the reform of family law in Islam.

427 _____. "Invalid and Void Marriages in Hanafi Law." Bul-
     letin of the Schools of Oriental & African Studies, 13
     (1950), 357-66.

428 _____. Islamic Law in the Modern World. New York:
     New York University Press, 1959. One of the five es-
     says deals with Islamic marriage law.

429 _____. "Recent Developments in Sharia Law." The Mus-
     lim World, 42 (1952), 33-47. Why reforms of inheri-
     tance laws are slower than reforms of marriage and di-
     vorce laws.

430 Badran, Badran Abu al-'Aynayn. Ahkam al-zawaj wa-al-
     talaq fi al-Islam. Cairo: Dar al-ma'arif, 1964. The
     revised and augmented third edition of a standard work
     on Islamic marriage law.

431 al-Bahansawi, Salim. "Family Laws Between the Lack of
     Women's Strength and the Ulama's Helplessness" (in
     Arabic). al-Mujtama', 275 (Nov. 1975).

432 Borrmans, M. "Statut personnel et droit familial en pays
     musulman." Proche Orient Chrétien, 2 (1973), 133-47.
     A brief review of all the new family codes in Muslim
     countries.

433 Brunschvig, R. "De la filiation maternelle en droit musul-
     man." Studia Islamica, 9 (1958), 49-60.

434 Bultaji, Muhammad. Dirasat fi ahkam al-usrah. Cairo:
     Maktabat al-habab, 1974. Comparative studies of family
     laws both shar'i and non-shar'i.

435 Castro, Francesco. "Illiceità della fecondazione artificiale
     in diritto musulmano secondo una recente pubblicazione
     dello Shaykh Muhammad Gawad Mughniyah." Oriente
     Moderno, 4 (1974), 222-225.

436 Chabbi, Belgacem. "Réflexion sur la condition juridique de
     la femme arabo-musulmane; matriarcat et concubinage."
     Paper delivered at the Neuvième Congrès de l'Institut
     International de Droit d'Expression Française, Tunis,
     May 27-June 2, 1974.

437 Chehata, Chafik. "L'Evolution moderne du droit de la famille
     en pays d'Islam." Revue des Etudes Islamiques, 1

(1969), 103-114.

438 _____. "La Conception de la famille musulmane dans les
récentes réformes législatives en matière de mariage."
Rapports généraux du VII Congrès International de droit
comparé de 1966. Stockholm. 55-66.

439 Durupty, M. "La Convention de New York du 10 décembre
1962 sur le consentement au mariage, l'âge minimum du
mariage et l'enregistrement des mariages." Revue Tunisienne de Droit, 1968, 45-51.

440 al-Faghali, Bakhus. Fi al-zawaj. Beirut: al-Rabitah al-
kahanutiyah, 1959. A commentary of the new 1949 marriage law and its comparison with Western marriage
laws.

441 Gannagé, P. "L'Evolution du droit de la famille au Proche-
Orient et en Afrique du Nord." Travaux et Jours, 4
(1962), 53-68.

442 Ghasasi, al-'Arbi. "Family in muslim law." (In Arabic),
Da'wat al-haqq, 9 (Nov. 1971), 20-24.

443 Guémard, F. La Condition juridique des femmes mariées en
droit musulman. Aix en Provence: n.p., 1915.

444 Hadidi, Mustafa Muhammad. "Marriage and Dowry in Islam"
(in Arabic). al-Hadi al-Islami, 1 (April 1967), 85-87.

445 Hasab Allah, 'Ali. al-Zawaj fi al-shari'ah al-islamiyah.
Cairo: Dar al-fikr al-'arabi, 1971.

446 Hasan, Lutfi. al-Zawaj fi al-Islam wa-azwaj al-nabi Muhammad. Cairo: Matba'at al-bahiyah al-misriyah, 1938.
The duties of the muslim woman and a short biography
of each one of the Prophet's wives.

447 Hasan, Zaynab. "The Family Between Islamic and Positive
Law." al-Musawwar, June 18, 1975, 72-74.

448 Ibrahim, Ahmad. "Recent Developments in Muslim Family
Law in the Arab Countries and in Pakistan." World
Muslim League Magazine, 12 (1967), 10-15.

449 Ibrahim, Muhammad Isma'il. Min shari'at al-Islam wa-
Sunnatih, al-zawaj. Cairo: Dar al-fikr al-'arabi, 1971.

450 al-Juburi, Husayn Khalaf. Firaq al-nikah wa-bayan ahkamiha
fi al-shari'ah al-islamiyah. Baghdad: Dar al-hurriyah
lil-tiba'ah, 1974.

451 Kerrou, Hédi. "The Marriage of the Muslim Woman With a

Non Muslim Man and the New York Convention" (in Arabic). al-'Amal, 4773 (Jan. 21, 1971), 6; 4774 (Jan. 22,
1971), 4; 4775 (Jan. 23, 1971), 3, 9.

452 Khalid, Hasan. Ahkam al-ahwal al-shakhsiyah fi al-shari'ah
      al-islamiyah. Beirut: al-Maktab al-tijari lil tiba'ah
      wa-al-nashr, 1964.

453 Khuda Bakhsh, Salahuddin. Marriage and Family Life Among
      the Arabs. Lahore: Orientalia, 1953.

454 Lathan, J. "Ibn 'Abd al-Ra'uf on the Law of Marriage: A
      Matter of Interpretation. " Islamic Quarterly, 1 (1971),
      3-16.

455 Mar'i, Ibrahim al-Disuqi. Bahth Mujaz hawla tanzim al-
      usrah wa-ra´y al-Islam fih. Cairo: Idarat al-masajid,
      1967. The religious aspects of birth-control.

456 al-Nahi, Salah al-Din. Mudawwanah qawanin al-ahwal al-
      shakhsiyah al-hadithah. Baghdad: Sharikat al-tab' wa-
      al-nashr al-ahliyah, 1958.

457 Qurra'ah, Mahmud 'Ali. al-Hayah al-zawjiah min al-
      wajihatain al-tashri'iyah wa-al-ijtima'iyah. Cairo: Dar
      al-kitab al-'arabi, 1947.

458 Roussier, J. "L'Annulation du mariage vicié en droit
      musulman malékite et le sort de la dot. " Revue Algé-
      rienne, 72 (1956), 113-127.

459 _____. "La Preuve du mariage en droit musulman. "
      Recueils de la Société Jean Bodin, 18 (1963), 201-204.

460 al-Sanhuri, Muhammad Ahmad Faraj. al-Usrah fi al-tashri'
      al-islami. Cairo: Ministry of National Guidance, n.d.
      A very conservative work.

461 Schacht, Joseph. "Adultery as an Impediment to Marriage in
      Islamic and in Canon Law. " Proceedings of the 22nd
      Congress of Orientalists, Istanbul, September 15-22,
      1951. Vol. II. Leiden: E. J. Brill, 1957, 237-241.

462 al-Shahawi, Muhammad 'Abd al-Fattah. al-Usrah fi al-
      mujtama' bayna al-shari'ah al-islamiyah. Cairo: Dar
      al-'ilm, 1962.

463 Swan, G. "Monogamy in Islam. " Moslem World, 3 (1913),
      75-77.

464 Tannumra, T. "The Institution of Marriage in Islam" (in
      Japanese). Chuto-tsuho, 215 (March 1974), 26-32.

465 al-Tantawi, Mahmud Muhammad. al-Ahwal al-shakhsiyah fi
     al-shari'ah al-islamiyah. Cairo: Dar al-nahdah al-
     'arabiyah, 1972.

466 Verdier, Jean Maurice. "Les Grandes Tendances de l'évo-
     lution du droit des personnes et de la famille dans les
     pays musulmans." Revue Algérienne des Sciences Juri-
     diques, Economiques et politiques, 4 (Dec. 1968), 1051-
     1063.

Divorce

467 Abdel Hamid, Ibrahim. "Dissolution of Marriage in Islamic
     Law." Islamic Quarterly, 3 (1956), 165-175, 215-223;
     4 (1957), 3-10, 57-65, 97-113.

468 Ali, Muhammad. "Divorce in Islam." Islamic Review, 37
     (Aug. 1949), 5-9.

469 Anderson, J. N. D. "Recent Developments in shari'a Law,
     IV." Muslim World, 41 (1951), 186-8. About dowry,
     alimony, and custody of children.

470 _____. "Reforms in the Law of Divorce in the Muslim
     World." Studia Islamica, 1970, 41-52.

471 Bouarifi, A. "Les Divorces: un fléau." Révolution Afri-
     caine, 257 (Jan. 18, 1968), 18-21.

472 Chehata, Chafik. "Le Droit de répudiation (talaq) dans le
     droit positif des pays arabes." Proceedings, of the 27th
     International Congress of Orientalists, 1967, 1971. 249-
     250.

473 Dabbagh, 'Abd al-'Aziz. "Divorce Does Not Require a Judg-
     ment" (in Arabic). Da'wat al-haqq, 7 (April-May
     1966), 19-22. Against the reforms of Tunisian family
     law.

474 "Le Divorce: les faits." Révolution Africaine, 101 (Jan. 2,
     1965), p. 4-5.

475 "Does a Trip to Mecca (Outside of Hajj Time) Deprive the
     Wife of Her Alimony?" (in Arabic). al-Ahram, Nov. 19,
     1974, p. 8, col. 4.

476 Hobbalah, Mahmoud. "Marriage, Divorce, and Inheritance in
     Islamic Law." George Washington Law Review, 22 (Oct.
     1953), 24-31.

477 al-Husari, Ahmad. al-Nikah wa al-qadaya al-muta'alliqah
     bih. Cairo: Maktabat al-Kuliyah al-Azhariyah, 1967.

478 Mahmud, 'Abd al-Majid. Hady al-Islam fi al-zawaj wa-al
furqah. Cairo: Maktabat al-shabab, 1972.

479 Miku, 'Abd al-Nabi. "Divorce Must Be Judged" (in Arabic).
Da'wat al haqq, 9-10 (July-Aug. 1966), 19-24. An
answer to Dabbagh's article (see no. 473).

480 Wafi, 'Ali 'Abd al-Wahid. Bayna al-ta'ah wa-ta'addud al-
zawjat wa-al-talaq fi al-Islam. Cairo: Mu'assassat al-
matbu'at al-hadithah, 1960.

Family Planning

481 Abu Zahrah, Muhammad. "Family Planning and Birth Control." Al-Azhar Academy of Islamic Research. The
Second Conference of the Academy of Islamic Research.
Cairo, 1965, 195-225. The author reviews legal reforms
in Arab countries. Very conservative in outlook; against
divorce reform and birth control.

482 Djemal, H., and A. Bourani. "Analyse comparative des
questionnaires sur la planification familiale dans les pays
arabo-musulmans." Revue Tunisienne des Sciences Sociales, 17-18 (1969), 337-360.

483 Farag, Fakhry M. al-Mar'ah wa-falsafat al-tanasuliyat.
Cairo: Elias A. Elias, 1924.

484 El-Hamamsy, Laila Shukry. "Islamic Society and Family
Planning: Are They Incompatible?" UNICEF News, 78
(Dec. 1973-Jan. 1974), 36-41.

485 "Is It Permissible for Female Pilgrims to Take Contraceptive Pills During the Hajj?" (in Arabic). al-Ahram,
Dec. 7, 1974, p. 10, col. 1.

486 J. G. "L'Islam face à la prévention des naissances." Confluent, 50-52 (1965), 302-314.

487 el Madani, Hédi. "Le Contrôle des naissances et l'Islam."
Confluent, 50-52 (1965), 323-327.

488 Makdur, Muhammad Salam. Nazrat al-Islam ila tanzim al-
nasl. Cairo: Dar al-nahdah al-'arabiyah, 1966. Family
planning in Islam.

489 Mar'i, Ibrahim al-Disuqi. Brief Study of Islam and Family
Planning. Cairo: Egyptian Family Planning Association, 1970. A translation of his Arabic book in which
the author endeavored to show that Islam does not oppose
family planning.

490 Nasiri, M. "A View of Family Planning in Islam Legisla-
     tion. " Islamic Review and Arab Affairs, 3 (March-April
     1969), 11-18.

491 Nazer, Isam. Islam and Family Planning. 2 vols. Beirut:
     IPPF, 1974.

492 Qamhawi, Wali. Tanzim al-nasl. Beirut: Dar al-'ilm lil-
     malayin, 1954.

493 Schieffelin, Olivia, ed. Muslim Attitudes Toward Family
     Planning. New York: Population Council, 1967. State-
     ments of religious and political leaders, excerpts from
     governmental documents and articles defining and explain-
     ing attitudes toward family planning in Muslim countries.

494 Schultz, T. Paul. "Fertility Patterns and Their Determi-
     nants in the Arab Middle East. " In Charles A. Cooper
     and Sidney S. Alexander, eds. , Economic Development
     and Population Growth in the Middle East. New York:
     American Elsevier Pub. Co. , 1972; 401-500. The au-
     thors recommend accrued female education as a means
     to implement birth control.

495 Seklani, Mahmoud. "La Fécondité dans les pays arabes:
     données numériques, attitudes et comportements. " Popu-
     lation, 15 (1960), 831-856.

496 al-Sharabasi, Ahmad. al-Din wa-tanzim al-usrah. Cairo:
     al-'alaqah al-'ammah, 1966.

497 _____. Islam and Family Planning. Cairo: Egyptian
     Family Planning Association, 1969. A very poor trans-
     lation of the preceding book. Gives a religious justifi-
     cation of birth control.

498 Zerruk, A. K. M. "Procreation and Family Planning in Is-
     lam. " Voice of Islam, 6 (1961), 311-316.

Polygamy

499 Abu-Gush, S. "Notes on Polygamy" (in Arabic). Majallah
     al-Akhbar al-Islamiyah, 3-4 (May 1971), 68-75.

500 'Attar, 'Abd al-Nasir Tawfiq. Dirasah fi qadiyat ta 'addud
     al-zawjat min al-nawahi al-ijtima'iyah wa-al-diniyah wa-
     al-qanuniyah. Cairo: Majma' al-buhuth al-islamiyah,
     1968. Studies on polygamy in its social, religious and
     legal aspects.

501 Berger-Vachon, V. "En pays d'Islam: l'interdiction de la
     polygamie est-elle religieusement licite?" Annales de

l'Université de Paris, 28 (1958), 281-93.

502   Daura, Bello.   "The Limit of Polygamy in Islam. " Journal
           of Islamic and Comparative Law, 3 (1969), 21-26.

503   Gallichan, Walter M.   Women under Polygamy.   New York:
           Dodd, Mead & Co. , 1915.   A world study of polygamy,
           concerned mostly with Muslim peoples.

504   Hinchcliffe, D.   "Polygamy in Traditional and Contemporary
           Islamic Law. "   Islam and the Modern Age, 3 (1970), 69-
           90.

505   Memmi, Albert.   "Polygamie et interprétation des civilisa-
           tions. "   Bulletin Economique de Tunisie, 49 (Feb. 1951),
           66-80.

506   "La Polygamie en Islam. "   Révolution et Travail, 74 (Jan.
           1965), 16.

507   Shaltut, Mahmud.   "The Plurality of Wives (Polygamy)" (in
           Arabic).   Majallat al Azhar, 1 (1960), 4-13.   The highest
           Egyptian Muslim authority opposes legal limitation of
           polygamy.

508   _____.   "Plurality of Wives in the Light of Social Cases:
           A Plan for the Limitation of Plurality" (in Arabic).
           Majallat al-Azhar, 2 (1960), 6-15.

509   Zafer, M. J.   "Polygamy. "   Islamic Literature, 7 (1955),
           423-429.   In defense of the practice.

                          Seclusion of Women

510   Cleugh, James.   Ladies of the Harem.   London: F. Muller,
           1955.

511   Cooper, Elizabeth.   The Harim and the Purdah.   New York:
           Century Co. , 1915?   The first four chapters are de-
           voted to a study of the Egyptian woman.

512   Dans l'ombre du harem.   Paris: Editions de la Revue
           Blanche, 1898.   A Circassian lady who prefers to re-
           main anonymous advocates the maintenance of the harem
           system because Oriental women are too irresponsible to
           take care of themselves.

513   Lens, A. R. de.   Le Harem entr'ouvert.   Paris: Calmann-
           Levy, 1919.   Social life in Morocco and Tunisia.   The
           author, a French woman, spent many years in the
           Maghreb.

514   Peters, Emrys. "Consequences of the Segregation of the
      Sexes Among the Arabs. " Paper presented at the Medi-
      terranean Social Science Council Conference, Athens,
      1966.

515   Reichardt, Annie. Girl Life in the Harem: A True Account
      of Girl Life in Oriental Climes. London: J. Ouseley
      Ltd. , 1908. The description of a few months in the life
      of a young girl in Damascus, at the time of her marriage.
      The book offers a detailed description of Oriental life,
      although it betrays prejudices and inexactitudes about Is-
      lam.

516   Tillion, Germaine. Le Harem et les cousins. Paris: Seuil,
      1966. A French ethnologist studies endogamic marriage
      in Mediterranean society, a pertinent analysis which
      raised strong criticism in some quarters.

517   Van Sommer, Annie, and Samuel M. Zwemer, eds. Day-
      light in the Harem. Edinburgh: Oliphant, Anderson &
      Ferrier, 1911.

518   Wessein-Szumlanska, Marcelle. Hors du Harem. Paris:
      Felix Juvens, 1905. Another plea in favor of the harem
      as the best place for Eastern women to stay since they
      are unable to fend for themselves.

(7) BIOGRAPHIES

519   'Abd Allah, Sufi and Nathmi Luqa. Nawabigh al-nisa .
      Cairo: Dar al-Hilal, 1964.

520   Ahmad, Anwar. Nisa´ khalidat. Cairo: al-Dar al-qawmiyah
      lil-tiba'ah wa-al-nashr, 1965.

521   Hasan, Muhammad Kamil. Sutur ma'a al-'azimat. Beirut:
      Dar al-buhuth al-'ilmiyah, 1969.

522   Kahhalah, 'Umar Rida. A'lam al-nisa´ fi 'alamay al-'Arab
      wa-al-Islam. Damascus: al-Matba'ah al-hashimiyah,
      1959, 5 vols. Extensive biographical dictionary of
      learned women, originally published in Cairo in 1940.

523   al-Kumyali, Sadiq. Shakhsiyat al-mar´ah fi al-Islam. Hush
      al-Rafiqah, 1972.

524   al-Kuzbari, Salma al-Haffar. Nisa´ mutafawwiqat, Beirut:
      Dar al-'ilm lil-malayin, 1961. Biographies of famous
      women, the only contemporary Arab woman being sing-
      er Umm Kulthum.

525   Musbah Haidar, Sharifa.   Arabesque.   London: Hutchinson,
      1954.   The autobiography of the daughter of the Sherif of
      Mecca, who spent most of her youth in Istanbul.

526   Sakakini, Widad aud Tamadh Tawfiq.   Nisa´ shahirat min al-
      sharq wa-al-gharb.   Cairo: Dar ihya´ al-kutub al-
      'arabiyah, 1959.   The first half of the book is devoted
      to Eastern women and includes the lives of ten Arab
      women outstanding in literature, social services and the
      arts.

(8) EDUCATION

527   Adibe, Nasrine.   "How the Arab Women are Educated."
      Paper delivered at the Conference on Development in the
      Arab World, New York, Oct. 1-3, 1976.

528   Algaiara, A.   "Education and the Arab Woman" (in Arabic).
      al-Qalam, 2:3 (Nov. 1965), 32-43.

529   Bashmil, Muhammad Ahmad.   La ya fatat al-hijaz!   Beirut:
      n.p., 1962.   A guide book of conduct for the Muslim
      woman.

530   al-Bayhani, Muhammad ibn Salim al-Kaddadi.   Ustadh al-
      mar´ah.   Cairo: Matba'at al-Madani, 1973.   A guide
      for Muslim women.

530a al-Bustani, Butros.   "The Education of Women" (in Arabic).
      al-Rawa´i', 22 (1929), 1-24.   Text of a lecture given in
      1849, one of the earliest "modern" statements in favor
      of female education.

531   Chaudhry, A. G.   "The Place of Women in Higher Islamic
      Education."   Iqbal, 3 (1953), 68-101.

532   Dali, Yahia Mohamed.   "L'Evolution des musulmans par
      l'instruction de la femme."   En Terre d'Islam, April
      1928, 71-73.

533   Gilmour, Andrew.   The Necessity of Scriptural Education, in
      Connection with the Condition and Character of Females
      in Pagan and Mahommedan Countries.   Greenock: A.
      Laing, 1839.   One of the earliest work by a Presbyteri-
      an missionary bent on converting Muslims, it includes
      all the current prejudices of the time.

534   Jreisat, Jamil, and Andrea Brunais.   "Women's Education in
      a Developing Arab Society."   Paper delivered at the
      Conference on Development in the Arab World, New York,
      Oct. 1-3, 1976.

535 Mas'ad, M. N. 'Woman and Education" (in Arabic).
     Masarra, 24 (1950), 542-546.

536 al-Sa'id, al-Sa'id Mustafa. al-Mar'ah wa-al-ta'al im al-
     jama'i. Alexandria: Jami'at al-iskindiriyah, 1955.

537 El-Sanabary, Nagat Morsi. "Comparative Study of the Dis-
     parities of Educational Opportunities for Girls in the
     Arab States. " Unpublished Ph.D. dissertation, Univer-
     sity of California, Berkeley, 1973. Attributes the lag
     in girls' education to various factors, among them the
     traditional cultural barrier to women's education and
     economic constraints of developing countries.

538 _____. 'Female Education and Manpower Needs in the
     Arab World. " Paper delivered at the Conference on is-
     sues in Human Resource Development, Kuwait: Dec. 28-
     31, 1975.

539 Shahin, A. "Towards a Practical, Rational Upbringing" (in
     Arabic). al-Ma'rifah, 103 (1970), 3-17.

540 "University Women in a Changing Society. " Panel discussion,
     Conference for Women, American University of Beirut,
     April 22, 1967.

541 Vivarez, Mario. L'Instruction et la femme musulmane.
     Algiers: n.p., 1895.

542 Wahaib, Abdul Amir. "Education and Status of Women in the
     Middle East with Special Reference to Egypt, Tunisia and
     Iraq. " Unpublished Ph.D. dissertation, Southern Illinois
     University, 1970. A short dissertation of five chapters.
     The situation in each country is examined in a separate
     chapter.

542a Youssef, Nadia Haggag. "Education and the Upsurge of Fe-
     male Modernism in the Muslim World. " Journal of In-
     ternational Affairs, 2 (1977), n.p.

(9) LITERARY WORKS BY OR ABOUT WOMEN

543 'Abd al-Rahman, 'A'ishah (Bint al-Shati'). al-Adibah al-
     'arabiyah ams wa-al-yawm. Cairo: Jami'at Omdurman
     al-Islamiyah, 1967.

544 _____. al-Sha'irah al-'arabiyah al-mu'asirah. Cairo:
     Jami'at al-duwal al-'arabiyah: Ma'had al-dirasat al-
     'arabiyah al-'aliyah, 1962/63.

545 Ben Halima, Hamadi. Les Principaux Thèmes du théâtre

arabe contemporain (de 1914 à 1960). Tunis: Publication de l'Université de Tunis, Faculté des Lettres et des Sciences Humaines, 1969. The author deals principally with Egyptian plays, see "Les Thèmes de l'affectivité," 47-105, and "Les Thèmes sociaux," 165-210.

546 Boisnard, Magali. Les Endormies. Paris: Sansot, 1909.

547 Boullata, Kamal, ed. Women of the Fertile Crescent: An Anthology of Arab Women's Poems. Washington, D. C.: Three Continents, 1976. Includes a biobibliography of each poet.

548 Catrice, Paul. "Femmes écrivains d'Afrique du Nord et du Proche-Orient." L'Afrique et l'Asie, 59 (1962), 23-44.

549 al-Ibyari, Fathi. al-Jins wa al-waqi'iyah fi al-qissah. Cairo: al-dar al-qawmiyah lil-tiba'ah wa-al-nashr, 1966.

550 _____. al-Umm fi al-adab. Cairo: al-Dar al-qawmiyah lil-tiba'ah wa-al-nashr, 1966.

551 al Jindi, Anwar. Adab al-mar'ah al-'arabiyah. Cairo: Matba'at al-risalah, 196-? Gives succinct information on many feminine figures of the Egyptian press and literature.

552 Loya, Arieh. "Poetry as a Social Document: The Social Position of the Arab Woman as Reflected in the Poetry of Nizar Qabbani." International Journal of Middle East Studies, 4 (1975), 481-494.

553 Mahmud, Muhammad. al-Shi'r al-nisa'i al-'asri wa-shahirat nujumih. Cairo: Matba'at dar al-turqi, 1929. Gives a short biographical notice on Wardah al-Yaziji, 'A'ishah Taymur, Aminah Najib and Malak Hifni Nasif, with a few excerpts from their works.

554 al-Maqdisi, Anis. "Woman and Modern Arab Literature" (in Arabic). al-Abhath, March 1951, 19-34.

554a Mikhail, Mona N. Images of Islamic Women: Fact and Fiction. Washington, D. C.: Three Continents Press, 1978.

555 Qabbani, Nizar. Yawmiyat imra'a la mubaliya. Beirut: Manshurat Nizar Qabbani, 1969. The author assumes a female identity to write this book because Arab women are unable to speak for themselves to demand freedom to love.

556 Shalhat, Yusuf Basil. Fi al-lughah wa-al-ijtima'. Aleppo: Majallat al-dad, 1931. A collection of essays on language and sociology dealing with contemporary problems.

557 Wadi, Taha 'Imran. Surat al-mar´ah fi al-riwayah al-
        mu'asirah. Cairo: Markaz Kutub al-sharq, 1973.

558 Ware, Lewis. "The Male Imperative and Women's Emanci-
        pation in the Middle East. " Paper delivered at the Tenth
        Annual Meeting of the Middle East Studies Association,
        Los Angeles, November 10-13, 1976. An analysis of the
        views of Jurji Zaydan who, despite his liberalism, failed to
        come out strongly in favor of improving women's conditions.

(10) WOMEN'S CONGRESSES AND POLITICS

559 'Abd al-Rahman, 'A´ishah, (Bint al-Shati´). al-Mafhum al-
        Islami li-tahrir al-mar´ah. Cairo: Jami'at Omdurman
        al-Islamiyah, 1967.

560 Adham, Mahmud. "The Story of the Struggle of the Arab
        Woman for her Freedom" (in Arabic). Akhir Sa'ah.
        August 1975.

561 The Afro-Arab Inter-Parliamentary Women's Conference.
        "The Role of Women in Economic Development. " Cairo:
        May 18-23, 1974.

562 Afro-Asian Women's Conference. Reports, Messages,
        Speeches, Resolutions. Cairo: Amalgamated Press of
        Egypt, 1961.

563 "The Afro-Asian Women's Union Discusses the First Women's
        Parliamentary Conference" (in Arabic). al-Ahram, May
        12, 1974, p. 8, col. 2.

564 "Arab Women's Conference Held in Cairo During the Feast"
        (in Arabic). al-Ahram, Oct. 11, 1974, p. 14, col. 1.

565 "The Arab Women's Federation. " Women Today, June 1965,
        78-86.

566 "The Arab Women's League Started Yesterday Its Meeting to
        Which Participate 18 Arab Countries" (in Arabic). al-
        Ahram, Nov. 5, 1974, p. 8, col. 1.

567 Bensalem, Kamaleddine. "About the 7th Congress of the
        Union of Arab Women ... " (in Arabic). al-Shabab, 2
        (April-June 1971), 16.

568 Castagné, Joseph. "Le mouvement d'émancipation de la
        femme musulmane en Orient. " Revue des Etudes
        Islamiques, 3 (1929), 161-226.

569 Chadjaré, H. "Le Deuxième Congrès musulman général des

femmes d'Orient à Téhéran. Introduction: Le féminisme oriental. " Revue des Etudes Islamiques, 7 (1933), 45-48. [See also item 586.]

570   "Le Congrès féministe arabe de Beyrouth. " Revue de Presse, 71 (1963).

571   "Il congresso femminile di Baghdad. " Oriente Moderno, 11 (Nov. 1932), 525.

572   Drewes, Gerardus W. J. "The Beginning of the Emancipation of Women in the Arab World. " In Nederlands-Arabische Kring, 1955-1965. Leiden: Brill, 1966; 47-68. The impact of Qasim Amin's books.

573   Fahmy-Bey, Mme J. (Jehan d'Ivray). "L'Orient et le féminisme. " Le Lotus, 1 (April 1901), 46-50.

574   Fuleihan, Louise. "The Arab Women's Congress (Cairo) Dec. 10-20, 1944. " Moslem World, 4 (1945), 316-323.

575   al-Gamal, 'Ali Hamdi. "The Parliamentary Conference of Afro-Asian Women Defines the Role of Women in An Effective Afro-Asian Strategy" (in Arabic). al-Ahram, May 9, 1974, p. 5, col. 1.

576   Gaudry, M. "A propos du Congrès International des Femmes Méditerranéennes. " Afrique Française, 1932, 712-718.

577   Graziani, J. "The Momentum of the Feminist Movement in the Arab World. " Middle East Review, 2 (1974-75), 26-33.

578   "A Group of Women Among Arab Worker Delegates Meets in Tunis, Starting December 14, to Discuss Women's Working Conditions in the Arab World" (in Arabic). al-Ahram, Nov. 3, 1974, p. 10, col. 1.

579   Hussein, Aziza. "The Woman's International Year" (in Arabic). Education of Masses, 3 (May 1975), 133-150. Abstract in English, pp. 170-171.

580   "International Committee of Afro-Asian Women" (in Arabic). al-Ahram, Oct. 26, 1974, p. 8, col. 1.

581   International Islamic Conference, Rabat, Morroco, 1971. Islam and Family Planning. A Faithful Translation of the Arabic Edition of the Proceedings of the International Islamic Conference Held in Rabat (Morocco), December, 1971. Beirut: International Planned Parenthood Federation, Middle East and North Africa Region, 1974. 2 vols.

582   "La Journée internationale de la femme. " El-Djeich, 94

(March 1971), 45-46.

583   "La Journée internationale des femmes. " El-Djeich, 23
      (March 1965), 14-15.

584   "La Journée internationale des femmes. " L'Algérien en
      Europe, 166 (March 16-31, 1973), 13.

585   Lébédew, Olga de [Olga Lébédeva]. "Les Nouveaux Droits de
      la femme musulmane. " In Verhandlungen des XIII. In-
      ternationalen Orientalisten-Kongresses. Hamburg. Sep-
      tember, 1902. Leiden: E. J. Brill, 1904; 314-19.

586   Massé, H. Le Deuxième Congrès musulman général des
      femmes d'Orient à Téhéran. Paris: Geuthner, 1935.
      Reprint from Revue des Etudes Islamiques, 7 (1933), 49-
      141, 419-423. [See also item 569.]

587   al-Mu'tamar al-Islami. al-Islam wa-tanzim al-usrah. Bei-
      rut: International Planned Parenthood Federation, Middle
      East and North Africa Region, 1973. Religious aspects
      of birth control.

588   Mu'tamar al-Mar'ah al-'Arabiyah wa-al-Tanmiyah al-
      Qawmiyah. al-Taqrir al-niha'i. Cairo, 1972. A con-
      gress held in Cairo, September 24-30, 1972, organized
      by UNICEF in collaboration with the League of Arab
      States, Direction of Social Affairs and Youth, Interna-
      tional Center for Adult Vocational Education in the Arab
      World.

589   N'Daw, Aly Kheury. "Vers de nouveaux horizons. " Jeune
      Afrique, 712 (Aug. 31, 1974). About Panafrican women's
      organization and its new secretary, the Algerian Fathia
      Bettahar.

590   "L'Ordre du jour du comité exécutif du Congrès de l'Union
      féministe orientale. " En Terre d'Islam, 45 (1931), 120-
      124. The congress was held in Damascus in November
      1930.

591   "Parliamentary Conference of Women from Arab and African
      States in Cairo" (in Arabic). al-Ahram, Feb. 8, 1974,
      p. 8, col. 6.

592   Raccagni, Michelle. "A Background to Feminism in Egypt
      and Tunisia. " American Research Center in Egypt News-
      letter, 94 (1975), 9-10.

593   _____. "The Conference on the Role of Women in the
      Islamic Family. " American Research Center in Egypt
      Newsletter, 96 (1976), 14-17. The conference was or-
      ganized by the International Islamic Center for Population

Studies and Research of al-Azhar University in December 1975.

594 _____ . "Feminism in the Arab World: A Comparison Between Egypt and Tunisia. " Ph.D. dissertation in progress, New York University.

595 "Recommendations of the Second Congress of Arab Girl Scouts" (in Arabic). Jil wa Risalah, 2-3 (Aug. -Sept. 1968).

596 Rushdi, Inji, and Aminah Shafiq. "The Biggest Feminine Meeting in Cairo: The Afro-Asian Women Parliamentary Conference Convenes Tomorrow" (in Arabic). al-Ahram, May 17, 1974, p. 3.

597 Shafiq, Aminah. "The Afro-Asian Women Parliamentary Conference in its Second Day" (in Arabic). al-Ahram, May 20, 1974, p. 3, col. 1.

598 Thabit, Munirah. "La Jeunesse et le féminisme. " L'Egyptienne, 157 (July-Aug. 1939), 17-21. Speech of M. Thabit as the Egyptian delegate to the International Feminist Alliance Congres, 13 July, 1939.

599 Ulrix, A. "Féminisme et Islam. " Revue des Missions de l'Abbaye de Saint-André-lès-Bruges, 1938, 226ff.

600 'Uthman, Mahjah. "Women's Rights or National Liberation" (in Arabic). Ruz al-Yusuf, 2398 (May 27, 1974), 22-23.

601 Vacca, Virginia. "Il congresso femminile a Damasco. " Oriente Moderno, 1930, 360-61.

602 _____ . "Il congresso femminile di Baghdad. " Oriente Moderno, 1 (1932), 525.

603 _____ . "Il V congresso dell'Unione femminile araba a Beirut." Oriente Moderno, 6 (1934), 280-81.

604 _____ . "Ordini del giorno del comitato esecutivo del congresso dell'Unione femminile orientale. " Oriente Moderno, 1 (1931), 55-56.

605 Wanisi, Zuhur. "About the 7th Congress of the General Union of the Arab Women" (in Arabic). El-Djeich, 87 (June 1971), 36-37.

II

ALGERIA

(1) GENERAL

606   "A la rencontre de deux civilisations. " El-Moudjahid, March
      11, 1967.

607   Abu Hamida, Ibrahim. "Isn't Like This That We Want Our
      Women to Be?" (in Arabic). El-Djeich, 38 (May 1967),
      19-21.

608   "L'adjouza au banc des accusées. " El-Moudjahid, Jan. 26,
      1968.

609   "L'Adolescente algérienne. " Révolution Africaine, Dec. 12,
      1964, 6-7.

610   Algeria. Ministère de l'Information. The Algerian Women.
      Algiers, 197-. Edited by the Ministry of Information in
      collaboration with Malek Haddad for the text, and
      Dominique Darbois, Louisa Ghelem and Farid Djemaa
      for the pictures.

611   "Algeria Celebrates the Day of the African Woman" (in Ara-
      bic). Ahdath wa-watha'iq, 26 (Aug. 1, 1967), 7-10.

612   Aminah. "Encounter With Najat Amudi" (in Arabic). El-
      Moudjahid, 598 (Feb. 6, 1972), 22-23.

613   _____. "Inspiration from March 8" (in Arabic). El-
      Djazairia, April 1970, 17-20.

614   _____. "When Woman Holds the Carte Blanche" (in Ara-
      bic). El-Djazairia, Jan. 1970, 11-13.

615   Amrouche, Fadhma Aïth Mansour. Histoire de ma vie.
      Paris: Domaine Maghrébin, 1968. The mother of writ-
      ers Jean and Marguerite Amrouche tells about her life
      and constant struggle against poverty and prejudices.

616   Auclert, Hubertine. Les Femmes arabes en Algérie. Paris:

Société d'Editions Littéraires, 1900.

617 Benatia, Farouk. "La Délinquance juvénile féminine." Algérie-Actualité, 173 (Feb. 9, 1969), 67.

618 Benhadji Serradj, M. "Quelques Usages féminins populaires à Tlemcen; suivis d'une note sur quelques procédés divinatoires traditionels dans la région de Tlemcen." IBLA, 55 (1951), 279-92.

619 Blanc, A. "L'Evolution intellectuelle, morale et sociale de la jeune fille musulmane en Algérie." Revue de Psychologie des Peuples, 13 (1958), 306-323.

620 Boisnard, Magali. "Nos Soeurs musulmanes." Bulletin de la Sociéte de Géographie d'Alger, 4th trim., 1909.

621 Boudjédra, Rachid. La Vie quotidienne en Algérie. Paris: Hachette, 1971. A lively description of the daily life of a couple of small shopkeepers.

622 Bugéja, Marie. Nos Soeurs musulmanes. Algiers: Editions France-Afrique, 1931.

623 "Caractéristiques et rôle de la femme dans la société." El-Moudjahid, March 13, 1967.

624 Carret, Jacques. La Femme musulmane. Algiers, 1958. Reprint from Bulletin de Liaison et de Documentation of the Service de l'Action Administrative et Economique de la Délégation Générale du Gouvernement en Algérie, no. 57-10/58-15.

625 Chelli, Mounira. "Les Mémoires d'une algérienne rangée." Jeune Afrique, 334 (June 4, 1967), 66-67.

626 Daumas, Eugène. "La Femme arabe." Revue Africaine, 56 (1912), 1-154.

627 _____. Women of North Africa. San Diego, Calif.: A. G. H. Kreiss, 1943. General Daumas participated in the conquest of Algeria.

628 Djedda, Zohra. "La Promotion sociale de la femme algérienne." Révolution et Travail, 106 (March 3, 1966), 5.

629 "Le donne algerine." Rassegna del Mondo Arabo, 1 (Jan. 1969), 25-40.

630 "Dossier sur le problème de la femme algérienne." Information Rapide 4 (Nov. 1963). Data issued by the "Social Secretariat" of Algiers.

631 "Les Droits de la femme dans une civilisation. " El-Moudja-
     hid, Feb. 21, 1967.

632 "The Emigrant Woman and the Pressing Necessity to
     Strengthen National Personality and Culture" (in Arabic).
     Afaq, 40 (Feb. -March 1973), 30-33.

633 Etudes Sociales Nord-Africaines. La Femme musulmane.
     Paris: Cahiers Nord-Africains 27, 1958.

634 "L'Evolution de la femme. " El-Moudjahid, March 10, 1967.

635 "L'Evolution de la femme algérienne. " Revue de Presse, 75
     (1963).

636 Fauque, L. P. "La Femme dans la société algérienne. "
     L'Afrique et l'Asie, 66, 2-14; Hommes et Migrations, 698
     (June 15, 1967), 1-10.

637 "La Femme africaine. " Révolution Africaine, 182 (July 28,
     1966).

638 La Femme algérienne. Paris: Etudes Sociales Nord-Afri-
     caines, 1969.

639 "La Femme dans le domaine social. " La République, Nov.
     19, 1968.

640 "La Femme et la jeunesse dans l'Algérie d'aujourd'nui. "
     France-Algérie, 17 (April-May 1967), 8-11.

641 "La Femme musulmane. " El-Djeich, 24 (April 1965), 29-31;
     25 (May 1965), 28-30.

642 "La Femme retrouvera sa place. " El-Djeich, 48 (April
     1967), 14-19.

643 "La Femme sera le devenir du monde arabe: ce que pense
     une universitaire algérienne. Propos d'Assia Djebar re-
     ceuillis par Monique Hennebelle. " L'Afrique Littéraire
     et Artistique, Feb. 1969.

644 "For a Better Comprehension of Relations Between Men and
     Women" (in Arabic). El-Djazairia, 31 (1973), 17.

645 Gastineau, B. Les Femmes et les moeurs de l'Algérie.
     Paris: Librairie Michel Lévy, 1861.

646 Gaudry, Mathéa. La Société féminine au Djébel Amour et au
     Ksel. Algiers: Société Algérienne d'Impressions Di-
     verses, 1961. Modestly defined by its author as a
     "study of North African rural sociology" it is actually an
     enormous compilation of information on such various

topics as how to build a tent, what are the various pieces
of jewelry, the tatoo designs, cooking recipes, weaving
methods, the various economic functions of women, magic,
witchcraft, abortive products and dances. Abundantly illustrated, it also includes a lexicon of usual words,
poems, and texts of judgments along with French transla-
tions on cases of "children asleep. "

647 Gordon, David C. "Algerian Women After Independence" (in
Arabic). Hiwar, 2-3 (March-April 1967), 179-196.

648 _____. Women of Algeria--An Essay on Change. Cambridge: Harvard University Press, 1968.

649 Hadri, Fatiha. "L'Algérienne et le sport. " El-Djazairia,
4-5 (Jan. 1971), 36-38; 9 (May 1971), 45-48.

650 _____. "Dossier no. 59: la femme algérienne en l'an X:
des résultats encourageants. " Révolution Africaine, 431
(July 21, 1972), 15-24.

651 _____. "Moeurs et société. Pourquoi la femme?" El-
Djazairai, 31 (1973), 12-18.

652 Hassène-Daoudji, Fatima. "L'Adolescente algérienne: être
à la hauteur des responsabilités qui lui incombent. "
Révolution et Travail, 76 (Feb. 11, 1965), 15.

653 Heggoy, Alf Andrew. "Cultural Disrespect: European and
Algerian Views on Women in Colonial and Independent
Algeria. " The Muslim World, 4 (Oct. 1972), 323-334.

654 Heim, Pierre. "La Condition de la femme musulmane:
l'Algérienne. " Eurafrica, 10 (Oct. 1968), 9-12.

655 Henablia, Zohra. "Etre femme en Algérie. " Faiza, 62
(Dec. 1968), 28-31.

656 Hennebelle, Monique. "La Femme sera le devenir du monde
arabe ... une interview d'Assia Djebar. " L'Afrique
Littéraire et Artistique, 3 (Feb. 1969), 62.

657 "How Does Society Perceive Women?" (in Arabic). El-
Djazairia, 34 (1973), 10-11.

658 Ibn Dada, Abd al-'Aziz. "Woman Between Evolution and
Permissiveness" (in Arabic). El-Djeich, 89 (Aug. 1971),
31-33.

659 Ihaddaden, Z. "Le Problème de la femme. " El-Moudjahid,
March 20, 1967.

660 "Interview with Mlle Sid Cara. " International Council of

51 General

Women Quarterly Review, April 1959, 51-52. Sid Cara was a member of the French Cabinet under the Fourth Republic.

661 J. D. "La Jeune Fille algérienne 1965, vue par elle-même." Hommes et Migrations, 623 (Oct. 24, 1965), 1-10.

662 "La Jeunesse algérienne, être consciente de son authenticité." Révolution Africaine, 176 (June 10, 1966), 10-11.

663 "La Jeunesse féminine algérienne (extraits de presse)." Revue de Presse, 92 (Feb. 1965).

664 Laadjal, L. "Des femmes prennent en main leur destin." Algérie-Actualité, 314 (Oct. 24, 1971), 22-23.

665 Lehrman, Hal. "Battle of the Veil in Algeria." The New York Times Magazine, July 13, 1958, 14, 16, 18.

666 Leila. "The Algerian Woman Between Tradition and Modernism" (in Arabic). El-Moudjahid, 606 (April 2, 1972), 22-24; 607 (April 9, 1972), 22-23.

667 _____. "The Emigrant Woman and Some Problems About Emigration" (in Arabic). El-Moudjahid, 649 (January 21, 1973), 12-13.

668 _____. "Where Is the Fighting Algerian Woman?" (in Arabic). El-Moudjahid, 583 (Oct. 24, 1971), 30-31.

669 Lesourd, M. "Les Femmes d'In Çalah mangeuses de chats à l'occasion de la fête Es Sabaa." Journal de la Société des Africanistes, 7 (1937), 33-35.

670 M. M. "Le Costume de la femme algérienne. Ce qu'il est aujourd'hui." Révolution Africaine, 296 (Oct. 1969).

671 Marchant, Annick. "A la rencontre des jeunes algériennes." Croissance des Jeunes Nations, 86 (March 1969), 21-28.

672 "Les Militantes de la beauté algérienne." Jeune Afrique, 566 (Nov. 1971), 50.

673 Mokarzel, S. A. Le Monde des femmes et son entrée dans la cité. Algiers: Secretariat Social d'Alger, 1967. Reprinted in Information Rapide, Dec. 8-10, 1967, 1-48.

674 Moll, Geneviève. "La Femme et la jeunesse dans l'Algérie d'aujourd'hui." France-Algérie, 17 (April-May 1967), 8-10.

675 M'rabet, Fadela. "Les Algériennes: défense d'aimer." Jeune Afrique, 354 (Oct. 22, 1967), 24-29.

676   Ouanisi, Zouhour.   "The Awakening of Woman: The Fields
      of Action and Opportunity Opened to Her" (in Arabic).
      El-Djeich, 71 (Feb. 1970), 22-23, 58.

677   _____.   "The Disquieting Question Asked by Men and Wo-
      men" (in Arabic).   El-Djeich, 47 (Feb. 1968), 19-20.

678   _____.   "A Picture of Our Social Diseases" (in Arabic).
      El-Djeich, 45 (Dec. 1967), 8, 4.

679   _____.   "The Power of Civilization and Its Benefit for
      Men and Women" (in Arabic).   El-Djeich, 48 (March
      1968), 14-15.

680   _____.   "The Road of Woman's Struggle: Home and
      Countryside" (in Arabic).   El-Djeich, 50 (May 1968), 28-
      30.

681   _____.   "Situation of the Algerian Woman Through His-
      tory" (in Arabic).   El-Djeich, 52 (July 1968), 53-55.

682   _____.   "To Place Woman in Front of Their Responsibili-
      ties" (in Arabic).   El-Djeich, March 1965, 15.

683   _____.   "Two Pictures of Our Social Reality" (in Arabic).
      El-Djeich, 43 (Oct. 1967), 5-6.

684   _____.   "Will There Be a Realistic and Decisive Answer?"
      (in Arabic).   El-Djeich, 35 (Feb. 1967), 18, 40.

685   _____.   "Woman Through Algerian History" (in Arabic).
      El-Djezairia, 1 (Jan. 1970), 5-8; 2 (Feb.-March 1970),
      7-10; 3 (April 1970), 9-13; 4 (May 1970), 8-12; 5-6
      (June-July 1970), 10-13; 8 (Aug. 1970), 6-9.

686   Ougouag-Kezzal, Ch.   "Un Exemple historique de la valeur
      morale des bijoux et leur symbolique chez les Arabes:
      La Taoussa."   Libyca (1969), 351-53.

687   "Portraits de femmes."   El-Moudjahid, March 9, 1968.

688   "Le Problème de la femme."   Révolution Africaine, 271
      (April 15, 1968).

689   Rafi, Samir.   "Le Corbusier et les 'Femmes d'Alger'."
      Revue d'Histoire et de Civilisation du Maghreb, 4 (Jan.
      1968), 50-66.

690   Rakibi, Nafisa.   "Do Our Clothes Betray Our Personality?"
      (in Arabic).   El-Djazairia, 3 (April 1970), 34-36.

691   Roberds, Frances.   "Moslem Women of North Africa."   The
      Moslem World, Oct. 1937, 362-369.   The author, an

American missionary, describes the slow progress of
women in the town of Constantine, and mentions the efforts made by some Tunisian women to educate other
women.

692   Roche, Millicent H.   "The Moslem Women of Algeria. "   The
      Moslem World, 23 (1933), 290-295.

693   Sara, Mouhoub.   "Jeunes Filles et femmes dans la ville. "
      Algérie-Actualité, 176 (March 2, 1969), 8-9; 177 March
      9, 1969), 10-11; 178 (March 16, 1969), 12-13; 200 (Aug.
      17, 1969), 6-7.

694   Touat, Larbi.   Le Monde des femmes et son entrée dans la
      cité.   Algiers: Secrétariat Social d'Alger, 1967.

695   Vasse, Denis.   "La Femme algérienne. "   Travaux et Jours,
      13 (1964), 85-102.   The impact of women's emancipation
      on traditional society.

696   "Le Vrai Problème. "   El-Moudjahid, March 4, 1967.

697   "Women Edge Into Social Mainstream. "   Christian Science
      Monitor, Sept. 24, 1970, p. 6, col. 1.

698   Yahyawi, 'Abd al-Qadir.   "The Role of the Algerian Woman
      in the Cultural Renaissance and the Economic Revolution"
      (in Arab'c).   El-Djazairia, 10 (Dec. 1970), 36-43.

(2) ISLAM

699   Ben Abdallah.   "L'Islam et la condition féminine. "   Monde
      Non Chrétien, 47-48 (July-Aug. 1958), 185-203.

700   Bukusha, Hamza.   " 'Abd al-Hamid Ibn Badis and Woman"
      (in Arabic).   El-Djeich, 37 (April 1967), 15, 27.

701   Chelli, Mounira.   "Une Algérienne parle: tout a commencé
      par une crise religieuse. "   Jeune Afrique, 329 (April 30,
      1967), 68-69.

702   de Salva, M. R.   "Il velo in Algeria: considerazioni sul
      vello della donna nei paesi arabi. "   Terzo Mondo,
      March-June, 1970, 97-109.   The veil in Algeria: con-
      siderations on the veiling of women in the Arab countries.

703   "En échange des recommandations divines. "   El-Moudjahid,
      Feb. 20, 1967.

704   "La Femme musulmane, la femme dans le mariage musulman
      selon le rite malékite, le donné actuel (Kabylie), signes

et causes d'évolution. " Etudes Sociales Nord-Africaines,
27 (Dec. 1952).

705   al-Haris, Sulayman. "Arab Broadcasting" (in Arabic). Jil
wa-Risalah, 12 (June 1968). A review of a broadcast
about Sheikh Ibn Badis, the Algerian reformer.

706   "In Remembrance of the Liberator of Woman" (in Arabic).
El-Djazairia, 4 (May 1970), 32-41. Commemorating the
30th anniversary of the death of Sheikh Ibn Badis, 1889-
1940.

707   Provansal, Danielle. "Le Phénomène maraboutique au Maghreb. " Genève-Afrique Acta Africana, 14:1 (1975), 59-
77. Includes a section on maraboutism and feminine
practices (pp. 71-74), and a brief bibliography.

708   La Réforme de la magistrature musulmane. Algiers: V.
Spielmann, 1924. A small brochure on French reforms
of the Algerian judicial apparatus.

709   "La Religion pour l'émancipation de la femme. " El-Moudjahid,
Feb. 18, 1967.

710   Roussier, Jules. "Application du chra au Maghreb en 1959;
mariage et divorce en Algérie. " Die Welt des Islams,
1-2 (1959-61), 25-55; 3-4 (1961), 248-254.

711   Tidjani, El Hachemi. "L'Association al-qiyam et les valeurs
islamiques. " Confluent, 42-43 (June-July 1964), 609-634.
The former Secretary General of the University of Algiers, then advisor to the Ministry of Agriculture, explains the aims of his association. He mentions that the
physiological and biological structures of the male brain
are superior to those of the female brain.

(3) KABYLE WOMEN

712   Aminah. "Family and Woman Condition in Kabylie" (in Arabic). El-Djazairia, 4 (May 1970), 17-21.

713   Ben Said, Si Ammar [called Boulifa]. Recueil de poésies
kabyles (texte Zouaoua): traduites, annotées et précédées
d'une étude sur la femme kabyle. Algiers: A. Jourdan,
1904. The introduction (pp. 7-69), includes an apology
for the condition of the Kabyle woman in answer to Hano-
teau's Les Us et coutumes des Kabyles.

714   "Les Bijoux chez les femmes du Mzab. " Le Monde Colonial
Illustré, 34 (June 1926), 127.

715 Bourdieu, Pierre. "The Sentiment of Honour in Kabyle Society." In J. G. Peristiany, ed. Honour and Shame: The Values of Mediterranean Society, Chicago: University of Chicago Press, 1966, 193-241.

716 Bousquet-Lefèvre, Laure. La Femme kabyle. Paris: Recueil Sirey, 1939. [See entry 741.]

717 _____. Recherches sur la condition de la femme kabyle. Algiers: La Typo-litho & J. Carbonnel Imprimeries Réunies, 1929. Thesis on the legal status of women in Greater Kabylia and Kabyle custom law.

718 Brès, H. "La Femme kabyle," Le Christianisme Social, 1932.

719 C. E. B. "Commérages autour d'une tasse de café." IBLA, 50 (1950), 193-202. The verbatim report of some lively gossip among three old women.

720 Callens, M. "La Femme kabyle." En Terre d'Islam, Jan. 1929, 12-35.

721 Carret, Jacques. "Le Particularisme ibadite au Mzab." L'Afrique et l'Asie, 1960, 38-46.

722 Charroin, J. "Femmes kabyles dans la famille patriarcale." Etudes Sociales Nord Africaines, 7-8 (1950), 28-31.

723 Coulon, Alfred. "La Femme kabyle." Bulletin de la Société de Géographie d'Alger et de l'Afrique du Nord, 35 (1930), 553-575.

724 Farrag, Amina. "Mechanism of Social Control Amongst the Mzabite of Beni-Isguen." Unpublished M.A. thesis, London University, 1969.

725 _____. "Social Control Amongst the Mzabite Women of Beni-Isguen." Middle Eastern Studies, 7 (1971), 317-328.

726 François, S. M. "Politesse féminine kabyle." IBLA, 53 (1951), 35-55. An extremely thorough article including a considerable amount of Berber vocabulary from the region of Tizi Ouzou.

727 G. C. "Les Femmes du Mzab." Le Monde Colonial Illustré, 83 (July 1930), 173.

728 Gaudry, Mathéa. La Femme chaouia de l'Aurès; étude de sociologie berbère. Paris: P. Geuthner, 1929.

729 _____. La Société féminine au Djebel Amour et au Ksel:

étude de sociologie rurale nord-africaine. Paris: P. Geuthner, 1961.

730 Genevois, Henri. Superstition, recours des femmes kabyles. Fort-National, Fichier de Documentation Berbère, no. 100, 1968.

731 Goichon, Amélie M. "La Conservation du groupe mozabite et la religion de ses femmes." Revue de Philosophie, 33 (1926), 290-321.

732 _____. "La Vie féminine au Mzab." Revue du Monde Musulman, 1925, 27-138.

733 _____. "La Vie féminine au Mzab." Revue des Etudes Islamiques, 4 (1930), 231-87, 517-95.

734 _____. La Vie féminine au Mzab; étude de sociologie musulmane. Paris: P. Geuthner, 1927.

735 Keun, Odette. Les Oasis dans la montagne. Paris: Calmann-Levy, 1919. About the life of women in the Aurès mountains and Tunis.

736 Lanfry, J. "Mariage--retour de la femme au domicile de ses parents sans répudiation." Fichier de Documentation Berbère, 1969, 1-49.

737 Lefèbvre, G. "La Toilette féminine dans deux villages de Petite Kabylie." Libyca, N.S. 11 (1963), 199-220.

738 Milliot, L. "Une Réforme du statut de la femme kabyle." Afrique Française et Renseignements Coloniaux, 1931, 681-83.

739 Morand, A. "Le Statut de la femme kabyle et la réforme des coutumes berbères." Revue des Etudes Islamiques, 1927, 47-94.

740 Raineau, M. "Chez les musulmanes non voilées de la Kabylie." La Géographie, 60 (1933), 168-74.

741 Tergoule, Léon de. "La Femme kabyle." IBLA 1 (1941), 69-86. Review of Bousquet-Lefèvre's book [entry 716].

742 Vigier, R. "La femme kabyle: quelques remarques sur le décret du 19 mai 1931." Revue des Etudes Islamiques, 1 (1931), 1-19.

(4) SAHARA WOMEN

743   Barrère, G. "Le Veuvage à Ideles (Ahaggar)." Travaux de
      l'Institut de Recherches Sahariennes, 24 (1965), 177-82.

744   Nouet, G. "L'Oeuvre de civilisation dans la préfecture
      apostolique du Sahara." Le Monde Colonial Illustré,
      March 1926, 58. Monsignor Nouet extols the work of the
      white fathers who have set up workshops to teach young
      girls and women carpet weaving.

745   Pommerol, Mme. Jean. Among the Women of the Sahara.
      London: Hurst & Blackett, 1900.

746   _____. Une Femme chez les Sahariennes (entre Laghouat
      et In-Salah). Paris: E. Flammarion, 1900.

747   Wakefield, Frances M. "Twareg Women of the Sahara."
      The Muslim World, Jan. 1949, 6-10.

748   Watson, A. Dorothy. "Women of the Western Sahara Desert."
      The Muslim World, April 1949, 97-101. Describes ways
      of life in the Algerian south, around Toggourt and the
      changes which have taken place since the 1930's.

(5) VILLAGE WOMEN

749   Boubekeur, F.; F. Bouderka; L. Hanifi; and L. Reziouk.
      "Les Femmes des hautes plaines constantinoises vues
      par elles-mêmes." Revue Algérienne des Sciences
      Juridiques, Economiques et Politiques, 53 (1974), 161-
      64.

750   Bousquet, G. H. "Promenades sociologiques III: les noms
      patronymiques féminins des douars Tacheta et Zougerra."
      Revue Africaine, 93 (1949), 335-38.

751   Corrèze, Françoise. Femmes des Mechtas: témoignage sur
      l'Est algérien. Paris: Editeurs Français Réunis, 1976.

752   "La Femme rurale ignorée mais active." El-Djazairia, 9
      (May 1971), 15-18.

753   Hadri, Fatiha. "La Femme et la révolution agraire." El-
      Djazairia, 31 (1973), 8-12.

754   _____. "La Femme rurale à l'ordre du jour." El-
      Djazairia, no. 29, I-VIII (1973), dossier no. 13.

755   Leila. "The Rural Woman and the Agrarian Revolution" (in

Arabic). El-Moudjahid, 588 (Nov. 28, 1971), 22-23.

756 Mas'udah. "Some Information About the Situation of the Wo-
     man in the Sawra Area" (in Arabic). El-Djazairia, 34
     (1973), 16-18.

757 "La Participation de la femme rurale au développement
     économique et social. " Rencontres et Documents, 11
     (1968).

758 "Quatre-vingt-cinq jeunes filles à la conquête de la Saoura. "
     Révolution Africaine, 116 (April 17, 1965).

(6) THE FAMILY

General

759 Afredj, R. "Colloque sur la protection familiale en milieu
     rural. " Algérie-Actualité, 389 (April 1-7, 1973), 7-8.

760 Aminah. "The Situation of the Algerian Family" (in Arabic).
     El-Moudjahid, 604 (March 19, 1972), 24-25.

761 _____. "Traditional Childbirth and Its Practice in Alger-
     ian Society" (in Arabic). El-Moudjahid, 607 (April 9,
     1972), 24, 32.

762 Azemni, A. "La Famille algérienne devant les problèmes
     sociaux modernes. " IBLA, 14 (1951), 27-34.

763 Bensaadi, Nefissa. "L'Exode rural, ou l'éclatement de la
     famille traditionnelle. " Algérie-Actualité, 264 (Nov. 8,
     1970), 7-9; 265 (Nov. 15, 1970), 8-9; 266 (Nov. 22,
     1970), 6-7; 267 (Nov. 29, 1970), 10-11; 268 (Dec. 6,
     1970), 6-7.

764 Bouzar, Mohammed. "Famille dans le désarroi. " Algérie-
     Actualité, 185 (May 4, 1969), 11-13.

765 Dejeux, Jean. "Connaissance du monde féminin et de la
     famille en Algérie (essai de synthèse documentaire),
     1947-1967. " Revue Algérienne des Sciences Juridiques,
     Economiques et Politiques, 4 (1968), 1247-1311.

766 Descloîtres, R. , and Laid Debzi. "Système de parenté et
     structures familiales en Algérie. " Annuaire de l'Afrique
     du Nord, 1963, 23-59.

767 Desparmet, J. Coutumes, institutions, croyances des indi-
     gènes de l'Algérie. Algiers: J. Carbonel, 1939. Third
     edition of a book originally published in 1905 to teach
     Arabic by direct method. The second half of the book is

devoted to marriage and family life.

768 Fauque, L. P.   Stades d'évolution de la cellule familiale
     d'Algérie.   Algiers: Délégation Générale du Gouverne-
     ment, 1959.

769 "La Femme dans la famille contemporaine." Algérie-
     Actualité, 522 (Oct. 19, 1975), 6-9, 12.

770 Francisi, A. "Algeria: grave crisi nell'ambito dell'istituto
     familiare." Oriente Moderno, 1-2 (1968), 111-113. The
     crises which plague Algerian family life.

771 Gaudefroy-Demonbynes, Maurice. Les Cérémonies du mariage
     chez les indigènes de l'Algérie. Paris: Maisonneuve,
     1901.

772 _____. "Les Cérémonies du mariage chez les indigènes
     de l'Algérie." Revue des Traditions Populaires, 1902,
     603-605; 1907, 49-60.

773 Genevois, Henri. La Famille; notes recueillies dans la ré-
     gion de Michelet, suites rimées, récits. Fort National:
     Fichier de Documentation Berbère, 1962.

774 "Les Incidences des lois sociales sur la famille musulmane."
     Le Fonctionnaire Algérien, Feb. 1951, 12-14.

775 Laadjal, L. "La Fille-mère et son enfant." Algérie-
     Actualité, 320 (Dec. 5, 1971), 4-5.

776 _____. "Les Mères et leurs enfants d'abord." Algérie-
     Actualité, 427 (Dec. 23, 1973), 18-19.

777 Lechani. "La Famille indigène en Algérie." En Terre
     d'Islam, 49 (1931), 253-57; 50 (1931), 295-300.

778 Leila. "Family Structure in Algeria" (in Arabic). El-
     Moudjahid, 648 (Jan. 14, 1973), 24-25.

779 _____. "The General Situation of the Algerian Family"
     (in Arabic). El-Moudjahid, 647 (Jan. 7, 1973), 22-23,
     25.

780 _____. "Talk With Dr. Belkhodja Nadjia: The Necessity
     of Organizing the Family for the Protection of Mother
     and Child" (in Arabic). El-Moudjahid, 589 (Dec. 5,
     1971), 24-27.

781 Letellier, G. "La Famille algérienne devant les problèmes
     sociaux modernes." Amina, 25-26 (1941).

782 Morand, Marcel. La Famille musulmane. Algiers:

Typographie A. Jordan, 1903.

783   Najjar, Rashid.   "The Family Between Stability and Instabil-
      ity" (in Arabic).   al-Qabas, April-May, 1968, 176-81;
      Oct. 1968, 39-44; Jan. -Feb. 1969, 179-83.

784   "Notes sur la famille en Sektana.   (Annexe de Taliouine). "
      Revue Algérienne, 1 (1952), 116-31.

785   Saadia and Lakhdar.   L'Aliénation colonialiste et la résistance
      de la famille algérienne.   Lausanne: Editions de la Cité,
      1961.

786   Slimane, Rahmani.   "La Grossesse et la naissance au Cap
      Aokas. "   Revue Africaine, 81 (1938), 217-45.

787   "La Société algérienne, la cellule familiale. " El-Djazairia,
      11 (July 1971), 13-16.

788   "Woman: The Situation of the Family" (in Arabic).   El-
      Moudjahid, 545 (Jan. 1971), 34-35.

789   Zehraoui, A.   Les Travailleurs algériens en France: étude
      sociologique de quelques aspects de la vie familiale.
      Paris: Maspero, 1971.

Family Law

790   "About Family Law" (in Arabic).   El-Djazairia, Jan. 1970,
      4.

791   Allag, Mme.   "La Famille et le droit en Algérie dans le
      contexte maghrébin. "   Revue Algérienne des Sciences
      Juridiques, Economiques et Politiques, 1974, 157-160.

792   Borrmans, M.   "Perspectives algériennes en matière de
      droit familial. "   Studia Islamica, 37 (1973), 129-53.

793   Bousquet, G.   "La Législation française et son influence sur
      le droit de la famille indigène. "   Revue Algérienne,
      Tunisienne et Marocaine de Législation et de Jurispru-
      dence, Aug. -Sept. 1930, 190-202.   An appeal of a law
      professor to modify the application of customary law
      toward a stricter observation of orthodox law in order
      to improve the condition of women, for instance in child
      marriages.

794   _____, and Jahier.   "L'Enfant endormi, notes juridiques,
      ethnographiques et obstétricales. "   Revue Algérienne,
      Tunisienne et Marocaine de Législation et de Jurispru-
      dence, Feb. 1941, 17-36.   The authors analyze why the
      popular belief that a child may have fallen asleep in the

womb is still very widespread.

795 Guiho, P. "Les Conflits entre la loi française et le status personnel des musulmans algériens en matière de mariage. " Université d'Alger-Annales Juridiques, Politiques, Economiques et Sociales, 3-4 (1955), 139-205.

796 Najjar, Rachid. "The Regime of Marriage in the 1909 Law" (in Arabic). El-Djeich, 42 (Sept. 1967), 40-41.

797 "Opinion on the Position of the Union of Algerian Women About Personal Status" (in Arabic). El-Djeich, 115 (Oct. 1973), 27-29.

798 "La Position de l'Union Féminine sur le project de loi sur la famille. " El-Djazairia, 35-36 (1973), 28-30.

799 Salah-Bey, Mohamed-Chérif. "Droit de la famille et problèmes idéologiques. " Revue Algérienne des Sciences Juridiques, Economiques et Politiques, 1974, 97-110.

800 Zeys, Ernest. Droit mozabite: le nil, du mariage et de sa dissolution. Algiers: A. Jourdan, 1891.

Marriage and Divorce

801 "A propos des mariages mixtes. " Documentation Française-Articles et Documents (O. 1370), 1963.

802 A. G. "Le Divorce. " Révolution Africaine, Dec. 26, 1964, 6-8.

803 Aouissi, Cheikh Mechri. "Les Causes classiques de l'instabilité du mariage. " Revue Algérienne de Sciences Juridiques, Economiques et Politiques, 1968, 1091-1099.

804 Benatia, Farouk. "Réflexions sur le mariage. " Algérie-Actualité, 192 (1969), 10-11.

805 Bousquet, G. H. "Annonces matrimoniales islamiques. " Revue Africaine, 89 (1945), 117-19.

806 _____. "Remarques sur quelques curieuses bida´ observées chez les musulmans d'Algérie. " Welt des Islams, 3 (1953), 34-35. The author mentions curious innovations, specially in marriage matters: advertising, rings, intermarriages.

807 _____, and Jahier. "A quel âge le mariage musulman peut-il être légalement consommé?" Revue Algérienne, 1942.

808/9 _____, and M. Noureddine. "Notes sur des usages relatifs à la dot dans la région d'Aumale. " Revue Africaine, 91 (1947), 301-04.

810   Dulout, Fernand. "De la répudiation dans les coutumes
kabyles. " Revue Algérienne, Tunisienne et Marocaine
de Législation et de Jurisprudence. Aug. -Sept. 1941,
100-110.

811   Foudil, Abdelkader. "De quelques causes modernes d'instabilité du mariage. De la procédure en matière de divorce et du rôle du juge. " Revue Algérienne de Sciences
Juridiques, Economiques et Politiques, 1968, 1101-1105.

812   Francisi, A. "Algeria: inchiesta sul divorzio. " Oriente
Moderno, 1 (1965), 37-41. Inquiry on the problem of divorce in Algeria.

813   "Freedom of Choice in Algerian Marriages. " The Muslim
World, 3 (July 1965), 279-281. Excerpts of Revue de
Presse of Dec. 1964, translated by E. H. D., and quot-
ing author Fadela M'rabet, Mrs. Khemisti (deputy), and
Grand Mufti Baba Ameur, whose daughter refused the
prospective husband he had chosen for her and married
someone else.

814   Haroun, Mohamed Ali. "Les Causes modernes d'instabilité
du Mariage. " Revue Algérienne de Sciences Juridiques,
Economiques et Politiques, 4 (Dec. 1968), 1128-1138.

815   Kehi, C. "Le Mariage mixte algérien. " Faculté d'Alger-
Annales Juridiques, Politiques, économiques et sociales,
3-4 (1955), 29-51.

816   _____. "Les Mariages mixtes. " Revue Algérienne,
Tunisienne et Marocaine de Législation et de Jurisprudence, 1938.

817   Khalil, Sidi. Mariage et répudiation, translated by E. Fa-
gnan. Algiers and Paris, 1909.

818   Koura, Salah-Eddine. "Le Divorce et la répudiation en droit
musulman (charia) et le droit positif algérien. " Revue
Algérienne des Sciences Juridiques, Economiques et
Politiques, 1974, 111-12.

819   Leila. "The Bride Trousseau Between Tradition and Modern
Life" (in Arabic). El-Moudjahid, 594 (Jan. 9, 1972), 30-
31.

820   "Le Mariage avec les étrangères--Le problème de la dot. "
Revue de Presse, 115 (May 1967), 4.

821 "Le Mariage des jeunes algériennes." Revue de Presse,
      1963, fasc. 74.

822 Mille, Pierre. "Dans 'l'autre' Algérie: un grand mariage
      à Biskra." Le Monde Colonial Illustré, 180 (June 1938),
      103. The wedding of M. Cheraga and Mlle. Smaia, both
      holders of the baccalaureate, set up in the most fashion-
      able Western style, is viewed as a triumph of France's
      civilizing mission.

823 "Opinions sur le mariage mixte." Revue de Presse, 1963,
      fasc. 79.

824 Ougouag-Kezzal, Ch. "Le Costume et la parure de la
      mariée à Tlemcen." Libyca, 1970, 253-68.

825 _____. "Le Sadaq et le mariage suivant le 'Urf' (rite) de
      Sidi Ma'ammar." Libyca, 1971, 235-41.

826 Peroncel-Hugoz, J-P. "Les Mariages avec les étrangers
      sont vivement dénoncés." Le Monde, Aug. 15, 1970, 2.
      There are about 25,000 mixed couples in Algeria. Mrs.
      Zhor Ounissi, head of the review El-Djezairia, would
      like mixed marriages outlawed.

827 Portier, L. "Débat public sur les mariages mixtes en
      Algérie." Terre Entière, 24 (July-Aug. 1967), 67-81.

828 Roussier, Jules. "Mariage et divorce en Algérie." Die
      Welt des Islams, 3-4 (1961), 248-254.

829 Schoen, Col. [of the] Comité National pour les Musulmans
      français. "Note sur le mariage et le divorce des
      musulmans d'origine algérienne." ESNA, 665 (1966).

830 Tourniol, Renée. "Une noce à Ouargla." Le Monde Colonial
      Illustré, 36 (Aug. 1926), 192.

831 Zerari, Z. "Trop de divorces: une enquête sociale."
      Algérie-Actualité, 181 (April 6, 1969), 48.

                          Family Planning

832 Dejeux, Jean. "La Régulation des naissances: essai de
      réponse à une question angoissante des femmes algé-
      riennes." Comprendre, 24 (Oct. 1960).

833 Kassiba, Ahmad. "The Opinion of the Ulama on Birth Con-
      trol in Algeria" (in Arabic). El-Djeich, 94 (Jan. 1972),
      12, 45-47.

834 "La Limitation des naissances au niveau d'un hôpital d'Alger:

Interview. " Confluent, 50-52 (1965), 328-331.

835 "Un Problème social: les maternités. " Revue Africaine,
    210 (Feb. 20, 1967).

836 Régulation des naissances, opinions et attitudes des couples
    algériens. Algiers: Association Algérienne pour les
    Recherches Démographiques, Economiques et Sociales,
    1968.

837 Semihi, M. "Le Couple algérien face à la limitation des
    naissances. " Algérie-Actualité, March 2, 1969, 6-7.

838 Tabah, L. "Une Enquête sur la fécondité en Algérie. Ap-
    plications de l'analyse factorielle des correspondances. "
    Population, 1972, 729-68.

839 Vallin, J. "Influence de divers facteurs économiques et
    sociaux sur la fécondite de l'Algérie. " Population, 1973,
    817-42.

840 Von Allman-Joray, M. , and F. Von Allman-Joray. "Atti-
    tudes concernant la taille de la famille et la régulation
    des naissances: présentation et essai d'interprétation
    des résultats préliminaires de l'enquête socio-démogra-
    phique algérienne. " Population, 26:2 (March 1971), 47-
    78.

(7) EDUCATION

841 "Accès des jeunes filles et des femmes à l'éducation dans
    les zones rurales. " Etudes et Documents d'Education,
    51 (1964), 62.

842 Benatia, Farouk. "L'Enseignement au féminin: l'enseigne-
    ment authentique de la femme. " Algérie-Actualité, 210
    (1969), 10-11.

843 _____ . "La Lycéenne à la recherche de sa personnalité. "
    Algérie-Actualité, 179 (March 23, 1969), 4-5.

844 Djabali, Melle. "Rapport sur l'instruction des filles indi-
    gènes. " La Voix des Humbles, 1938. The author, a
    former elementary school teacher in Sétif, suggests ways
    of improving female education.

845 Gaudry, Mathéa. "L'Instruction de la femme indigène en
    Algérie. " Afrique Francaise, 45 (Dec. 1935), 731-36;
    46 (Jan. 1936), 28-34.

846 Genevois, Henri. Education familiale en Kabylie. Fort

National: Fichier de Documentation Berbère no. 89,
1965.

847   Illio, Sylviane. L'Enseignement des métiers féminins en
      Algérie. Paris: Imprimerie A. Marchand, 1937.

848   "Les Jeunes Algériens et le problème de la mixité. " Docu-
      ments Nord-Africains, 589 (Dec. 31, 1964).

849   Leila. "The Female Student and Voluntary Service in the
      Agricultural Revolution" (in Arabic). El-Moudjahid, 655
      (March 4, 1973), 18-21.

850   _____ . "Talk With Female Students" (in Arabic).   El-
      Moudjahid, 585 (Nov. 7, 1971), 26-27.

851   _____ . "Voluntary Work ... and the Integration of Se-
      condary School Girls in True Social Life" (in Arabic).
      El-Moudjahid, 660 (April 8, 1973), 14.

852   "La Mixité: Faux problème?" Revue de Presse, 112 (Feb.
      1967).

853   "The Mother is Also an Educator" (in Arabic). El-Djazairia,
      4 (May 1970), 13-16.

854   Raineau, Michel. "La Vie et la mort de la Princesse des
      Sables. " Le Monde Colonial Illustré, 123 (Nov. 1933),
      172-73. Bibliographical article on Amélie Tedjani, wife
      of Ahmed Tedjani, then El Bachir Tedjani, both heads
      of the Tedjania brotherhood. Her philanthropic activities
      included the foundation of the first school/workshop for
      Algerian girls.

855   Salah, Muhammad Tahar. "La Mixité. " El-Djazairia, 34
      (1973), 28-31.

856   "Scolarisation des jeunes filles en Algérie. " El Djeich,
      Sept. 1968, 17-19.

857   "La Scolarisation des jeunes filles en Algérie. " An-Nasr,
      October 1, 1968.

858   "La Scolarisation des jeunes filles musulmanes en Algérie. "
      Documentation Nord-Africaine, 410 (1960).

859   "Le Volontariat des étudiantes. Une expérience riche en
      enseignements. " El-Djazairia, 25 (Sept. 1972), 18-22.

860   Zerdouni, Nefissa. Enfants d'hier. L'éducation de l'enfant
      en milieu traditionnel algérien. Paris: Maspero, 1970.

861   Ziad, Mohamed. "Etudiantes--wali d'Alger: à bâtons

rompus. " Algérie-Actualité, 354 (July 30, 1972), 8.

(8) LITERARY WORKS BY OR ABOUT WOMEN

862   Bentami, Rosalie. L'Enfer de la casbah. Algiers: Impri-
       merie du Lycée, n.d.

863   Bittari, Zoubeida. O mes soeurs musulmanes, pleurez!
       Paris: Gallimard, 1964. The unhappy marriage and
       subsequent divorce of a young woman.

864   Borrmanns, M. "La Femme algérienne--Les Algériennes."
       In Faivre, Charles, ed., Les Etrangers d'Auvergne,
       Paris: Etudes Sociales Nord-Africaines, 1969.

865   Boudjedra, Rachid. La Répudiation. Paris: Denoël, 1969.
       The first novel of a young Algerian author who had to
       publish it abroad because of the touchiness of its topic.

866   Bugéja, Marie. Du vice à la vertu: roman d'une naïlia.
       Paris: Nouvelles Editions Argo, 1932. Daughter and
       wife of prominent colons, Marie Bugéja was very much
       interested in the condition of Algerian women.

867   Cazes, Jeanine. Soumicha, la fille du soleil. Algiers:
       Esquirol, 1936. This novel describes the problems of
       mixed marriages.

868   Debèche, Djamila. Leïla, jeune fille d'Algérie. Algiers:
       Imp. Charras, 1947.

869   Dejeux, Jean. "Romans sur les milieux féminins algériens."
       ESNA, Feb-March, 1961, 53-61; also in Confluent,
       Sept.-Oct. 1961, 519-527.

870   Djebar, Assia. Les Alouettes naïves. Paris: Julliard,
       1967. The conflict between people and between couples
       as experienced by Nfissa, the heroine.

871   _____. Femmes d'Alger. In press. Gathering of short
       stories.

872   Duchêne, Ferdinand. Les Barbaresques: Kamir, roman
       d'une femme arabe. Paris: Albin Michel, 1926. The
       vicissitudes of a young Kaybyle woman reduced to prosti-
       tution after an unhappy marriage.

873   _____. Les Barbaresques: la Rek'ba, histoire d'une
       vendetta kabyle. Paris: Albin Michel, 1927. The mur-
       der of a woman after two unhappy marriages starts a
       vendetta.

874 _____. Les Barbaresques: Thamil'la. Paris: Albin
      Michel, 1923. This novel, very successful in its time,
      received the Grand Prix Littéraire de l'Algérie in 1921
      and was translated in English and Spanish.

875 Faure-Sardet, Jeanne. Fille d'Arabe. Paris: Editions
      Eugène Figuière, 1935. The French-Algerian author re-
      ceived several literary prizes. Her novel describes the
      problems of mixed marriages.

876 Géniaux, Charles. ... Les Musulmanes. Paris: Ernest
      Flammarion, 1920. Reprint of the 1909 edition of a
      novel inspired by the author's sojourn in Algeria, about
      female emancipation and mixed marriages.

877 Géniaux, Claire. ... Le Cyprès. Paris: P. Lafitte, 1918.
      A novel about mixed marriages.

878 Ibn Habib, Cheikh. Vrouwenleven en-lieven in een arabischen
      harem, wit het arabisch vertaald door J. S. Hubrechts.
      Amsterdam: C. Daniëls, 1905.

879 La Rochère, Eugénie (Mistral). Stéphanie Valdor--Etudes de
      moeurs arabes. Tours: Alfred Mame et Fils, 1869.
      Madame de la Rochère, wife of an army officer, lived in
      Algeria in the early days of French colonization. Her
      works offer glimpses of life in Algeria as it was shortly
      after the French conquest.

880 "Marie-Rose: La femme dans le roman des trente dernières
      années." Le Monde, April 7, 1972, p. 16. Women in
      the Algerian novel between 1942 and 1972.

881 Mikhail, Mona N. "Images of Women in North African Liter-
      ature--Myth or Reality?" American Journal of Arabic
      Studies, 3 (1975), 34-47. An analysis of Assia Djebar's
      Les Alouettes Naïves and Rachid Boudjedra's La Répudi-
      ation.

882 Mortimer, Mildred P. "La Femme algérienne dans les ro-
      mans d'Assia Djébar." The French Review, April 1976,
      759-763.

883 Pommerol, Mme. Jean. Un Fruit, et puis un autre fruit.
      Paris: Calmann-Levy, 1910. Madame Pommerol, who
      made a long sojourn in the Sahara, first wrote her book
      in the Tamashek language, then rewrote it in French for
      publication.

884 "La Promotion de la femme à travers les textes littéraires."
      Revue de Presse, 117 (July-Aug. 1967), 3.

885 Rhaïss, Elissa. Le Mariage de Hanifa. Paris: Librairie

Plon, 1926. A good description of traditional life in Muslim and Jewish milieux.

886 al-Sharqawi, 'Abd al-Rahman. Ma'sat Jamila. Cairo: Dar al-ma'arif, 1962. A drama about Jamila Bouhaired, an Algerian tortured by the French in 1958.

(9) THE WORKING WOMAN

887 A. G. "L'Algérienne au travail." Révolution Africaine, Oct. 17, 1964, 6-8.

888 "Algérie: femmes de ménage; Manque de formation et méconnaissance des droits de l'aide ménagère." Aicha, 13-14 (Aug. 1971), 27-30. How cleaning women are being taken advantage of.

889 Aminah. "What is Hidden Behind Woman's Work?" (in Arabic). El-Djazairia, 8 (Aug. 1970), 14-18.

890 _____. "With the Cleaning Women" (in Arabic). El-Djazairia, (June-July 1970), 25-28.

891 _____. "Why Does the Working Woman Take So Many Sick Leaves?" (in Arabic). El-Moudjahid, 606 (April 2, 1972), 25, 32.

892 _____. "Woman in Traditional Craftsmanship" (in Arabic). El-Djazairia, 36 (1973), 6-8.

893 "An Attempt to Conciliate Work and Home" (in Arabic). El-Djazairia, 32 (1973), 10-12.

894 "Arrêté du 7 Novembre 1963 relatif aux accoucheuses rurales." Journal Officiel de la République Algérienne, 90 (Dec. 3, 1963), 1267.

895 "Arrêté du 7 Novembre 1963 relatif aux accoucheuses rurales (rectificatif)," Journal Official de la République Algérienne, 91 (Dec. 6, 1963), 1284.

896 "Arrêté du 18 Novembre 1963 relatif à l'admission dans les centres féminins de formation professionnelle des adultes, des jeunes filles de 14 à 16 ans." Journal Officiel de la République Algérienne, 90 (Dec. 3, 1963), 1268.

897 "Arrêté du 2 Décembre 1963 portant organisation d'un stage de formation accélérée d'aides physiothérapeutes." Journal Officiel de la République Algérienne, 93 (Dec. 13, 1963), 1307.

898   "Arrêté interministériel du 17 Juillet 1967 fixant les tarifs
      maximums que peuvent percevoir les praticiens médecins,
      chirurgiens-dentistes et sage-femmes pour les actes
      professionnels dispensés en clientèle privée. " Journal
      Officiel de la République Algérienne, 83 (Oct. 10, 1967),
      881.

899   Baha' al-Din, Ahmad. "The fatma" (in Arabic). El-Dja-
      zairia, 5 (May 1970), 14-16. "Fatma" is the traditional
      French appellation for the native maid in North Africa.

900   Benatia, Farouk. "L'Algérienne et le travail salarié. "
      Algérie-Actualité, 215 (1969), 4-5.

901   _____. "Femmes en prison. " Algérie-Actualité, 182
      (April 13, 1969), 6-7.

902   _____. Le Travail féminin en Algérie (Département
      d'Alger). Algiers: Société Nationale d'Edition et de
      Diffusion, 1970. A very thorough work full of useful in-
      formation, statistics and tables.

903   Benattig, Rachid. "Volontariat. Beaucoup de choses peuvent
      être faites ... avec la brigade féminine dans les douars
      des communes de Djendel et Oued-Cheurfa. " Algérie-
      Actualité, 287 (April 18, 1971), 8-9.

904   " 'C'est par le travail que la femme peut s'épanouir et
      s'intégrer à la société', " affirme Mme Chentouf, secré-
      taire générale de l'U. N. F. A. " El-Moudjahid, April 29,
      1967.

905   'Décret Num. 63-398 du 7 Octobre 1963 portant création de
      diplôme d'Etat en médecine, pharmacie, chirurgie den-
      taire et de sage-femme de la République Algérienne,
      Démocratique et Populaire. " Journal Officiel de la Ré-
      publique Algérienne, 76 (Oct. 16, 1963), 1042.

906   'Décret num. 63-428 du 7 Novembre 1963 portant suppres-
      sion de l'ordre des médecins et de l'ordre des chirur-
      giens dentistes, de l'ordre des sage-femmes et de l'ordre
      des pharmaciens. " Journal Officiel de la République
      Algérienne, 83 (Nov. 8, 1963), 1130.

907   Dermenghem, Emile. Le Pays d'Abel. Paris: Gallimard,
      1960. Part 2, "Les Filles de la douceur, " deals with
      prostitution as practiced by the Ouled Nail.

908   Duchesne, Edouard Adolphe. De la prostitution dans la ville
      d'Alger depuis la conquête. Paris: J. B. Baillère,
      1853.

909   "L'Exploitation des femmes de ménage et des enfants. " El-

Moudjahid, April 12, 1967.

910   "Une Femme au comité de gestion de la COGEHORE." Ré-
       volution Africaine, 107 (Feb. 13, 1965).

911   "La Femme dans l'édification économique du pays." Révo-
       lution Africaine, 114 (April 3, 1965).

912   "Une Femme élue à la tête du syndicat U.G.T.A. pour
       défendre les droits des ouvrières victime de discrimina-
       tion. L'évolution de la femme algérienne face à l'édifi-
       cation du socialisme." Révolution et Travail, 25 (Feb.
       13, 1964).

913   "La Femme et le travail." An Nasr, July 30, 1965; Aug. 1,
       2, 3, 4, 5, 1965. An inquiry which appeared in a daily
       newspaper from Constantine.

914   "Les Femmes et le travail." Révolution et Travail, 101
       (Nov. 5, 1965), 7.

915   "Les Femmes responsables dans l'autogestion." Révolution
       Africaine, 103 (Jan. 16, 1965), 6-7.

916   "Les Femmes sont au travail." Révolution Africaine, 123
       (June 5, 1965).

917   Hadri, Fatiha. "La Femme et l'artisanat." El-Djazairia,
       29 (1973), 6-11.

918   Hennebelle, G. "La Situation de la femme en Algérie-
       Théâtre." L'Afrique Littéraire et Artistique, 13 (Oct. 1970).

919   J. D. "Jeunes Travailleuses algériennes." Hommes et Mi-
       grations, 640 (Feb. 28, 1966), 80.

920   "J.F.L.N. quatre vingt cinq jeunes filles à la conquête de la
       Saoura." Révolution Africaine, 116 (April 17, 1965), 8-9.

921   "La Leçon d'un Premier Mai; Le Travail féminin, une exi-
       gence pour toute une société." El-Djazairia, 9 (May
       1971), 36-41.

922   Leila. "About the Problems of the Working Woman" (in
       Arabic). El-Moudjahid, 654 (Feb. 25, 1973), 22-23.

923   _____. "The Administration: The Best Place of Work
       for Woman" (in Arabic). El-Moudjahid, 554 (April 4,
       1971), 34.

924   _____. "Commemoration of March 8: The Algerian Woman
       Asserts Her Position in the Battle for Labor and Production"
       (in Arabic). El-Moudjahid, 603 (March 12, 1972), 24-25.

925 _____. "Female Unionization in Algerian Public Enter-
prises" (in Arabic). El-Moudjahid, 660 (April 8, 1973),
12-13.

926 _____. "Teaching: Is It the Best Profession for Women?"
(in Arabic). El-Moudjahid, 553 (March 28, 1971), 34.

927 _____. "The Union Woman Asks for Real Unionizing Opportunities Lest Her Participation Be In Name Only" (in
Arabic). El-Moudjahid, 661 (April 15, 1973).

928 Lepoil, Maurice. Faut-il abolir la prostitution? Algiers:
Imprimerie V. Heintz, 1947.

929 Makki, Raqiq Ala' al-Din. "Woman and Theater" (in Arabic).
El Moudjahid, 595 (Jan. 16, 1972), 34-35.

930 Maurin, Ch. "L'Evolution de la femme dans la casbah
d'Alger." Terres d'Afrique, 25 (1946), 31-49. The
place of female work in the social evolution of the casbah.

931 Ouanisi, Zouhour. "The Problem of Women Between Work,
Perdition and Neglect" (in Arabic). El-Djeich, 88 (July
1971), 16-20.

932 Ougouag-Kezzal, Ch. "Bref Aperçu historique sur la bro-
derie arabe: sur une vieille brodeuse au coeur d'Alger."
Libyca, 1969, 343-49.

933 Pauline-Marie, Sister. "Le Tissage dans la vie féminine au
Mzab." Bulletin de la Société Neuchâteloise de Géographie, n.s. 8, 15-30.

934 "Pour la libération de la femme par le travail." Révolution
Africaine, 111 (March 13, 1965).

935 "Premier séminaire de la travailleuse algérienne." Révolution et Travail, 45 (July 2, 1964).

936 "Rapports entre la femme algérienne et son travail." Révolution Africaine, 134 (Aug. 21, 1965).

937 "Le Rôle de la femme." Révolution et Travail, 107 (April
10, 1966).

938 "Talks With Madame Jamila J. Responsible for the Labor
Office" (in Arabic). El-Djazairia, 3 (April 1970), 21-24.

939 Touili, Mohamed. "La Prostitution en Algérie avant la révolution." Révolution Africaine, 288 (Nov. 22, 1968),
54-55.

940   "Le Travail des femmes. " Révolution et Travail, 116 (May
       30, 1967).

941   "Le Travail est le meilleur gage pour l'émancipation de la
       femme. " Révolution et Travail, 138 (Oct. 29, 1969), 8.

942   "Le Travail féminin dans le développement d'Alger: 1965-
       1968. " Révolution Africaine, 360 (January 15, 1971), 31-
       32.

943   "With the Working Woman" (in Arabic). El-Djazairia, 1
       (Jan. 1970), 14-17; 2 (Feb. 1970), 18-22.

944   "Woman and Work" (in Arabic). El-Djazairia, 33 (1973), 6-
       9.

945   "Woman's Participation to the Development of the Country"
       (in Arabic). El-Moudjahid, Feb. 27, 1967.

946   "The Working Woman Between Two Duties" (in Arabic).   El-
       Djeich, 113 (Aug. 1973), 48-50.

947   Zerdouni, N. La Femme algérienne face au problème de
       l'emploi. Montrouge: Institut Social de Montrouge,
       1963.

(10) WOMEN'S CONGRESSES AND FEMINISM

948   "A propos de l'émancipation de la femme. " El-Moudjahid,
       March 18, 1967.

949   "Les Algériennes réclament leur émancipation. " Hommes et
       Migrations, 755 (Dec. 9, 1968).

950   "Après quatre ans d'indépendance: Premier Congrès de
       l'U.N.F.A. " Révolution Africaine, 196 (Nov. 2, 1966),
       15; Nov. 25, 1966, 18-19.

951   Armand, M. L. "Féminisme. " En Terre d'Islam, 17
       (1936), 324-332. About the current developments in
       Egypt and the work of Marie Bujéja in Algeria.

952   Arnaud, G. "Une Algérienne se révolte. " Terre Entière,
       Jan. -Feb. 1970, 76-99.

953   "L'Assemblée Générale des Femmes. " L'Algérien en Europe,
       181 (Dec. 16, 1973), 4-12.

954   "Au colloque sur la F.P.A. : la promotion féminine concré-
       tisée. " Révolution Africaine, 129 (July 17, 1965).

955   Bensaadi, Nefissa.   "Y-a-t-il un problème de la femme?"
       Algérie-Actualité, 262 (Oct. 25, 1970), 7-9.

956   Bernheim, Nicole.   "Les Femmes du Maghreb sur la rude
       voie de l'indépendance--Les Ambiguités algériennes."
       Le Monde, Jan. 4, 1969, 6.   The author comes to the
       conclusion that liberation was not for everybody.

957   "Billets et courrier des lecteurs: l'émancipation de la
       femme."   Revue de Presse, 113 (March 1967).

958   Bitat, Z., and M. Belmihoud.   "Existe-t-il un problème de
       la femme algérienne?"   Confluent, 32-33 (1963), 493-99.

959   Boumedienne, Houari.   "Speech to the First Congress of Al-
       gerian Women" (in Arabic).   al-Jami'ah, 14-15 (Dec.
       1966-Jan. 1967), 49-52.

960   Bouri, Antar.   "U.N.F.A.: pour une action dynamique."
       Révolution Africaine, 44 (Jan. 7, 1973), 8-9.

961   "Clôture du séminaire des cadres de l'U.N.F.A."   Révolu-
       tion Africaine, April 8, 1968, 6-7.

962   "Congrès de l'U.N.F.A."   Révolution Africaine, 196 (Nov.
       2, 1966).

963   "Le Congrès, notre point de départ."   Révolution Africaine,
       197 (Nov. 18, 1966).

964   Dionisi, Bianca.   "A proposito del III Congresso dell'Union
       Nationale des Femmes Algériennes."   Oriente Moderno,
       55 (Jan.-Feb. 1975), 62-66.   About the third National
       Congress of Algerian Women held in Algiers in April
       1974.

965   "Dossier no. 14--Le Conseil national de l'Union Nationale
       des Femmes Algériennes."   El-Djazairia, 30 (1973), 26-
       42.

966   "L'Emancipation de la femme vue par une européenne."   El-
       Moudjahid, March 21, 1976.

967   "Emancipation et radotages ou les 'femmes savantes.' "   El-
       Moudjahid, Jan. 20, 1968.

968   "Entretien avec Mme Chentouf, secrétaire générale de
       l'U.N.F.A."   El-Moudjahid, Feb. 9, 1967.

969   "La Femme algérienne contre les rétrogrades."   Révolution
       et Travail, 107 (March 10, 1966), 6.

970   "La Femme et son émancipation: la femme: où va-t-elle?"

El-Moudjahid, March 9, 1967.

971 "Huit Mars: Journée Internationale de la Femme; Il ne
suffit pas de jeter le voile. " Révolution Africaine, 367
(March 5, 1967), 7.

972 Ihaddaden, Z. "Emancipation ou dépersonnalisation. " El-
Moudjahid, March 18, 1966.

973 "L'Interprétation des droits de la femme. " El-Moudjahid,
March 1, 1967.

974 "Journée internationale des femmes. " El-Djeich, 23 (March
1965).

975 "Journée internationale des femmes. " El-Djeich, 36 (April
1966).

976 Leila. "After the Last Congress of the Feminist Union,
What?" (in Arabic). El-Moudjahid, 654 (Feb. 25, 1973),
24.

977 _____. "The Woman Mujahidah at the Fourth Mujahidun
Conference Declares ... " (in Arabic). El-Moudjahid,
666 (May 20, 1973), 10-11.

978 Lewis, Flora. "No Revolution for the Woman of Algiers. "
New York Times Magazine, Oct. 29, 1967, 28-29, 117-
120. As one Algerian man told the author: "We are all
for the emancipation of women ... except maybe for our
sisters. "

979 M'rabet, Fadela. La Femme algérienne--Les Algériennes.
Paris: François Maspero, 1969. Despite her sacrifices
during the War of Independence, the Algerian woman is
far from having gained the recognition of all her rights.

980 Nasser, Mesaoud. "L'Emancipation de la femme: encore du
chemin à accomplir. " Révolution Africaine, 212 (March
6, 1967), 24-25.

981 Ouanisi, Zouhour. "The Women's Union; A Step for a New
Departure" (in Arabic). El-Djeich, 62 (May 1969), 55-
56.

982 "One Step Forward" (in Arabic). El-Djazairia, 3 (April
1970), 2-3.

983 "La Participation de la femme à la vie sociale: vers une
communauté anti-féministe. " El-Moudjahid, Feb. 22,
1967.

984 "Plaidoyer pour la femme. " El-Moudjahid, 5 (Feb. 1971),

11; 12 (Feb. 1971), 11.

985 Raineau, Michel. "En Algérie: deux aspects de la femme
     musulmane d'aujourd'hui. " Le Monde Colonial Illustré,
     115 (March 1933), 42-43. Two Algerian civil servants
     explain why they are in favor of female emancipation.

986 "Renouvellement des instances. Conférence nationale et
     congrès de l'U. N. F. A. ; un souffle nouveau. " Révolution
     Africaine, 368 (March 12, 1971), 4-5.

987 Saidani, S. "Position U. N. F. A. ; La Vie de l'organisation. "
     El-Djazairia, 31 (1973), 19-24.

988 "La Situation de la femme en Algérie: tragédie ou comédie? "
     Jeune Afrique, 507 (Sept. 22, 1970), 38-40.

989 "Text of the Report of the National Union of Algerian Women"
     (in Arabic). El-Djazairia, 3 (1973), 9.

990 "U. N. F. A. et perspectives de la femme algérienne. " Révo-
     lution Africaine, 173 (May 20, 1966).

991 "U. N. F. A. : la femme doit prendre ses responsabilités. "
     El-Djeich, 124 (Sept. 23, 1973).

992 "U. N. F. A. (Union Nationale des Femmes Algériennes). "
     Révolution Africaine, 242 (Oct. 2, 1967), 18-19.

993 "Union Nationale des Femmes Algériennes; démocratie et
     efficacité. " Révolution Africaine, 320 (April 11, 1970),
     12.

994 "World Women's Day and the Algerian Woman" (in Arabic).
     El-Djazairia, 33 (1973), 2-3, 20-28.

(11) WOMEN AND POLITICS

995 Abu-Zayd, Hikmat. al-Tarbiyah al-islamiyah wa-kifah al-
     mar´ah al-jaza´iriyah. Cairo: Maktabah al-anjlu-al-
     misriyah, 196-.

996 Arnaud, Georges, and Jacques Verges. Pour Djamila Bou-
     hired. Paris: Editions de Minuit, 1958.

997 "Une Autre Promotion de la femme algérienne. " Révolution
     Africaine, 108 (Feb. 20, 1965).

998 Benatia, Farouk. "L'O. N. U. veut que des you-you éclatent
     ... Pour prouver quoi? " Révolution Africaine, 285
     (Nov. 1, 1968), 30-33.

An Algerian sociologist studies the participation of the
Algerian woman in the Revolution.

999   Boumedienne, Houari. "La Femme est un élément actif
       dans la société algérienne. " Révolution Africaine, 163
       (March 12, 1966).

1000   Buzayyan, Diraji. "The Arab Woman in the War of Libera-
       tion" (in Arabic). El-Djeich, 45 (Dec. 1967), 9-10.

1001   "Le Colonel Boumedienne invite les femmes à participer
       aux municipalités. " Le Monde, Aug. 23, 1966, 5.

1002   "Les Elections communales: toutes les candidates élues à
       Alger. " El-Moudjahid, Feb. 7, 1967.

1003   "Les Elues: déployer tous nos efforts dans l'intérêt de la
       collectivité. " El-Moudjahid, Feb. 9, 1967.

1004   Fanon, Frantz. L'An V de la révolution algérienne.   Paris:
       François Maspero, 1962.   Fanon, who worked in Al-
       giers as a psychiatrist, analyzes the attitude of the Al-
       gerian woman during the War of Liberation.

1005   Fauque, L. P. "L'Oeuvre française émancipatrice de la
       femme musulmane d'Algérie. " Bulletin de Liaison et
       de Documentation des Affaires Algériennes, Jan. -Feb.
       1962, 16-17.

1006   "La Femme algérienne doit lutter pour élever son niveau. "
       El-Moudjahid, June 27, 1968.

1007   "La Femme algérienne entre officiellement dans la vie
       publique. " El-Moudjahid, Feb. 10, 1967.

1008   "La Femme dans la commune. " Révolution Africaine, 206
       (Jan. 20, 1967), 15.

1009   "La Femme et la vie politique en Algérie. " Maghreb, 39
       (May-June 1970), 32-41.

1010   "La Femme et l'édification de l'Algérie socialiste. " Revue
       de Presse, 1963, fasc. 76.

1011   "Les Femmes ont été nombreuses à voter. " El-Moudjahid,
       Feb. 6, 1967.

1012   Ghudban, Muhammad. "Social reflexions" (in Arabic). al-
       Mar'ah, 8 (Aug. 1967).   The opinion of a Libyan jour-
       nalist on the Algerian woman and the Palestinian ques-
       tion.

1013   Heggoy, Alf Andrew. "Algerian Women and the Right to

Vote: Some Colonial Anomalies. " The Muslim World, 3 (July 1974), 228-235.

1014   Honoré-Laine, Geneviève. "A l'heure de la révolution al-gérienne-Attitudes féminines. " Documents Nord-Africains, 540 (Nov. 4, 1963), 1-5.

1015   Leila. "The Role of Women in Our Socialist Society" (in Arabic). El-Moudjahid, 60 (Feb. 27, 1972), 22-23.

1016   _____. "Women Between Yesterday's and Today's Revolution" (in Arabic). El-Moudjahid, 584 (Oct. 31, 1971), 67-69.

1017   _____. "Women on Municipal Election Day" (in Arabic). El-Moudjahid, 548 (Feb. 21, 1971), 34.

1018   al-Mar'ah fi ma'arakat al-Jaza'ir. Cairo: Dar al-dimuqratiyah al-jadidah, 1958.

1019   Marchand, H. "La Musulmane algérienne et la réconciliation franco-musulmane. " Compte-Rendus de l'Académie des Sciences d'Outre-Mer, 1959, 269-282.

1020   Ouanisi, Zouhour. "The Absence of Women from the Battlefield" (in Arabic). El-Djeich, 5 (Aug. 1969), 58-60.

1021   _____. "The Algerian Woman Before and After November 1, 1954" (in Arabic). El-Djeich, 44 (Nov. 1967), 20-21, 30.

1022   _____. "The November Révolution and the Beginnings of a Woman's Personality" (in Arabic). El-Djeich, 80 (Nov. 1970), 19-22.

1023   _____. "The Progress of Révolution ... and Its Sick and Lost Half" (in Arabic). El-Djeich, 18 (Aug. 1965), 20-22. Despite the revolution, one half of the Algerian people are not free.

1024   _____. "The Situation of the Algerian Woman and Her Political, Economic and Social Activity" (in Arabic). al-Wihdah al-'arabiyah, 31 (Oct. 1, 1973), 44-47.

1025   _____. "Women and the Anniversary of November" (in Arabic). El-Djeich, 68 (Nov. 1968), 34-35.

1026   "Pour elles la lutte continue. " Révolution Africaine, Oct. 1964, 6-9.

1027   "Pour un référendum: plaidoyer pour les femmes. " El-Moudjahid, March 6, 1967.

1028   "Quatre Questions aux femmes qui représentent les femmes."
        El-Moudjahid, April 13, 1968.

1029   Rakibi, Nafisa. "Women ... and the Second Revolution" (in
        Arabic). El-Djazairia, 1 (Jan. 1970), 20-23.

1030   "Le Rôle de la femme dans l'Algérie nouvelle. " Croissance
        des Jeunes Nations, 10 (April 1962), 15-17.

1031   "Le Rôle de la femme dans l'Algérie nouvelle. " Revue de
        Presse, 1962, fasc. 65.

1032   Sissani. "Sur la voie de la mobilisation. " Révolution Afri-
        caine, 479 (April 27, 1973), 14-15.

1033   "Trente Mille Femmes luttent pour leur droit. " Révolution
        Africaine, 130 (July 24, 1965).

1034   "L'Union Franco-Musulmane des Femmes d'Algérie. " Docu-
        ments Algériens, 21 (June 10, 1948).

1035   Vandevelde, Hélène. La Femme et la vie politique et so-
        ciale en Algérie depuis l'indépendance. Université
        d'Alger, Faculté de Droit et des Sciences Economiques,
        Mémoire de D. E. S. Sc. Pol. 1968.

1036   "Woman and Revolution" (in Arabic). El-Djazairia, 1 (Jan.
        1970), 1-2.

1037   "Woman and the New Struggle" (in Arabic). El-Djeich, 109
        (April 1973), 21-23.

1038   "Woman Inside and Outside the Community" (in Arabic).
        El-Djazairia, 32 (1973), 20-21.

1039   "The Young Woman and National Social Service" (in Arabic).
        El-Djazairia, 32 (1973), 2-3.

III

BAHRAIN

1040 Hansen, Henny Harald. Investigations in a Shi´a Village in
Bahrain. Copenhagen: National Museum of Denmark,
1967. (Ethnographical Series 12.)

1041 _____. "The Pattern of Women's Seclusion and Veiling
in a Shi´a Village." Folk 3 (1961), 23-42.

1042 Harfouche, Jamal. "The Family Structure in the Changing
Middle East and the Pre-School Children." Beirut:
UNICEF, 1968. (PSWG/PSC/14.)

IV

EGYPT

(1) GENERAL

1043   Abbate, Pasha. "Fixité de la race dans la femme égypti-
       enne. " Bulletin de la Société de Géographie d'Egypte,
       6 (1906), 461-70.

1044   'Abd al-Majid, Fa´izah. al-Mar´ah fi mayadin al-kifah.
       Cairo: Mu´assasah al-misriyah al-'ammah lil-ta´lif
       wa-al-nashr, 1967.

1045   'Abd al-Nabi, Hidayah. "Our Expectations for the Year
       2000: A Woman as Ambassador and as Assistant
       Foreign Minister" (in Arabic). al-Ahram, July 30,
       1976, p. 7, col. 3.

1046   Abdelhalim, I. H. "Factors Relating to the Attitude of
       Adults Towards Relations Between the Sexes in a
       Specific Culture. " International Journal of Social Psy-
       chology, 2 (1956), 196-206. Inquiry conducted by in-
       terviewing 300 educated Egyptians.

1047   Abdel Kader, Soha. A Report on the Status of Egyptian
       Women, 1900-1973. Cairo: American University in
       Cairo, Social Research Center, 1973. An informative
       work, although references are not always accurately
       given.

1048   Abou-Saif, Laila. "The Contemporary Egyptian Women in
       the Mass Media. " Paper delivered at the Ninth Annual
       Meeting of the Middle East Studies Association, Louis-
       ville, Ky. , Nov. 19-22, 1975.

1049   Abu-Lughod, Janet, and Lucy Amin. "Egyptian Marriage
       Advertisements: Microcosm of a Changing Society. "
       Journal of Marriage and Family Living, 2 (May 1961),
       127-38. One hundred marriage ads offer a glimpse of
       Egyptian society.

1050   al-Adhami, 'Abd al-Qadir ibn 'Ali al-Husayni. Mir´at al-

nisa´ fima hasan minhuna wa-sa´. Cairo: al-Matba'ah
al-mahmudiyah al-tijariyah (1933/1934).

1051   Allen, Roger. "Writings of Members of 'the Nazli Circle. ' "
        Journal of the American Research Center in Egypt, 8
        (1969-70), 79-84.

1052   Amine, Rhoda Gordon. Seven Years in the Sun. London:
        R. Hale, 1959. The English wife of an Egyptian, the
        author makes many pertinent observations on Egyptian
        customs, women's condition and family life.

1053   "L'ammirazione di une scrittrice araba egiziana per il
        Duce. " Oriente Moderno, 9 (Sept. 1935), 475-76.
        About a letter sent to al-Ahram by a female reader ex-
        pressing her admiration for Mussolini who seemed more
        interested in the fate of the peasants than an Egyptian
        minister who had recently visited the countryside.

1054   "Are Women More Intelligent Than Men?" (in Arabic). al-
        Ahram, June 5, 1974, p. 9, col. 1.

1055   al-Ashmawi, 'Abd al-Qadir. "Le Chemin le meilleur?"
        La Patrie, Jan. 16 and Jan. 30, 1947. Several per-
        sonalities discuss the best way to improve the life of
        the Egyptian woman.

1056   _____. "L'Egyptienne et les partis politiques. " La
        Patrie, May 29, 1947.

1057   Badawi, Ahmad. "The Egyptian Woman from al-Tahtawi to
        Qasim Amin" (in Arabic). al-Majallah, 1957, 113ff.

1058   Badre, Zoë Rafia. "Egypt's 'New Woman. ' " Asia, 39
        (1939), 533-35.

1059   Baha al-Din, Ahmad. "A Campaign to Incite Women to
        Register on Electoral Lists" (in Arabic). al-Ahram,
        Nov. 10, 1974, p. 10, col. 1.

1060   Bahjat, Ahmad. "The Charm of Egypt's Face" (in Arabic).
        al-Ahram, July 23, 1976, p. 2, col. 3.

1061   _____. "Khadijah Afandi and the Story of the Egyptian
        Woman" (in Arabic). al-Ahram, Feb. 15, 1974, p. 4,
        col. 5.

1062   al-Baradi'i, Muhammad Mustafa. "And This Shame, We
        Refuse!" (in Arabic). al-Ahram, March 20, 1976, p.
        9, col. 1. About the difficulties met by women trying
        to use crowded public transportation.

1063   Basyuni, Jawdah. "Reactionary Stand Rejected by Girls" (in Arabic). Ruz al-Yusuf, July 19, 1965, 52-53.

1064   Belzoni, Mrs. Short Account of the Women of Egypt, Nubia
and Syria. London: John Murray, 1821. Mrs. Belzoni
accompanied her husband in his exploration of Egypt
from 1815 to 1819. She traveled alone to Palestine,
and judged the condition of the Palestinian woman to be
better than that of the Egyptian.

1065   al-Bindari, Muhammad. al-Mar'ah wa-markazuha al-ijtima'i
fi al-dawlah. Cairo: Maktabat al-adab, 1944.

1066   al-Bisi, Sana'. "He ... and She" (in Arabic). al-Ahram,
July 30, 1976, p. 7, col. 1. About the ways Egyptian
women choose what they need.

1067   _____. "She ... " (in Arabic). al-Ahram, June 25, 1976,
p. 7, col. 1. On the behavior of women in the face of
death.

1068   _____. "She and Marriage" (in Arabic). al-Ahram,
June 4, 1976, p. 7, col. 1.

1069   "Breaking Arab Male Dominance." Christian Science Monitor, July 22, 1974, p. 7, col. 1.

1070   "Brides for Sale in Egypt." Littell's Living Age, 46 (1855),
676-79. A visit to slave dealers in Cairo.

1071   al-Bulaqi, Muhammad Ahmad Hasanayn. Kitab al-jalis al-
anis fi al-tahdir amma fi tahrir al-mar'ah min al-
talbis. Cairo: Matba'at al-ma'arif al-ahliyah, 1899.
A polemical book written in answer to Qasim Amin's
Tahrir al-mar'ah, trying to demonstrate that woman is
inherently inferior to man.

1072   al-Buluk, 'Adil. "Woman is Still at the Mercy of Man" (in
Arabic). Akhir Sa'ah, 2121 (June 18, 1975). An interview with Naguib Mahfuz in which the novelist denounces the present divorce and inheritance laws.

1073   Central Agency for Public Mobilisation and Statistics. Population and Research Studies Centre. International Women's Year 1975. The Egyptian Woman in Two De-
cades, 1952-1972. A very informative booklet with much
statistical data.

1074   "Changes in the Seating of Women in Cairo Buses" (in Arabic). al-Ahram, July 18, 1974, p. 8, col. 4.

1075/6 Chennells, Ellen. Recollections of an Egyptian Princess
By Her English Governess. Edinburgh: William
Blackwood & Sons, 1893. Miss Chennells enjoyed her

stay in Egypt and was a good observer of the khedivial family's life for five years.

1077   "The Conference on Woman and Combat Will Open Tomorrow" (in Arabic). al-Ahram, Nov. 15, 1974, p. 12, col. 1.

1078   Cooper, Elizabeth. The Women of Egypt. London: Hurst & Blackett, 1914.

1079   "Delegations of Women's Organizations Visit the Wounded and the Invalids" (in Arabic). al-Ahram, Jan. 2, 1974, p. 7, col. 1.

1080   Diab, Fuad. "Measuring Public Opinion in Cairo Toward Granting Political Rights to the Egyptian Woman." In Malik, Loweis, ed., Readings in Social Psychology in Arab Countries, Cairo: al-Dar al-qawmiyah, 1969.

1081   al-Diftirdar, Hashim, and Muhammad 'Ali al-Zurbi. Hayat al-mar'ah fi al-siyasah wa-al-ijtima'ah. Cairo, 1949.

1082   Dodd, Peter C. "Youth and Women's Emancipation in the United Arab Republic." Middle East Journal, 2 (1968), 159-72.

1083   "The Egyptian Woman Between Two Phases" (in Arabic). al-Nida', May 8, 1951, p. 20.

1084   "The Egyptian Woman in Figures" (in Arabic). al-Ahram, May 29, 1976, p. 7, col. 2.

1085   Un Egyptien. "Le mal national," par un égyptien. Le Lotus, 3 (June 1901), 121-129.

1086   "Eighty Girls From the Youth Organization of the Arab Socialist Union Arrived at Ismailia to Prepare the Stadium" (in Arabic). al-Ahram, Aug. 20, 1974, p. 8, col. 1.

1087   "Exchange of Visits Between Women from Egypt and Yemen" (in Arabic). al-Ahram, Sept. 14, 1974, p. 8, col. 1.

1088   F. G. "Epouse de Mourad Bey, Nefissa El Mouradiah a joué un grand rôle dans la résistance à l'invasion étrangère." Le Progrès Egyptien, July 26, 1975, p. 2.

1089   Fahmy-Bey, Mme J. L'aventure Saint-Simonienne et les femmes. Paris: Félix Alcan, 1930. Describes the efforts of French Saint-Simonian women to improve Egyptian health services and their unsuccessful attempts to improve the condition of the Egyptian women.

1090   _____ . L'Egypte éternelle. Paris: La Renaissance du
           Livre, 1921. The observations of the author, the
           French wife of an Egyptian official, after a lengthy so-
           journ in Egypt.

1091   Faraj, Fakhri. al-Mar´ah wa-falsafat al-tanasuliyat. Cai-
           ro: Matba'at al-'asiriyah, 1924. Faraj was a physi-
           cian whose liberal ideas, expressed at a lecture, made
           him the subject of a legal suit in 1929.

1092   Fauconney, J., and H. Manini. La Femme en Orient et en
           Extrême Orient: sa condition sociale. Paris: Vernier,
           1901.

1093   "Feminist Leaders Being Briefed on the Kilometer 101
           Agreement" (in Arabic). al-Ahram, Jan. 20, 1974,
           p. 8, col. 1.

1094   Fergany, Nader. "Egyptian Women and National Develop-
           ment: A Demographic Background." Paper presented
           at the Seminar on Arab Women in National Development,
           Cairo, Sept. 24-30, 1972.

1095   "Figures About Women in Our Country" (in Arabic). al-
           Ahram, May 7, 1976, p. 7, col. 3.

1096   "The First Bibliography on the Arab Woman" (in Arabic).
           al-Ahram, Aug. 25, 1976, p. 10, col. 1.

1097   "The First Feminine Group From the Reconstruction Groups
           Went to Suez Yesterday" (in Arabic). al-Ahram, July
           17, 1974, p. 8, col. 1.

1098   "The First Girls Conference Ends Its Session" (in Arabic).
           al-Ahram, July 23, 1974, p. 8, col. 4.

1099   "The First Survey on the Role of the Egyptian Woman in
           History" (in Arabic). al-Ahram, June 4, 1976, p. 7,
           col. 4.

1100   Franke, Elisabeth. "Frauen und Mädchen in Ägypten."
           Missionspädagogische Blätter, 3 (May 1913), 44-47.

1101   _____ . Hinter dem Schleier! Frankfurt am Main:
           Verlag Orient, 1908.

1102   Frederick, Pauline. Ten First Ladies of the World. New
           York: Meredith Press, 1967. Includes a chapter on
           Mrs. 'Abd al-Nasir.

1103   Gad, 'Atiyat Mahmud. al-Mar´ah fi al-mithaq. Cairo:
           Dar al-qawmiyah lil-tiba'ah wa-al-nashr, 1962. Women
           in the Egyptian National Charter.

1104   "The Gains of the Egyptian Woman" (in Arabic). al-Ahram,
        Sept. 15, 1976, p. 3, col. 7.

1105   "The Gains of the Egyptian Woman During International
        Women's Year" (in Arabic). al-Ahram, Jan. 14, 1976,
        p. 12, col. 1.

1106   "The Gains of the Egyptian Woman in the Corrective Revo-
        lution" (in Arabic). al-Ahram, May 14, 1976, p. 7,
        col. 1.

1107   Gérard de Nerval. The Women of Cairo; Scenes in the
        Orient. London: G. Routledge, 1929.

1108   Gordon, D. H. "The Zar and the Bhut: A Comparison."
        Man, 29 (1929), 153-55.

1109   Gornick, Vivian. In Search of Ali Mahmoud: An American
        Woman in Egypt. New York: E. P. Dutton, 1973.

1109a Gran, J. "Impact of the World Market on Egyptian Women."
        MERIP Reports, 58 (July 1977), 3-7.

1110   Gued Vidal, Fina. Safia Zaghloul. Cairo: R. Schindler,
        1946. The biography of "the mother of the nation,"
        wife of nationalist leader Sa'd Zaghlul, by her childhood
        friend.

1111   Guerville, A. B. de. La Nouvelle Egypte. Paris: Li-
        brairie Universelle, 1905. Good reportage. Chapter
        X (pp. 183-200) is devoted to women.

1112   Gyomai, Imré. Les Petites Filles des Pharaons. N. p.,
        n. d.

1113   el-Hamamsy, Laila Shukry. "The Changing Role of the
        Egyptian Woman." In Lutfiyya, Abdullah M., and
        Charles W. Churchill, eds., Readings in Arab Middle
        Eastern Societies and Cultures, Paris: Mouton, 1958.

1114   _____. "The Changing Role of the Egyptian Woman."
        Middle East Forum, 3 (1958), 24-38.

1115   _____. "Egypt." In International Institute of Differing
        Civilizations INCIDI; Women's Role in the Development
        of Tropical and Sub-tropical Countries; Brussels, 1959;
        Report of the XXXIth Meeting, Held in Brussels on 17th,
        18th, 19th and 20th September 1958; 229-241. A good
        study of the labor laws applying to women.

1116   Hasan, Zaynab. "Dr. 'A´ishah Ratib: Let Our Slogan Dur-
        ing the Women's Year Be: Rights Will Not Be Lost If
        Assiduously Pursued" (in Arabic). al-Musawwar, July 18,

1975, 21.

1117   _____. "In the World of Woman, Her Problem in Mexico as Well as Here: The Man Remains Master of the
House" (in Arabic). al-Musawwar, June 20, 1975, 20-
21.

1118   al-Hay´ah al-'Ammah lil-Isti'lamat. Egyptian Women: A
Long March From the Veil to October 6, 1973. Cairo:
Ministry of Information, State Information Service, 1974.

1119   Heikal, Ateya. La mujer egipcia. Bilbao: Ediciones de
Conferencias y Ensayos, n.d. Text of a lecture given
at the Instituto Hispano-Arabe, Madrid.

1120   _____. "La mujer egipcia. " Cuadernos de Estudios
Africanos, 1952, 49-62.

1121   Hirschfeld, Magnus. Men and Women; The World Journey
of a Sexologist. New York: AMS Press, 1974. A reprint of the translation of Die Weltreises eines Sexual-
forschers, first published in 1935. It includes a section on the Arab world.

1121a   Hori, S. "My Impression of Egyptian Women: Part 1" (in
Japanese). Chuto-tsuho, 246 (Feb. 1977), 21-36.

1122   Hussein, Aziza. "The Role of Women in Social Reform in
Egypt. " The Middle East Journal, 4 (Fall 1953), 440-
50.

1123   Idris, Yusuf. "The Secret Regime of the Egyptian Woman"
(in Arabic). al-Ahram, Oct. 10, 1975, 9.

1124   "In Honor of Five Alexandria Ladies Given Certificates for
Services Rendered" (in Arabic). al-Ahram, Oct. 14,
1974, p. 10, col. 1.

1125   "An Invitation to Egypt to Participate to the Ceremonies of
Woman's Year" (in Arabic). al-Ahram, June 27, 1974,
p. 8, col. 1.

1126   'Izzat, Samir. "Women in the World of Theft for the First
Time" (in Arabic). Ruz al-Yusuf, July 5, 1965, 24-25.
As women break into many male preserves, they also
start emulating men in crime.

1127   al-Jam'iyah al-Misriyah lil-Dirasat al-Ijtima'iyah. Maktab
al-Buhuth al-Ijtima'iyah. Dirasah ijtima'iyah lil-usrah
bi-hayy al-Sayyidah Zaynab. Cairo, 1956. A social
inquiry in a very popular Cairene district.

1128   al-Jishi, Bahiyah. "Face to Face with Aminah al-Sa'id" (in Arabic). al-Bahrayn al-Yaum, 282 (Sept. 9, 1974), 20-23. The famous journalist deplores the reluctance of Arab women to use their political rights.

1129   Kamil, Murad. La Situation de la femme en Egypte par rapport au culte de Marie. N. p. , n. d. Text of a lecture given in Lisbon. Pamphlet in the Library of the Dominican Institute, Cairo. (20th cent.)

1130   Katibah, Habib. "Social Trends in Egypt. " The Open Court, 916 (Sept. 1932), 632-46.

1131   Kennedy, John G. "Circumcision and Excision in Egyptian Nubia. " Man, 5 (June 1970), 175-91. Also: American University in Cairo, Social Research Center, Reprint no. 11.

1132   _____. "Nubian Zar Ceremonies as Psychotherapy. " Human Organization, 4 (Winter 1967), 185-94. Also: American University in Cairo, Social Research Center, Reprint no. 7.

1133   Khalifah, Ijlal. "al-Sahafah al-nisa´iyah fi Misr, 1892- 1939. " Unpublished M.A. thesis, Cairo University, 1965. The history of the Egyptian feminine press from its beginning until the eve of the second World War.

1134   _____. "al-Sahafah al-nisa´iyah fi Misr, 1940-1965. " Unpublished Ph.D. dissertation, Cairo University, 1969. The history of the Egyptian feminine press from 1940 to 1965. The following newspapers are dealt with: Ana wa-Inta, Chic, Fatat al-Ghad, Bint al-Nil, Hawwa´, Fatayat Misr, and Hiya.

1135   Khoury, R. "Le zar et la métapsychique. " Cahiers d'Histoire Egyptienne, 8 (1956), 198-205.

1136   Labib, Zaynab, and Mustafa Fahmi. Rasa´il ijtima'iyah bayna misri wa-misriyah. Cairo: al-Maktabah al- anglu-al-misriyah, 1947.

1137   Lane, Edward W. The Manners and Customs of the Modern Egyptians. London: J. M. Dent & Sons, 1963. A classic, first published in 1836, which includes much valuable information on Egyptian women in the first half of the 19th century.

1138   Lane-Poole, Stanley. Social Life in Egypt; A Supplement to Picturesque Palestine: A Description of the Country and Its People. London: J. S. Virtue, 1884. Having visited Egypt soon after the British invasion, the au- thor observed the condition of women in this country and thought it was the "fatal spot" in Islam.

1139   Laoust, Henri. "L'Evolution de la condition sociale de la
        femme musulmane en Egypte." Afrique Française, 3
        (1935), 171-76.

1140   Le Balle, R. "La Condition privée de la femme égyptienne
        musulmane." L'Egypte Contemporaine, 141 (1933), 415-
        34.

1141   Leon, E. de. "Bridal Reception in the Harem of the
        Queen." Lippincott's Monthly Magazine, 16 (1875), 379-
        83. A description of the marriage of Fatmah Hanim,
        daughter of Isma'il Pasha, with Tusun Pasha.

1142   Lichtenstadter, Ilse. "The Muslim Women in Transition,
        Based on Observations in Egypt and Pakistan." Sociolo-
        gus, 1 (1957), 23-28.

1143   _____. "The 'New Woman' in Modern Egypt; Observa-
        tions and Impressions." Muslim World, 38 (July 1948),
        163-71.

1144   Lord, Edith Elizabeth. "Changing Roles of Women in Two
        African Muslim Cultures." In Dana Raphael, ed.
        Being Female: Reproduction, Power and Change. The
        Hague: Mouton, 1975; 249-53.

1145   Maghraby, Marelene. "Zamala, Sadaka and Hobb: Concep-
        tions of Relations Between the Sexes Among Urban Cairo
        Youth and Adults." Unpublished M.A. thesis, Ameri-
        can University in Cairo, 1973.

1146   Makosch, Ulrich, et al. Salaam Fatima! Frauen der
        erwachenden Welt. Leipzig: Verlag Leipzig, 1972.

1147   Mansur, Anis. "Fashion and Its Effects on Women" (in
        Arabic). al-Ahram, May 5, 1976, p. 14, col. 8.

1148   Markaz al-Abhath wa-al-Dirasat al-Sukkaniyah. al-Mar'ah
        al-misriyah fi 'ishrin 'am. Cairo, 1972.

1149   Maslahat al-Isti'lamat. al-Mar'ah al-misriyah. Cairo,
        1952.

1150   el-Masry, Youssef [i.e. Jacques Baulin]. Daughters of Sin:
        The Sexual Tragedy of Arab Women. New York:
        Macfadden-Bartell, 1963. A translation of entry 1151.

1151   _____. Le Drame sexuel de la femme dans l'Orient
        Arabe. Paris: Laffont, 1962. A violent indictment
        against the present conditions of the Arab woman, cur-
        rent prejudices and female excision, more specifically
        devoted to the Egyptian woman.

89   General

1152 Mas'ud, Mahmud. Dunya al-mar'ah. Cairo: Sharikat al-
      tawzi' al-misriyah, 1951.

1153 Mazhar, Isma'il. al-Mar'ah fi 'asr al-dimuqratiyah.
      Cairo: Matba'at al-hadithah, 1949. The author was a
      liberal lawyer and well-known historian.

1154 Meinardus, O. "Mythological, Historical and Sociological
      Aspects of Female Circumcision Among the Egyptians."
      Acta Ethnographica Academiae Scientiarium Hungaricae,
      16 (1967), 387-97.

1155 al-Misri, Fatimah. al-Zar: dirasah nafsiyah, tahliliyah
      anthrubulujiyah. Cairo: al-Hay'ah al-misriyah al-
      'ammah lil-kitab, 1975. Psychoanalytic and anthropo-
      logical study of the zar.

1156 Mito, Muhammad A. S. "The Social Change of Daughters'
      Position in Egyptian Middle Class Families in Alexan-
      dria." Unpublished thesis, Alexandria University, 1953.

1157 Mohammed, Laila. "Rôle social de la femme." La Ré-
      publique Algérienne, May 12, 1951. Study of the
      Egyptian woman in a special issue of the paper.

1158 Mohsen, Safia K. "The Egyptian Woman: Between Modern-
      ity and Tradition." In Matthiasson, Carolyn J., ed.,
      Many Sisters: Women in Cross-Cultural Perspectives.
      New York: Free Press, 1974. Conservative attitudes
      of both sexes cannot be changed by legislation alone.

1159 Mu'assasat al-Ahram. 'Alam al-mar'ah. 5 vols. Cairo,
      1974.

1160 Muhanna, Majidah. "Is There a Battle Against Women in
      the Local Assembly Elections?" (in Arabic). al-Ahram,
      Oct. 26, 1975, p. 11. The supervisor of the regional
      elections denies women nominees were left out.

1161 _____. "The Opinions of An American Scholar on the
      Problems of the Rural Women, Her Children and Her
      Husband, the Problems of the City Woman and the
      Laws of Personal Status" (in Arabic). al-Ahram, June
      18, 1976, p. 7, col. 5.

1162 _____. "The Straight Road for the Volunteer Woman
      Worker" (in Arabic). al-Ahram, Jan. 9, 1974, p. 3,
      col. 7.

1163 Mukhtar, Bahirah. "About the Image of the Arab Woman
      on Radio and Television" (in Arabic). al-Ahram, Jan.
      3, 1976, p. 5, col. 1.

1164   Murad, Mahmud. Hiwar ma'a Huda 'Abd al-Nasir. Cairo:
        Matba'at al-Ahram al-tijariyah, 1975. An interview
        with the daughter of the late President Nasser.

1165   Muwafi, Yusra. "The Man is At the Head and Without Him
        We Cannot Survive" (in Arabic). al-Ahram, Jan. 17,
        1976, p. 5, col. 1.

1166   Nassar, Husni. Huquq al-mar'ah. Alexandria: Dar nashr
        al-thaqafah lil-tiba'ah wa-al-nashr, 1966. Reprint of
        the 1958 edition. The author, a magistrate, examines
        the rights of women in various countries but more
        specifically in Egypt, from a constitutional, economic
        and sociological point of view.

1167   Nelson, Cynthia. "Changing Roles of Men and Women: Il-
        lustrations from Egypt." Anthropological Quarterly, 2
        (1968), 57-77.

1168   Nizzoli, Amalia. Memorie sull'Egitto. Milano: Libreria
        Pirotta e C. 1841. The author, niece of a doctor of
        Muhammad 'Ali and wife of an Austrian consul, stayed
        in Egypt from 1819 to 1828. She visited the daughter
        of Muhammad 'Ali, wife of the Defterdar, and inter-
        viewed the wife of Abdin Bey who told her her life.

1169   el-Ouazzane. Encyclopédie de l'amour. Vol. IV: Egypte
        moderne arabe et Copte. Paris: Daragon, 1913.

1170   Palmer, M. Reeves. " 'al-Sufur'-'The Unveiled' (a weekly
        newspaper for Moslem women). " The Moslem World,
        8 (1918), 168-71. A brief analysis of the type of
        articles appearing in an Egyptian paper.

1171   Penfield, F. B. "Les femmes en Egypte." Revue de
        l'Islam, 4 (1899), 187-88.

1172   "The Permanent Bureau of the Arab Women Union Discusses
        Topics of Its Next Conference" (in Arabic). al-Ahram,
        Feb. 21, 1974, p. 10, col. 2. One of the main topics
        was the role of women in the October 1973 War.

1173   Pierre, Robert. "L'Evolution de la femme musulmane en
        Egypte. " En Terre d'Islam, 61 (July-Aug. 1933), 277-
        87; 62 (Sept.-Oct. 1933), 297-310.

1174   "President al-Sadat Asks Women to Make Use of Their
        Spare Time in His Speech to Cooperatives and Private
        Organizations" (in Arabic). al-Ahram, Feb. 27, 1974,
        p. 4, col. 4.

1175   "Problèmes féminins en Egypte." Revue de Presse, 118
        (Sept.-Oct. 1967).

1176 Qasim Amin. Les Egyptiens: Réponse à M. le duc
      d'Harcourt. Cairo: Jules Barbier, 1894. In his first
      book, Qasim Amin, later the champion of Egyptian
      women's rights, justifies the use of the veil as a safe-
      guard for women and criticizes the promiscuity of Euro-
      pean women.

1177 al-Qissi, Layla. "Sadiqah, the Bride Who Died As a Mar-
      tyr on the Day of Her Wedding for the Sake of Egypt"
      (in Arabic). al-Musawwar, Aug. 15, 1975, 58-59.

1178 Raccagni, Michelle. "The Image of Women in a Few Con-
      temporary Egyptian Plays and Movies." Paper delivered
      at the Tenth Annual Meeting of the Middle East Studies
      Association, Los Angeles, Nov. 10-13, 1976.

1179 Ragai, Doria (Shafik) and Ibrahim 'Abduh. al-Mar'ah al-
      misriyah min al-fara'unah ila al-yawm. Cairo:
      Matba'at Misr, 1955.

1180 Raghib, Muhammad 'Atiyah. al-jara'im al-jinsiyah fi al-
      tashri' al-jina'i al-misri. Cairo: Maktabat al-nahdah
      al-misriyah, 1957. Criminal law and sexual crimes.

1181 Rashid, Fatmah Ni'mat. "Une Enquête originale." La
      Bourse Egyptienne, March 17, 1944. In answer to a
      male colleague who made fun of the ignorance of women,
      Mrs. Rashid did not have to search long to meet igno-
      rant men.

1182 _____. "Un Mot à Fikri Abaza." La Patrie, Dec. 17,
      1935. In defense of journalist Ceza Nabarawi who wrote
      in French, since French was a good propaganda tool
      abroad.

1183 _____. "Om al-Masriyine." Cairo Calling, Jan. 22,
      1949, 6-7. Article extolling Safiyah Zaghlul, wife of
      Wafdist leader Sa'd Zaghlul.

1184 _____. "Perspectives pour la femme...." La Patrie,
      July 10, 1947.

1185 Rizq, 'Aidah. "What Is the Meaning of This Public Con-
      sensus?" (in Arabic). al-Ahram, May 24, 1976, p. 5,
      col. 2. Why so many people importune women in the
      streets.

1186 Rodriguez Mellado, I. "Notas sobre la evolución social de
      la mujer egipcia." Cuadernos de Estudios Africanos,
      1952, 49-62.

1187 Sabri, Mustafa. Qawli fi al-mar'ah wa-muqaramatu bi-
      aqwal muqaladah al-gharb. Cairo: al-Matba'ah al-

salafiyah, 1254 A. H. (1925-1926).

1188 Sa'd, Fu'ad, and Samiah Mitwali. "Heated Debate at the
End of the Meeting on the Evolution of the Regime"
(in Arabic). al-Ahram, Sept. 27, 1974, p. 6, col. 5.

1189 al-Sadat, Sakinah. "Feelings, Desires and Blames From
My Readings" (in Arabic). Hawwa', 979 (June 28,
1975), 39.

1190 al-Sa'dawi, Nawal. al-Mar'ah wa-al-jins. Cairo: Dar al-
sha'b, 1972; Beirut: al-Mu'assasah al-'arabiyah lil-
dirasat wa-al-nashr, 1972. A very controversial book
whose unexpurgated version had to be published in Lebanon.

1191 _____. "A Window in the Wall Between Man and Woman" (in Arabic). al-Ahram, Oct. 20, 1976, p. 9,
col. 1. About the role of woman and her activity in
society.

1191a Said, Amina. "The Renaissance of Women in Egypt. " In
M. L. Roy Choudhury, Egypt in 1945, Calcutta; n. p. ,
1946.

1192 al-Sa'id, Aminah. "The Woman Found Her Leadership During the October War" (in Arabic). al-Hilal, Oct. 1974,
74-81.

1193 Saint-Elme, Ida de. La Contemporaine en Egypte. 6 vols.
Paris: Ladvocat, 1831. The author, who led a very
eventful life during the Napoleonic Wars, traveled ex-
tensively in the East. Her observations on Egyptian
women are distributed through the six volumes of her
travelogue.

1194 Sedki, L. K. "Egyptian Women. " African Women, 3 (Dec.
1959), 53-55.

1195 al-Shahidi, 'Ali Hamdi. Umm al-dunya, al-mar'ah wa-
halitha min ahd al-khilafah ila al-an. Cairo: n.p. ,
1903. A history of the Arab woman by a partisan of
the veil and very limited education for women. See
his Amrina lillah [entry 1786].

1196 Shahin, Zeinab Mohamed. "Conformists, Manipulators and
Rebels: Problems of Self-Conception Among Women in
a Changing Culture. " Unpublished M.A. thesis, American University in Cairo, 1975.

1197 Shalabi, Mahmud. Sirr al-mar'ah. Cairo: Matba'at al-
I'timad, 1945.

1198   "The Shy Girls of Egypt" (in Arabic).   Ruz al-Yusuf, July
       19, 1965, 51-52.

1199   Sidqi, 'Abd al-Rahman.   "The Inclination to Freedom of
       Our Modern Girls and Its Influence on the Evolution of
       Relations with Men" (in Arabic).   al-Hilal, April 1971,
       40-49.

1200   Siham, B.   Frauenbildung und Frauenbewegung in Ägypten.
       Wuppertal: Kölner Arbeiten zur Pädagogik, 1968.

1201   Smock, Audrey Chapman, and Nadia Haggag Youssef.   "The
       Changing Role and Status of Women in Egypt. "   Unpub-
       lished report.   Cairo: American University in Cairo,
       Social Research Center, 1975.

1202   "Some Speakers at the Conference on the Constitutional
       Charter Ask For the Draft of Women" (in Arabic).   al-
       Ahram, June 19, 1976, p. 4, col. 8.

1203   Sulayman, Bahijah Bayumi.   al-Mar'ah.   Cairo: Matba'at
       al-Tawakkul, 1946.

1204   "There Is No Heroine Like Her" (in Arabic).   al-Ahram,
       Sept. 26, 1976, p. 9, col. 8.   About the difficulties en-
       countered by women in public transportation.

1205   Tomiche, Nada.   "La Femme dans l'Egypte moderne. "
       Etudes Méditerranéennes, Summer 1957, 99-111.

1206   _____ .   "The Position of Women in the UAR. "   Journal
       of Contemporary History, 3 (1968), 129-43.

1207   _____ .   "The Situation of Egyptian Women in the First
       Half of the Nineteenth Century. "   In William R. Polk
       and Richard L. Chambers, eds. , Beginnings of Moderni-
       zation in the Middle East: The Nineteenth Century.
       Chicago: University of Chicago Press, 1968, 171-184.

1208   Tugay, Emine Foat.   Three Centuries: Family Chronicles
       of Turkey and Egypt.   London: Oxford University
       Press, 1963.   The autobiography of a granddaughter of
       Khedive Ismail which includes much information on
       women of the khedivial family and the aristocracy.

1209   "A $2,000 Prize for a Song on the Role of Woman in the
       Arab World" (in Arabic).   al-Ahram, July 28, 1976,
       p. 14, col. 5.

1210   United Arab Republic.   Ministry of National Guidance.
       State Information Service.   The Role of Women in the
       United Arab Republic.   Cairo, n.d.

1211   Vaucher-Zananiri, Nelly. "Le Rôle des femmes dans la
       RAU. " Preuves-Informations, 16 (Jan. 3, 1961).

1212   "Vis-à-vis the Art: Woman Is as Responsible as Man" (in
       Arabic). al-Ahram, May 27, 1976, p. 5, col. 2.

1213   Voilquin, Suzanne. Souvenirs d'une fille du peuple ou La
       Saint-Simonienne en Egypte (1834-36). Paris: Sauzet,
       The memoires of a disciple of Saint-Simon who tried
       to spread instruction and medical care among Egyptian
       women.

1214   "What Is In Egypt's Report for the International Women's
       Year" (in Arabic). al-Musawwar, June 20, 1975, 21.

1215   "Wolf-Whistle Can Bring Prison. " Christian Science Moni-
       tor, Oct. 17, 1972, p. 11, col. 5 (Western ed.); p. 14,
       col. 5 (Mid-western ed.). About penalties incurred for
       importuning women in the streets.

1216   "Women Express Their Opinion at a Round-Table About the
       Evolution of the Political Regime" (in Arabic). al-
       Ahram, Sept. 26, 1974, p. 4, col. 6.

1217   "The Women of Our Country in Figures" (in Arabic). al-
       Ahram, May 7, 1976, p. 7, col. 3.

1218   "The Women of Our Country in Figures" (in Arabic). al-
       Ahram, May 21, 1976, p. 7, col. 6. About the in-
       crease in the number of working women in recent years.

1219   Yusuf, Ahmad. al-Mar'ah al-misriyah. Cairo: Dar al-
       ma'arif, 1932.

1220   Yusuf, Mahmud. al-Jins al-rashiq. Cairo: Matba'at al-
       hurriyah, 1942.

1221   _____. al-Nisa' mala'ikah. Cairo: Matba'at al-
       hurriyah, 1948.

1222   _____. Tabi'at al-mar'ah. Cairo: Matba'at al-
       hurriyah, 1945.

(2) ISLAM

General

1223   'Abd al-Rahman, 'A'ishah (Bint al-Shati'.) al-Mafhum al-
       islami li-tahrir al-mar'ah. Cairo: Jami'at Omdurman
       al-islamiyah, 1967.

1224   Abd al-Raziq, Mustafa. "L'Influence de la femme dans la

vie du cheikh Mohamed Abdou. " L'Egyptienne, 40
(Aug. 1928), 2-8.

1225   "al-Azhar, Islam and the Role of Women in Islamic Society,
       An Unislamic Pronouncement. " Islamic Review, 8
       (Aug. 1952), 3-4.

1226   "Donna: parere di el-Azhar sulla funzione della donna nella
       societa. " Oriente Moderno, 5 (1956), 351.

1227   Fikri, 'Ali. al-Mar'ah al-ashya'. Cairo: Maktabat al-
       Shabab, 1928.

1228   Hilmi, 'Abbas. al-Mar'ah, intiqad ijtima'i. Cairo: n. p.,
       1915. In a very old fashioned style the author exhorts
       women not to unveil or wear make-up.

1229   Husayn, Ahmad. al-Zawaj wa-al-mar'ah fi al-Islam.
       Cairo: Dar al-kitab al-misriyah, 1946.

1230   Imam, 'Abd Allah. "Does This Sheikh Speak in the Name of
       God?!" (in Arabic). Ruz al-Yusuf, May 31, 1965, 38-
       41.

1231   _____. "The Imam 'Ali Ayat Allah Kashif al-Ghata' De-
       clares ..." (in Arabic). Ruz al-Yusuf, June 7, 1965,
       42-43.

1232   al-Jabri, 'Abd al-Mit'al Muhammad. al-Mar'ah fi al-
       tasawwur al-islami. Cairo: Maktabat al-wahbah, 1975.
       Extensive comments on Islamic traditions concerning
       women, recommends female education.

1233   Jomier, J. "Un Livre récent sur la femme. " Mélanges
       de l'Institut Dominicain d'Etudes Orientales, 1 (1954),
       150-59. Review of al-Mar'ah bayn al-bayt wa-al-
       mujtama' by Muslim brother al-Bahi al-Khuli.

1234   Kernkamp, W. J. A. De Islam en de Vrouw, Bijdrage Tot
       de Kennis van het Reformisme Naar Aanleiding van
       M. R. Rida's "Nida' lil-djins al-latif." Amsterdam:
       N. V. Noord-Hollandische Uitgeversmaatschappij, 1935.

1235   Khalid, Khalid Muhammad. From Here We Start. Wash-
       ington, D. C.: American Council of Learned Societies,
       1953. This controversial book by a modernist sheikh
       includes a section on women, 149-161.

1236   al-Khuli, al-Bahi. al-Mar'ah bayn al-bayt wa-al-mujtama'.
       Cairo: Dar al-kitab al-'arabi, 1953. The author be-
       longed to the Muslim brotherhood.

1237   Linant de Bellefonds, Y. "A propos d'un livre récent du recteur d'al-Azhar. " Orient, 19 (1961), 27-42.

1238   Muhammad Rashid Rida. Nida´ ila al-jins al-latif. Cairo:
        Matba'at al-manar, 1351 A.H. (1932-1933). An appeal
        to the fair sex to acknowledge the rights Islam recog-
        nized women.

1239   Muhanna, Majidah. "Jihan al-Sadat: Islam Pioneered
        Women's Liberation" (in Arabic). al-Ahram, Dec. 21,
        1975, p. 6, col. 4. About the seminar on the role of
        woman in the Islamic family, sponsored by al-Azhar
        and inaugurated by Mrs. al-Sadat.

1240   Mukhtar, Bahirah. "Will a Female Swimming Champion Go
        to Hell?" (in Arabic). al-Ahram, Dec. 25, 1975, p. 4.
        About the controversies raised at the Seminar on the
        Role of Woman in the Islamic Family, organized by al-
        Azhar University.

1241   "A Muslim Women's Club" (in Arabic). al-Ahram, March
        3, 1976, p. 5, col. 3. About the establishment of
        Islamic courses at Munirah Khatir's in Misr al-Jadidah.

1242   Nabarawi, Ceza. "A une néophyte. " L'Egyptienne, 27
        (June 1927), 19-23. In answer to a recent convert to
        Islam who accused the Feminist Union of attacking re-
        ligion.

1243   Nançon, A. "La Condition des femmes dans l'Islam. "
        Revue de l'Islam, 4 (1899), 97-99, 113-17.

1243a   Nasif, Malak Hifni. al-Mar´ah al-muslimah al-'asriyah.
        Cairo: Dar al-Ansar, 1976. Articles and speeches
        concerning the behavior of modern muslim women.

1244   Radhi, 'Ali 'Abd al-Jalil. al-Mar´ah al-muslimah al-yawm.
        Cairo: al-Maktabah al-anglu-al-misriyah, 1954.

1245   al-Ra'i, Mustafa Muhammad. al-Mar´ah al-muslimah.
        Cairo: Matba'at al-mahallah al-shar'iyah, 1941.

1246   Rejwan, Nissim. "Social Reformers in Egyptian Islam. "
        New Outlook, 7 (Aug. 1964), 46-55.

1247   "Thirty Dresses Inside the Mosque of Sayyid al-Badawi for
        Women and Girls Entering the Mosque" (in Arabic).
        al-Ahram, July 22, 1974, p. 11, col. 4.

1247a   Timm, Klaus and Schahnas Aalami. Die muslimische Frau
        zwischen Tradition und Fortschritt: Frauenfrage und
        Familien-entwicklung in Ägypten und Iran. Berlin:
        Akademie Verlag, 1976.

1248   'Un, Kamal Ahmad.   al-Mar'ah fi al-Islam.   Tanta:
       Matba'at al-sha'rawi, 1955.

1249   Wajdi, Farid.   al-Mar'ah al-muslimah.   Cairo: Matba'at
       Hindiyah, 1911.   This book was written in answer to
       Qasim Amin's al-Mar'ah al-jadidah [entry 1749].

                                  Law

1250   'Abd al-Hamid, Muhammad Muhyi al-Din.   al-Ahwal al-
       shakhsiyah fi al-shari'ah al-islamiyah.   Cairo: Mu-
       hammad 'Ali Sabih, 1966.

1251   Anderson, J. N. D.   "The Problems of Divorce in the
       Sharia Law of Islam."   Royal Central Asian Journal,
       37 (April 1950), 169-85.

1252   _____.   "Recent Development in Sharia Law."   The Mus-
       lim World, 2 (1951), 113-26.   About marriage con-
       tracts in Egyptian family law and marriages below legal
       age.

1253   _____.   "Recent Developments in Sharia Law, VII."
       The Muslim World, 42 (April 1952), 124-40.   Analyzes
       the 1943 Egyptian law.

1254   al-Maraghi, 'Abd Allah Mustafa'.   Huquq al-mar'ah fi al-
       shari'ah al-Islamiyah wa-muqaranatuha bi-al-shara'i al-
       ukhra.   Cairo: al-Matba'ah al-salafiyah, 1928-1929.

1255   Mohamed, A. Z.   "Certains Aspects des relations conjugales:
       leurs particularités en droit musulman."   L'Egypte Con-
       temporaine, 327 (Jan. 1967), 79-124.

1256   Ragai, Doria (Shafik).   La Femme et le droit religieux de
       l'Egypte contemporaine.   Paris: Paul Geuthner, 1940.
       The first book of leading feminist Doria Shafik.

1257   Rossi, Ettore.   "Polemica in Egitto per una proposta di
       equiparare le donne agli uomini nelle successioni di
       diritto musulmano."   Oriente Moderno, 1 (1929), 53-54.
       About a law project which would have established equal-
       ity between men and women in inheritance matters.

1258   al-Sa'id, al-Sa'id Mustafa.   Fi mada isti'mal huquq al-
       zawjiyah wa-ma tataqayyadu bihi fi al-shari'ah al-
       islamiyah wa-al-qanun al-misri al-hadith.   Cairo: n. p. ,
       1936.

1259   Schacht, Joseph.   "L'Evolution moderne du droit musulman
       en Egypte."   Mélanges Maspero.   Cairo: Institut
       Français d'Archéologie Orientale, 1935-1940.   Vol. 3,

323-34.

1260   Vacca, Virginia. "Fetwa di al-Azhar sulla participazione
        delle donne alla vita pubblica." Oriente Moderno, 1
        (Jan. 1953), 40-41.

(3) THE RURAL WOMAN

1261   "About Women's Rights: Literacy Will Lead to the Evolu-
        tion of the Country Women" (in Arabic). al-Ahram,
        Nov. 17, 1974, p. 10, col. 1.

1262   Abu-Lughod, Janet. "Migrant Adjustment to City Life:
        The Egyptian Case." American Journal of Sociology,
        July 1961, 22-32.

1263   Ammar, Hamed. "The Aims and Methods of Socialization
        in Silwa." In John Middleton, ed. , From Child to
        Adult: Studies in the Anthropology of Education.   New
        York: Natural History Press, 1970; 226-49.

1264   'Ammar, Hamid Mustafa. Growing Up In An Egyptian Vil-
        lage. London: Routledge & Kegan Paul, 1954. The
        author returned to his native village of Silwa, in the
        province of Aswan, for this study, one of the best on
        Egyptian rural life.

1265   Ayrout, Henry Habib. The Egyptian Peasant. Trans. by
        John A. Williams. Boston: Beacon Press, 1963. The
        revised edition of a work originally published in French
        in 1938, for long the standard work on rural life in
        Egypt.

1266   Barclay, Harold B. "Study of an Egyptian Village Commu-
        nity." Studies in Islam, 4 (Oct. 1966), 201-26.

1267   el-Bayoumi, Soheir. "Sex Role Differentiation and Illness
        Behavior in the Egyptian Nile Delta Community."
        Paper delivered at the Ninth Annual Meeting of the
        Middle East Studies Association, Louisville, Ky. ,
        Nov. 19-22, 1975.

1268   Blackman, Winifred. The Fellahin of Upper Egypt; Their
        Religious, Social and Industrial Life Today. London:
        G. G. Harrap & Co. , 1927. One of the best docu-
        mented and most entertaining books written on rural
        Egypt; numerous data on women throughout the book.

1269   "A Blooming Face Among the Wheat Sheave" (in Arabic).
        al-Ahram, Sept. 30, 1976, p. 5, col. 5.

1270   Fakhouri, Hani. "The Zar Cult in an Egyptian Village."
        Anthropological Quarterly, Vol. 41, 49-56.

1271   Family Orientation and Consultation Office. Non-Registered
        Marriages in Mashala Village, Sharkia Governorate.
        Zagazig, 1966.

1272   al-Hilbawi, Mustafa 'Ali. Fi al-rif al-misri. Cairo: n.p.,
        1928. The fourth chapter describes the life of the
        peasant woman.

1273   Hussein, Aziza. "Emancipation Comes to Egypt's Villages.
        Women in Decision-Making." The Egyptian Gazette,
        July 6, 1975, p. 4.

1274   Ibrahim, Haridi. Haqiqat al-mar'ah al-rifiyah. Cairo:
        Matba'at al-watan, 1939.

1275   Karam, Emile. "Yesterday ... and Today" (in Arabic).
        al-Ahram, May 18, 1976, p. 5, col. 3. The author
        thinks that woman's condition has not changed in the
        countryside.

1276   Klunzinger, C. B. Upper Egypt: Its People and Its Prod-
        ucts. London: Blackie & Son, 1878. The author, a
        physician, made many good observations on women,
        family life, dancing girls, festivities, and the zar.

1277   al-Markaz al-duwali lil-tarbiyah al-assasiyah bi-al-'alam
        al-'arabi. Sirs al-Layyan. Bahth halat usrah rifiyah.
        Sirs al-Layyan, 1955. Results of an inquiry on the
        condition of the rural family.

1278   Mieville, W. "The Fellah's Yokemate." Fortnightly Re-
        view, 85 (1906), 1093-1105. A sympathetic description
        of the Egyptian peasant woman.

1279   Saunders, Lucie Wood. "Women, Men and Political Power
        in an Egyptian Village." Paper presented at the Ninth
        Annual Meeting of the Middle East Studies Association,
        Louisville, Ky., Nov. 19-22, 1975.

1280   "The Wedding Night" (in Arabic). al-'Alam al-'arabi, May
        10, 1947, 46-47.

1281   Willcoks, William. "Le Fellah et sa femme sur les terres
        incultes d'Egypte." Bulletin de la Société de Géogra-
        phie d'Egypte, n.s., 8 (1917), 167-88. The financial
        role of the peasant woman is compared to that of an
        outside money-lender.

1282   Work, Margaret. "Egypt's Peasant Women." The Muslim
        World, 35 (1945), 32-43.

(4) THE BEDOUIN WOMAN

1283   Ahmed, Abou Zeid. "Honour and Shame Among the Be-
            douins of Egypt." In J. G. Peristany, ed., Honour
            and Shame: The Values of Mediterranean Society.
            Chicago: University of Chicago Press, 1966, 243-60.

1284   Mohsen, Safia K. "The Legal Status of Women Among the
            Awlad 'Ali." Anthropological Quarterly, 3 (July 1967),
            153-66.

1285   _____. "The Legal Status of Women Among the Awlad
            'Ali." In Louise E. Sweet, ed., Peoples and Cultures
            of the Middle East. Garden City, N.Y.: Natural His-
            tory Press, 1970; vol. 1, 220-33.

1286   Work, Telford Hindley. "Bedouin Wedding Feast." Geo-
            graphical Magazine, 30 (Sept. 1957), 219-33.

(5) THE COPTIC WOMAN

1287   Abbott, Nabia. Arabic Marriage Among Copts. 2 vols.
            Leipzig: Brockhaus, 1941.

1288   Bishay, Sa'id Bishay, and Yusuf Salah Wadi'ah. Dirasat
            kitabiyah 'an makan al-mar'ah fi al-kanisah al-misriyah.
            Cairo: Dar al-jil lil-tiba'ah, 1973.

1289   Freeland, Anthony. "Egyptians and Turks at Home." St.
            James's Magazine, April-Dec. 1876, 65-78. The au-
            thor describes a Coptic wedding he attended.

1290   Ghrighurius, Bishop. al-Dars al-awwal lil-mar'ah. Cairo:
            Maktabat al-marhabah, 1973.

1291   Nasim, Sulayman. Usratuna fi zilal al-masihiyah. Cairo:
            Kanisat Mar Murqus al-qubtiyah al-urthuduksiyah bi-
            Shubra, 1971.

1292   Sawiris, Bishop. al-Mar'ah al-katiah. Alexandria: Makta-
            bat Kanisat Mar Girgis, 1969.

1293   Shinudah III, Patriarch of the Coptic Church. Shari'at al-
            zawaj al-wahidah fi al-masihiyah. Cairo: Lajnat al-
            ta'lif wa-al-tarjamah wa-al-nashr, 1967.

(6) MARRIAGE AND THE FAMILY

General

1294   'Abd al-Jawwad, Muhammad. Ahadith al-zawaj fi Misr.
        Cairo: Maktabat al-Ma'arif, n.d.   On the practical
        and moral aspects of marriage.

1295   Asaad, Ramses W. 'Social Survey of Egypt. " Civiliza-
        tions, 1 (1957), 47-56.

1296   al-Baradi'i, Muhammad Mustafa.   "Lest Motherhood Be-
        comes a Hobby" (in Arabic). al-Ahram, Jan. 17, 1976,
        p. 9, col. 1.   About educational programs preparing
        girls to become good mothers.

1297   al-Basyuni, Amirah 'Abd al-Mun'im. al-Usrah al-misriyah.
        Cairo: Dar al-katib al-'arabi lil tiba'ah wa-al-nashr,
        1967.

1298   al-Bisi, Sana'. "She ... " (in Arabic). al-Ahram, March
        21, 1976, p. 9, col. 1.   About the sacrifices of Egyp-
        tian mothers to raise their children.

1299   _____. "She ... " (in Arabic). al-Ahram, July 16,
        1976, p. 7, col. 1.   About the relationship between
        husband and wife after the discovery of adultery.

1300   "Did You Marry an Emigrant?" (in Arabic). Akhir Sa'ah,
        2183 (Aug. 25, 1976), 34-35.   About student marriages
        abroad.

1301   Douglass, Joseph H., and Katherine W. Douglass. "As-
        pects of Marriage and Family Living Among Egyptian
        Peasants. " Marriage and Family Living, 16 (1954),
        45-48.

1302   "Du mariage en Orient. " Presse Médicale d'Egypte, 16
        (Aug. 15, 1912), 241-43; 18 (Sept. 15, 1912), 273-75.

1303   Fu'ad, Ni'mat. Ila ibnati. Cairo: Maktabat al-Khanji,
        1956.

1304   Ghali, Pierre. Fiançailles, mariages, etc. Cairo: Edi-
        tions du Scorpion, 1944.

1305   al-Hasani, Kamal. al-Takhtit fi hayat al-usrah. Cairo:
        Wizarat al-shu'un al-ijtima'iyah.   'Ilaqat 'ammah, 1971.

1306   "Honoring the Beloved: The Housewife Is a Worker Because
        She Uses Her Hands" (in Arabic). al-Ahram, May 24,
        1976, p. 14, col. 1.

1307 "Honoring the Beloved: Where Do We Situate the Housewife Among the Masses?" (in Arabic). al-Ahram, May 21, 1976, l. 7, col. 4.

1308 Hussein, F. H. "Endogamy in Egyptian Nubia." Journal of Biosocial Science, 3 (1971), 251-57.

1309 "The Ideal Mother Is From Suhag" (in Arabic). al-Ahram, March 15, 1976, p. 8, col. 4.

1310 al-Jawhari, Muhammad Fa'iq. Fann al-zawaj wa-kayfa tatazawwajayni wa-law kunti armalah. Cairo: Matba'at al-tarbiyah al-badaniyah, 1932.

1311 ________. al-Hubb wa-al-zawaj. Cairo: n.p., 1931.

1312 al-Jiddawi, Zinat. Ummi: mukhtarat wa-rasa'il wa-umniyat. Cairo: al-Dar al-qawmi lil-tiba'ah wa-al-nashr, 1964.

1313 "La Journée des Mères en Egypte." La Bourse Egyptienne, May 10, 1950. About the first Mothers' Day in Egypt, observed after a campaign by the National Feminist Party of Fatmah Ni'mat Rashid.

1314 Junaydi, Muhammad Farid. Azmat al-zawaj fi Misr, asbabuha, nata'ijuha, 'ilajuha. Cairo: Matba'at Hijazi, 1933. The author believed there was a reluctance to marry affecting all classes of Egyptian society. He analyzed the reasons for this phenomenon. He and several personalities put forward some suggestions to remedy the situation.

1315 Lichtenstadter, Ilse. "An Arab Egyptian Family." The Middle East Journal, 4 (Fall 1952), 379-99.

1316 al-Mazini, Ibrahim. "My Mother" (in Arabic). al-Hilal, 1934, 17-21.

1317 Mu'assasat al-Ahram. al-Mar'ah wa-al-bayt, 1967.

1318 Musa, Salamah. Fann al-hubb wa-al-hayah. Beirut: Maktabat al-Ma'arif, 196-.

1319 al-Muti'i, Muhammad Bahit. Raf' al-aghlaq 'an mashru' al-zawaj wa-al-talaq. Cairo: al-Matba'ah al-salafiyah, 1345 (i.e. 1926/1927).

1320 Nasim, Sulaiman. al-Fatah wa-al-usrah wa-mantiq al-'asr min wijah al-nathir al-masihiyah. Cairo: Maktabat al-Mahabbah, 1973.

1321 "New Rules to Choose the Ideal Mother for 1976" (in Arabic).

al-Ahram, Feb. 3, 1976, p. 6, col. 1.

1322   Perkins, E. E. "Marriage Ceremony in Lower Egypt. "
       Man, 32 (1932), 63-66.

1323   Petersen, Karen K. "Demographic Conditions and Extended
       Family Household: Egyptian Data. " Social Forces, 4
       (June 1968), 531-37.   The author comes to the conclu-
       sion that patrilocal extended family households are actu-
       ally uncommon in Egypt.

1324   _____. "Family and Kin in Contemporary Egypt. " Un-
       published Ph.D. dissertation, Columbia University,
       1967.

1325   Rizk, Hanna. "Social Services Available for Families in
       Egypt. " Marriage and Family Living, 17 (Aug. 1955),
       212-17.

1326   Ross, Mary; Mona Khoury-Schmitz; and Zeinab Hefnawy.
       Preliminary Report on Visits to 23 Families in Agbour
       Soughra. Cairo: FAO, 1954. Inquiry on the feeding
       pattern of poor families in Lower Egypt.

1327   Sadiq, Zaynab. "Late Marriages" (in Arabic). Ruz al-
       Yusuf, July 19, 1965, 46-47.

1328   Salam, Muhammad Fahmi. al-Mar'ah wa-sirr al-sa'adah
       al-zawjiyah. Cairo: Sharikat istandard lil-tiba'ah,
       1951.

1329   "The Selection of the Ideal Mother by the Ministry of Social
       Affairs" (in Arabic). al-Ahram, March 5, 1976, p. 8,
       col. 4.

1330   "Starting to Select the Ideal Mothers to Honor Them on
       Mothers Day" (in Arabic). al-Ahram, March 3, 1976,
       p. 6, col. 8.

Family Law

1331   'Abd al-Jawwad, Muhammad. "Evolution du statut familial
       en droit égyptien. " L'Egypte Contemporaine, 314 (Oct.
       1963), 91-101.

1332   Asaf, J. "About Inheritance Between Spouses. " Mashriq,
       43 (1949), 98-118.

1333   al-Bindari, 'Abd al-Wahhab. Qadaya al-zawaj wa-al-talaq
       wafqa li-ahdath al-ahkam. Cairo: al-Matba'ah al-
       'alamiyah, 1969.

1334   "Common Law Marriage" (in Arabic).   Ruz al-Yusuf, Aug.
        30, 1965, 38-39.

1335   "Family Day Instead of Mothers Day" (in Arabic).   al-
        Ahram, March 27, 1976, p. 15, col. 8.   The whole
        family should be honored on a special day.

1336   Goadby, F. M.   "La Capacité de la femme mariée en droit
        égyptien. "   L'Egypte Contemporaine, 1915-16, 51-58.

1337   Haggag, Nadia.   "Change in Egyptian Family Life. "   Unpub-
        lished M.A. thesis, American University in Cairo,
        1958.

1338   al-Husayni, Muhammad Mustafa Shihatah.   al-Ahwal al-
        shakhsiyah fi ahkam al-zawaj wa-al-talaq.   Cairo:
        Matba'at dar al-ta'lif, 1967.

1339   Khalifah, 'Abd al-'Aziz.   al-Mushkilah al-Zawjiyah wa-
        asbabuha wa'ilajuha.   Cairo: Matba'at lajnat al-ta'lif,
        1948.

1340   al-Mahdi, 'Abd al-'Alim.   "Why Don't We Remember Agar,
        An Egyptian, and the Mother of the Arabs, on Mothers'
        Day?" (in Arabic).   al-Ahram, March 22, 1976, p. 5,
        col. 1.

1341   Nabarawi, Ceza.   "Une Loi n'a de valeur que par son appli-
        cation. "   L'Egyptienne, 65 (Jan. 1931), 5-8.   Against
        the marriage of young girls without official documents
        stating their age.

1342   _____.   "La Situation juridique de la femme égyptienne. "
        L'Egyptienne, 66 (Feb. 1931), 3-15.   Text of a lecture
        about polygamy, repudiation, inheritance inequality and
        testimony of women.

1343   Ratib, 'A'ishah.   "Women's Laws in Egypt" (in Arabic).
        al-Hilal, April 1971, 138-43.

1344   Rida, Husayn Ahmad Tawfiq.   al-Ahwal al-shakhsiyah lil-
        misriyin ghayr al-muslimun.   Cairo: Dar al-nahdah
        al-'arabiyah, 1967.

1345   Sadiq, Shukri.   al-Quwah al-hayawiyah aw al-mar'ah wa-al-
        zawaj.   Cairo: Dar al-ma'arif, 1910.

1346   al-Sayyid, 'Abd al-Fattah.   "De l'étendue des droits de la
        femme dans le mariage musulman et particulièrement
        en Egypte. "   Thesis. Paris, Recueil Sirey, 1922.
        The author, a former judge and professor at Cairo Law
        School, denounces abuses against women because of too
        rigorous an application of the law.   Includes translation

of the 1920 law on alimony, pp. 281-85.

1347   Sha'rawi, Huda. "La Quote-part de la femme dans l'héri-
       tage." L'Egyptienne, 45 (Jan. 1929), 2-5. Transla-
       tion of her article published in al-Ahram, Dec. 28,
       1929.

1348   Soliman, Mikhail. La Répression de l'adultère en Egypte.
       Paris: E. Sagot et Cie, 1925.

1349   Tanaghu, Samir 'Abd al-Sayyid. Ahkam al-usrah al-
       misriyah ghayr al-muslimun. Alexandria: Munsha'at
       ma'arif, 1968.

1350   Zuhayr, Su'ad. "Marriage of Pleasure Instead of Sin" (in
       Arabic). Ruz al-Yusuf, June 21, 1965, 37-39. About
       mut'ah marriage.

Divorce

1351   al-'Amri, Muhammad. "Divorce Egyptian Style" (in Ara-
       bic). Ruz al-Yusuf, July 26, 1965, 42-43.

1352   Ayrout, H. "Le Divorce déplaît." En Terre d'Islam, 10
       (1935), 275-76. The unpopularity of divorce among
       religious leaders.

1353   "Divorce Bill Touches Off Squabble." The Christian Science
       Monitor, April 15, 1974, p. 5, col. 1.

1354   "Divorce On the Increase Concerns Egyptians." The
       Christian Science Monitor, Sept. 24, 1973, p. 5, col.
       4.

1355   "Une Enquête de Révolution Africaine sur le divorce."
       Revue de Presse, 91 (Jan. 1965).

1356   Levi, I. G. "La Nuptialité et les divorces en Egypte."
       Bulletin de l'Institut d'Egypte, 21 (1939), 191-209.

1357   Mitchell, Loretta. "The Sorrow of Egypt." The Moslem
       World, Jan. 1913, 64-66.

1358   "Opinions sur le divorce." La Patrie, Jan. 2, 1947.

1359   Péroncel-Hugoz, J. P. "Divorce à l'égyptienne." Le
       Monde, June 6-7, 1976. On the attempts to reform
       the law of personal status.

1360   Sabri, Yahya. Mashakilna al-ijtima'iyah. Cairo: Matba'ah
       Hijazi, 1957. A brief survey of national problems, in-
       cluding a section on divorce and polygamy, 25-36.

1361   Walz, Jay. "Cairo to Abolish Casual Divorce. " New York
        Times, Feb. 23, 1960, 11. About the law project to
        force husbands to state their motives for divorce in
        court.

1362   Zaalouk, Malak el-Husseiny. "The Social Structure of Di-
        vorce Adjudication in Egypt. " Unpublished M.A. thesis,
        American University in Cairo, 1975.

                        Fertility and Family Planning

1363   Abu Lughod, Janet. "The Emergence of Differential Fer-
        tility in Urban Egypt. " Milbank Memorial Fund Quar-
        terly, 2 (1965), 235-53.

1364   _____. "Urban-Rural Differences As a Function of the
        Demographic Transition: Egyptian Data and An Analyti-
        cal Model. " American Journal of Sociology, March
        1964, 476-91.

1365   Badrawi, Malak, and Mona Ghaleb. "Mrs. al-Sadat Sug-
        gests Sterilization as a Solution for Egypt's Overpopu-
        lation Problem. " Caravan, Dec. 8, 1975, 6.

1366   el-Badry, M. A. 'Some Aspects of Fertility in Egypt. "
        Milbank Memorial Fund Quarterly, 1 (1956), 22-24.

1367   Blackman, Winifred S. "Fertility Rites in Modern Egypt. "
        Discovery, 28 (April 1922), 154-58.

1368   Gadalla, Saad. "Population Problems and Family Planning
        Programs in Egypt. " In Proceedings of the Eighth In-
        ternational Congress of Anthropological and Ethnological
        Sciences, Tokyo: Science Council of Japan, 1968; vol.
        3 (American University in Cairo, Social Research
        Center, Reprint no. 14).

1369   Garzouzi, Eva. Old Ills and New Remedies in Egypt.
        Cairo: Dar al-ma'arif, 1958.

1370   El-Hamamsy, Laila Shukry. "Characteristics of Clients of
        Family Planning Clinics in Cairo. " Paper delivered
        at the Family Planning Conference, United Arab Repub-
        lic Ministry of Social Affairs, 1968.

1371   _____. "Egypt's Family Planning Program From the
        Social Perspective. " Paper prepared for the United
        Nations Social Welfare Services Section, 1974.

1372   Hanna, Azmi T. , et al. "Family Planning Studies: The
        Teachers Survey. " Egyptian Population and Family
        Planning Review, 1 (June 1970), 17-66.

1373   Hussein, Aziza.   "Status of Women and Family Planning in
        a Developing Country, Egypt. " In Abdel R. Omran,
        ed. , Egypt: Population Problems and Prospects.
        Chapel Hill, N. C. : Carolina Population Center, Uni-
        versity of North Carolina, 1973, 181-86.

1374   Kamel, W. H. , et al.   "A Fertility Study in al-Amria. "
        The Egyptian Population and Family Planning Review,
        2 (1968), 83-100.

1375   Karni, A.   "Birth Control in the UAR. "   New Outlook, 5
        (1968), 20-30.

1376   Khalifa, Abd. Mohammed.   "Differential Fertility in Egypt:
        Multivariate Analysis. " Unpublished Ph. D. dissertation,
        University of North Carolina, Chapel Hill, 1971.

1377   Khazbak, Muhammad.   Tanzim al-nasl fi Misr.   Cairo: al-
        Dar al-qawmiyah lil-tab'ah wa-al-nashr, n. d.

1378   Marzouk, Girgis Abdo.   "Fertility of the Urban and Rural
        Population in Egypt. " L'Egypte Contemporaine, Jan.
        1959, 27-34.

1379   Rashid, Fatma Ni'mat.   "La Limitation de la natalité. "
        La Patrie, April 14, 1937.   Mrs. Rashid thinks that
        birth control would prevent the spreading of hereditary
        diseases and that even abortions could be performed.

1380   Rizk, Hanna.   "Fertility Patterns in Egypt. " In Institut
        International de Sociologie.   Actes du XVIIème Congrès
        International de Sociologie, Beirut, 23-29 September 1957.
        Vol. I, 651-66.

1381   _____.   "Fertility Patterns in Selected Areas in Egypt. "
        Unpublished Ph. D. dissertation, Princeton University,
        1959.

1382   _____.   "Population Growth and Its Effect on Economic
        and Social Goals in the United Arab Republic. " Popula-
        tion Review, 7 (Jan. 1963), 51-56.

1383   _____.   "Social and Psychological Factors Affecting Fer-
        tility in the United Arab Republic. " Marriage and
        Family Living, 1 (Feb. 1963), 69-73. Economic de-
        velopment cannot be implemented without social change.

1384   Sabagh, George.   "Differential Fertility in an Arab Coun-
        try. " Milbank Memorial Fund Quarterly, Jan. 1963,
        100-96.

1385   Sayf al-Nasr, 'Aliyah.   "... Because Husbands Refuse to
        Cooperate in Family Planning!" (in Arabic).   al-Ahram,

Jan. 4, 1976, p. 9, col. 1. The results of an inquiry conducted by the National Center for Social Research near Cairo.

1386 Shanawany, H. A. "Family Planning: An Equilibrium Response to Demographic Conditions in the United Arab Republic (Egypt). " Unpublished Ph. D. dissertation, Cornell University, 1967.

1387 Tomiche, Nada. "En Egypte: le gouvernement devant le problème démographique. " Orient, 3 (1957), 106-119.

1388 Toppozada, N. K. "Progress and Problems of Family Planning in the United Arab Republic. " Demography, 2 (1968), 590-98.

1389 Waterbury, John. "Chickens and Eggs: Egypt's Population Explosion Revisited. " American Universities Field Staff, North East Africa Series, May 1975, 1-17. Includes the figures of contraceptive users, marriage and divorce rates, analyzes Egyptian attitudes towards family planning.

1390 Zikry, Abdel-Khalik Mahmoud. "Socio-Cultural Determinants of Human Fertility in Egypt, U. A. R. " Unpublished Ph. D. dissertation, University of Syracuse, 1963.

1391 _____. "Urbanization and Its Effects on the Levels of Fertility of U. A. R. Women. " L'Egypte Contemporaine, 55 (Oct. 1964), 27-42.

Polygamy

1392 "En marge d'un projet: le Parti féministe contre la polygamie. " La Bourse Egyptienne, Feb. 19, 1945. Instead of restricting polygamy to those wealthy enough to support a second wife, F. N. Rashid wanted its complete abolition.

1393 Farrag, A. M. "Remarriages, Multiple Marriages and Polygamous Nuptiality Tables in the United Arab Republic, 1960. " In International Population Conference, London 1969; vol. 3, 2180-81.

1394 Rossi, Ettore. "L'Unione femminile egiziana chiede al Governo l'abolizione della poligamia. " Oriente Moderno, 9 (1935), 476. Includes the text of a letter from Huda Sha'rawi to Prime Minister Tawfiq Nasim Pasha asking for suppression of polygamy.

1395 Thabit, Munirah. "Polygamy and the Opinion of Sheikh al-Maraghi. " al-Misriyah, March 1, 1940. Mrs. Thabit advises young women to include in their marriage contract a clause authorizing them to obtain a divorce if their husband takes another wife.

Seclusion of Women

1396 Badran, Margot. "Institution of the Harim and Aspects of Harim Life in the Late and Early 20th Century Egypt." Paper delivered at the Eighth Annual Meeting of the Middle East Studies Association, Boston, Nov. 6-9, 1974.

1397 Biais, M. "L'Egypte vivante: Harems sans histoire." Correspondance d'Orient, Aug. 1, 1910, 89-92.

1398 _____. "L'Egypte vivante: Un harem arabe." Correspondance d'Orient, July 15, 1910, 73-78.

1399 _____. "L'Egypte vivante: Un harem turc." Correspondance d'Orient, June 15, 1910, 507-511.

1400 Fahmy-Bey, J. Au coeur du Harem. Paris: Félix Juven, 1911. Madame Fahmy-Bey, who wrote under the pseudonym of Jehan d'Ivray, was married to a high-ranking Egyptian official. A good and objective writer, she received the Prix de la Société des Gens de Lettres in 1927.

1401 Javidan, Princess. Harem Life. London: Noel Douglas, 1931. A good analysis of life in the harem by American born Djavidan Hanum, former wife of Khedive Abbas Hilmi II.

1402 Lott, Emmeline. Harem Life in Egypt and Constantinople. London: Richard Bentley, 1867. Miss Lott, a proper Victorian governess, did not like the East and her sojourn in the employment of the khedivial family did not dispel her prejudices.

1403 Nabarawi, Ceza. "A un député réactionnaire." L'Egyptienne, 156 (June 1939), 8-10. Answers a deputy who favored the claustration of women. Asks him how an educated orphaned young lady can support herself and her younger brothers: should she be reduced to begging or prostitution?

1404 Nizzoli, Amalia. Memorie sull'Egitto e specialmente sui custiomi delle donne orientali e gli harem, scritte durante il suo soggiorno in quel paese 1819-1828.

1405 Rushdi, Eugénie. Harems et musulmanes d'Egypte; lettres. Paris: Félix Juvens, 1902. French born Eugénie

Rushdi, was married to Rashid Pasha. She wrote under the pseudonym of Niya Salima. Her books are in-
valuable accounts of the life of the high Egyptian bourgeoisie.

(7) EDUCATION AND SPORTS

1406   Abu Zayd, Hikmat. Ma'alim al-ta´rikh, amam al-mar´ah
        al-'amilah. Cairo: Idarat al-ma'alumat al-'ammah li-
        wizarat al-shu´un al-ijtima'iyah, 1964.

1407   _____, et al. The Education of Women in the U.A.R.
        During the 19th and 20th Centuries. Cairo: National
        Commission for UNESCO, 1970. Gives various figures
        and statistics.

1408   Babazogli, Sophie. L'éducation de la jeune fille musulmane
        en Egypte. Cairo: Paul Barbey, 1928.

1409   al-Bagri, Isma'il. "Woman and Karate" (in Arabic). al-
        Ahram, Aug. 14, 1976, p. 12, col. 1.

1410   al-Baradi'i, Muhammad Mustafa. "What Do We Teach
        Girls?" (in Arabic). al-Ahram, Jan. 10, 1976, p. 9,
        col. 1. Questions whether young Egyptian women are
        properly educated to raise a family.

1411   "Contro l'invio di studentesse in Inghilterra per studiare la
        vita sociale." Oriente Moderno, 5 (May 1936), 295.
        The Egyptian government was willing to let girls stay
        in girls' institutions in England but not to study social
        life.

1412   Couvreur, A. Etudes de psychologie et de morale fémi-
        nines. Conferences faites aux dames egyptiennes.
        Cairo: Université Egyptienne, 1911. Text of the first
        lectures given to female students at the Egyptian Uni-
        versity, by a French lecturer.

1413   _____. La Femme aux différentes époques de l'histoire.
        Le Puy: Peyriller; Cairo: Université Egyptienne, 1910.
        Text of the first lectures given to female students at
        the Egyptian University.

1414   "Don't Prevent Married Women from Enrolling in Universi-
        ties" (in Arabic). al-Ahram, July 28, 1976, p. 9, col.
        6.

1415   Farid, Zaynab. "Tatawwur ta'lim al-banat fi Misr." Un-
        published M.A. thesis, 'Ain Shams University, 1961.

1416   _____. _____. Unpublished Ph.D. thesis, 'Ain
         Shams University, 1966.

1417   Hafiz, Tahani. "The Woman Teacher: In a School With
         Obedient Pupils" (in Arabic). al-Ahram, Jan. 4, 1976,
         p. 9, col. 1. According to this report women teachers
         know best how to handle unruly boys.

1418   Harby, Mohammed Khairy, and Z. M. Mehrez. "Education
         for Women in the United Arab Republic." Overseas
         Quarterly, 1 (Dec. 1959), 241-43.

1419   Hashim, Labibah. Kitab fi al-tarbiyah. Cairo: Matba'at
         al-ma'arif, 1911. Texts of lectures on education given
         to female students at the Egyptian University in 1911.

1420   Hilmi, Munirah Ahmad. Mushkilat al-fatat al-murahiqah
         wa-hajatuha al-irshadiyah. Cairo: Dar al-nahdah al-
         'arabiyah, 1965. A study of adolescent girls in Cairo's
         secondary schools.

1421   Hogan, Anthony. "Abla: Queen of the Nile." Aramco
         World Magazine, May-June 1975, 20-25. Reportage
         about Abla Khairy, the youngest swimmer to cross the
         English Channel.

1422   I. S. "L'Instruction des filles et l'école mixte." Le
         Progrès Egyptien, Nov. 30, 1975. The author of the
         article suggests that female graduates be prevented from
         working or marrying unless they pass a "certificate of
         aptitude to matrimonial life." A year of home eco-
         nomics courses would be better than the year of public
         service presently required in Egypt.

1423   "Legislation Enabling Women to Head Sports Clubs" (in
         Arabic). al-Ahram, Aug. 28, 1976, p. 12, col. 4.

1424   Leoncavallo. "L'Education des femmes en Egypte." Bulle-
         tin de l'Institut d'Egypte, 9 (1863), 45-49.

1425   Lichtenstader, Ilse. "Some Aspects of Public Elementary
         Education in Egypt." The Harvard Educational Review,
         3 (1952), 158-83. Mentions the efforts of al-Jami'ah
         al-sha'biyah to educate middle class women.

1426   Madkur, Muhammad Sallam and Ibrahim Amin 'Abduh. al-
         Azhar wa-al-fatah. Cairo: Matba'at al-futuh, 1936.
         Debate by the Muslim Brethren Youth Organization on
         the role of girls in religious studies at al-Azhar Uni-
         versity.

1427   al-Mahdi, 'Abd al-'Alim. "Memorandum of Four Hundred
         al-Azhar Students to the President of the Student Welfare

Committee" (in Arabic). al-Ahram, Jan. 23, 1976,
p. 5. The President of the Committee is Mrs. al-
Sadat.

1428   Markaz al-Tawthiq al-Tarbawi. Access of Girls and Women
to Education. Cairo, 1971.

1429   Merriam, Kathleen H. "The Impact of Modern Secular Education Upon Egyptian Women's Participation in Public
Life." Paper delivered at the Tenth Middle East
Studies Association Meeting, Los Angeles, November
10-13, 1976.

1430   Mihriz, Zaynab Mahmud. "A Brief Summary of Technical
and Vocational Education for Girls in the A.R.E." (in
Arabic). Abstract in: Education of the Masses, 3
(May 1975), 166-67.

1431   _____. Ta'lim al-fatah fi al-jumhiriyah al-'arabiyah al-
muttahidah. Cairo: Matba'at wizarat al-tarbiyah wa-
al-ta'lim, 1965.

1432   Muhammad Rashid Rida. "Bahithat al-Badiyah" (in Arabic).
al-Manar, 21 (1918), 108, 123-28. The obituary of
writer and teacher Malak Hifni Nasif. The only good
result Muhammad Rashid Rida sees in the incipient
Egyptian feminism is an increase in female education.

1433   Nabarawi, Ceza. "Le Gouvernement égyptien et l'enseignement des jeunes filles." L'Egyptienne, 61 (Sept. 1930),
2-5. Includes the answers of the Minister of Public
Instruction to a list of questions submitted by the paper.

1434   _____. "Les Progrès de l'instruction des filles en
Egypte." L'Egyptienne, 44 (Dec. 1928), 2-7. A short
but informative article replete with data, including statistics from reports of controllers of the Ministry of
Public Instruction.

1435   "One Hundred Girls Graduate from the Vocational Institute
In Electricity, Welding and Carpentry" (in Arabic). al-
Ahram, July 17, 1976, p. 16, col. 1.

1436   al-Qissi, Layla. "Woman's Illiteracy: Her Main Problem"
(in Arabic). al-Musawwar, July 25, 1975, 62-63.

1437   Rachad, Ahmad. "Rifaa Rafeh El Tahtaoui, 1801-1873."
L'Egyptienne, 151 (Jan. 1939), 9-20.

1438   Rashid, Fatmah Ni'mat. "Mes concitoyennes en deux
mots!..." La Patrie, Jan. 30, 1947. Denounces the
danger of marriage between partners of the same social
class with different educations.

1439   Sabr, Muhyi al-din. "The Woman's Education and Training
       in Relation to Social Development" (in Arabic). Educa-
       tion of the Masses, 3 (May 1975), 30-38, 171-172.

1440   Sukkary, Soheir. "Women and Education in Egypt: A Case
       Study of Vocational Education in An Egyptian Village. "
       Paper delivered at the Conference on Development in
       the Arab World, New York, October 1-3, 1976.

1441   Suleiman, Michael. "Sex Differences and Societal Values
       Among Elementary School Children in Egypt. " Paper
       presented at the Tenth Middle East Studies Association
       Meeting, Los Angeles, November 10-13, 1976.

1442   "Teaching of Sewing, Knitting and Embroidery to Retarded
       Girls" (in Arabic). al-Ahram, Jan. 7, 1974, p. 4,
       col. 4.

1443   United Arab Republic. Department of Planning and Research.
       Female Juvenile Institutions in Egypt. Cairo, 1969.

1444   "University Students Yesterday and Today" (in Arabic). al-
       Ahram, May 2, 1976, p. 12, col. 1.

1445   "Where is She?" (in Arabic). al-Ahram, May 9, 1976, p.
       5, col. 8. About barring women from pilot schools.

1446   "Woman Between Emancipation and Seclusion" (in Arabic).
       al-Hilal, 2 (Oct. 1, 1910), 106-109. The article recog-
       nizes that female emancipation and seclusion are now
       important problems. Includes a qasidah of Bahithat al-
       Badiyah.

1447   "Woman Participates in the Managing Committee of the
       Sport Clubs by Ministerial Decree" (in Arabic). al-
       Ahram, Aug. 5, 1976, p. 6, col. 2.

(8) LITERARY WORKS BY OR ABOUT WOMEN

1448   'Abd al-Hayy, Diyab. al-Mar´ah fi hayat al-'Aqqad. Cairo:
       Dar al-sha'b, 1969. An analysis of the opinion of al-
       'Aqqad on women as expressed in his various works.

1449   'Abd Allah, Sufi. Nisa´ Muharibat. Cairo: Dar al-
       ma'arif, 1951.

1450   'Abd al-Malik, Fluri. Ruh ha´imah. Alexandria: Dar al-
       ma'arif, 1969. A collection of poems.

1451   'Abd al-Qaddus, Ihsan. Ana hurrah. Cairo: Matabi' Ruz
       al-Yusuf, 1954. This book, whose heroine is a

university student living with her lover, caused quite a
stir at the time of its publication. Its author has since
written several other works in which he analyzes the
female personality.

1452   . Mudhakkirat zawjah. Cairo: n.p., n.d.

1453 'Abd el-Chahid, Guindi. "Le Mariage d'Aziza." La Revue
du Caire, 47 (Oct. 1942), 534-51.

1454 Abu al-Wafa, 'Abd al-Latif. Tahdib al-mar´ah wa-al-rajul
bi-al-amthal. Alexandria, Matba'at al-safir, 1936.

1455 Abu Ghazalah, Samirah Muhammad Zaki. Mudhakkirat fatah
'arabiyah. Cairo: Matba'at al-risalah, 1959.

1456 'Anbar, Muhammad 'Abd al-Rahim. al-Jins wa-al-adab.
Cairo: n.p., 1970. 2 vols. The second half of vol.
2 analyzes sex in the works of Tawfiq al-Hakim, Ihsan
'Abd al-Qaddus and Najib Mahfuz.

1457 al-'Aqqad, 'Abbas Mahmud. al-Insan al-thani aw-al-mar´ah.
Cairo: Matba'at al-Hilal, 1912. The title page bears
printed along the spine the Koranic quotation, "Man has
domination over woman," which sets the mood of this
short work and in which its author strongly believed.

1458 al-'Ashari, 'Abd al-Salam. Bahithat al-Badiyah (Malak
Hifni Nasif). Cairo: Wizarat al-tarbiyah wa-al-ta'alim
Idarat al-shu'un al-'ammah, 1958.

1459 Assaf, Antoine. "Aichat Asmat Taimour." L'Egyptienne,
Aug.-Sept. 1926, 198-202. Gives some interesting details on the life of Aishah al-Taymuriyah.

1460 Bahjat, Ahmad. Mudhakkirat zawj. Cairo: Dar al-ma'arif,
1969.

1461 al-Barquqi, 'Abd al-Rahman. Dawlat al-nisa´, mu'jam
thaqafi, ijtima'i, lughawi 'an al-mar´ah. Cairo:
Matba'at al-i'timad, 1954.

1462 Bellos, Nausicaa. Sous le voile d'Isis. Paris: Marcel
Blondin, 1934.

1463   , and Morik Brin. Karima ou la patrie avant
l'amour. Cairo: Les Amis de la Culture Française en
Egypte, 1940. Play extolling a nationalist heroine.

1464 Bint al-Shati´ ['A´ishah 'Abd al-Rahman]. Suwar min
hayatihinna. Twenty-four short stories depicting contemporary Arab women.

1465   al-Bisi, Sana´. "She ... " (in Arabic). al-Ahram, July 23, 1976, p. 7, col. 1. About the memoirs of a woman in her 70's.

1466   al-Bulaki, Mahmud Hamdi. Mufrih al-jins al-latif wa-suwar mushahir al-raqqasin. Cairo: n.p., 1904. "Poems in Egyptian Arabic in praise of favorite modern Egyptian dancing girls. "

1467   Caillard, Mabel. "Crime of Honour. " Ma'iya, 226 (Aug. 24, 1894), 123.

1468   Dumani, Georges. "Jeanne Arcache. " La Revue du Caire, Feb. 7, 1939, 106-110. Review of three books written by J. Arcache, an Egyptian who writes in French.

1469   "An Egyptian Diplomat Wins a Prize on His Book About the Egyptian Woman" (in Arabic). al-Ahram, May 24, 1976, p. 5, col. 6.

1470   Fahim, 'Adli. al-Hisab, ya madmuwazil. Cairo: Mu´assasat Ruz al-Yusuf, 1973. The life of a cafeteria waitress.

1471   Fawwaz, Zaynab bint 'Ali. al-Durr al-manthur fi tabaqat rabbat al-khudur. Bulaq: al-Matba'ah al-kubra al-amiriyah, 1899. A lenghty biobibliographical work on illustrious women, including a bibliography of 'A´ishah al-Taymuriyah, pp. 303-19.

1472   al-Hakim, Tawfiq. Himari wa-hizb al-nisa´. Beirut: Dar al-kitab, 1973.

1473   _____ . Jinsuna al-latif. In al-Hakim, Tawfiq. Masrahiyyat. Cairo: Lajnat al-ta´lif, wa-al-tarjamah wa-al-nashr, 1937. A play written for Huda Sha'rawi and played at her Feminist Union in 1935.

1474   _____ . al-Mar´ah al-jadidah. Cairo: Kitab al-yaum, 1952. Play originally written in 1923 but not staged until 1936.

1475   _____ . Masrah al-mujtama'. Cairo: Maktabat al-adab wa-matba'atuha, 1950. Among the collected plays in this volume, see: Ashab al-sa'adah al-zawjiyah, al-Na´ibah al-muhtaramah and Uridu hadha al-rajul.

1476   _____ . Rahib bayna nisa´. Cairo: al-Hai´ah al-misriyah al-'ammah lil-kitab, 1972.

1477   Haqqi, Yahya. "A Poor Woman" (in Arabic). al-Adab, April, 1973. Short story about a "poor little lady" who shrewdly exploits the pity she inspires.

1478   Hasan, Muhammad 'Abbas al-Fani. "An Elegiac Poetess at
        Times of Distress, 'A'ishah al-Taymuriyah" (in Arabic).
        al-Hilal, April 1974, 14-23.

1479   Haykal, Muhammad Husayn. Hakadha khuliqat. Cairo:
        Matabi' dar akhbar al-yaum, 1955. The heroine, who
        was an acquaintance of the author, is a very willful and
        determined woman, quite different from Haykal's first
        heroine.

1480   _____. Zaynab. Cairo: Maktabat al-nahdah al-misriyah,
        1967. Hailed as the first Egyptian novel at its first
        appearance in 1914, this work depicts the unfortunate
        life of a country girl.

1481   al-Ibyari, Fathi. al-Umm. Cairo: Mu'assasat akhbar al-
        yaum, 1972. Short stories on motherhood.

1482   Jamali, Muhammad Ra'fat. Mudhakkirat baghi. Cairo: al-
        Maktabah al-tijariyah, 1922. Great misfortunes befell
        the heroines of these short stories who seem totally un-
        able to cope with their problems.

1483   al-Jiddawi, 'Abd al-Mun'im. al-Jins wa-al-jarimah. Cairo:
        Dar al-hilal, 1973. Short stories based on actual sex-
        related crimes in Egypt.

1484   al-Jindi, Anwar. al-Mar'ah wa-al-hubb fi kitabina al-
        mu'asir. Cairo: Dar al-a'lam lil-tiba' wa-al-nashr,
        1955.

1485   Kher, Amy. Mes Soeurs. Cairo: R. Schindler, 1942.
        The autobiography of Amy Kher, born 1897 of an Egyp-
        tian father and an English mother, who lived in Egypt
        and Lebanon, had a salon in the 1930's and 40's and
        was a prominent writer in the French language.

1486   Le Gassick, Trevor. "Ihsan Abd al-Qaddus: Chief Expo-
        nent of Female Arab Attitudes?" Mid East, Nov.-Dec.
        1968, 24-26. Followed by a translation of "The Ideal
        Wife," 27-28.

1487   Mahjub, Fatimah. Nihayat shay. Cairo: Maktabat al-
        nahdah al-'arabiyah, 1962.

1488   Mahmud, Muhammad. al-Shi'r al-nisa'i al-'asri wa-
        shahirat nujumih. Cairo: Dar al-taraqqi, 1929. In-
        cludes very short biographical notices on Wardah al-
        Yaziji, 'A'ishah al-Taymuriyah, Aminah Nasib and
        Malak Hifni Nasif.

1489   Mahmud, Mustafa. 'Arba'in mushkilat hubb. Cairo: Dar
        al ma'arif, 1964.

1490   . I'tirafat 'ushshaq. Cairo: Dar al-nahdah al-'arabiyah, 1971.

1491 Mansur, Anis. Min awwal nazrah. Cairo: Dar al-sha'b, 1970.

1492   . Nadwah 'an al-mar'ah al-'amilah. Cairo: Jami'at al-Qahirah. Ma'had al-dirasat wa-al-buhuth al-ihsa'iyah wa-markaz al-hisab 'ilmi, 1969-70. Text of a lecture given at Cairo University.

1493   . Qalu. Cairo: Dar al-katib al-'arabi lil-tiba'ah wa-al-nashr, 1967.

1494 Miskuni, Yusuf. Min 'abqariyat nisa' al-qarn al-tasi' 'ashar. Baghdad: Matba'at al-ma'arif, 1947. Includes the biographies of Wardah al-Yaziji, 'A'ishah al-Taymuriyah and Zaynab Fawwaz.

1495 al-Misri, Ibrahim. Qulb al-mar'ah. Cairo: Dar al-hilal, 1970.

1496 Muhammad, Muhsin. al-Zawaj sanat alfayn. Cairo: Mu'assasat akhbar al-yaum, 1972.

1497 Muhammad, Zaynab. Mudhakkirat wasifah misriyah. Cairo: Dar al-ma'arif, 1927.

1497a Muhsin, Muhammad. Dafa' 'an al-zawjat. Cairo: Mu'assasat Akhbar al-yum, 1975.

1498 Musa, Salamah. "Talk with Miss Mayy" (in Arabic). al-Hilal, April 1928, 658-61. An interview with Mayy Ziyadah.

1499 Out-el-Kouloub. Harem. Paris: Gallimard, 1955. A series of descriptions of Egyptian typical scenes as the author witnessed them in her youth.

1500   . Ramza. Paris: Gallimard-Nouvelle Revue Française, 1958. Novel about a woman who succeeds in freeing herself after two unhappy marriages and devotes her time to work for female emancipation.

1501   . Les Trois Contes de l'amour et de la mort. Paris: Correa, 1940.

1502   . Zanouba. Paris: Gallimard, 1947.

1503   . "Le Zar." La Revue du Caire, Jan. 14, 1940, 131-37.

1504 Pickthall, Marmaduke. Veiled Women. London: Eveleigh

Nash, 1913.   The story of Barakah, an English governess who converts to Islam to marry a high class
Egyptian.   Despite her considerable assimilation to
harim life she is quite unhappy but resigned after she
has realized it is impossible for her to return to the
West.

1505   Qariyaqus, 'Abd al-Quddus.   Qissat al-niza' bayna al-
'uzubiyah wa-al-zawaj.   Cairo: Maktabat al-nahdah,
1949.

1506   Raccagni, Michelle.   "The Image of Woman in a Few Contemporary Egyptian Plays and Movies."   Paper delivered
at the Tenth Annual Meeting of the Middle East Studies
Association, Los Angeles, November 10-13, 1976.

1507   Rida, Jalilah.   Ana wa-al-layl.   Cairo: al-Nashr al-'arabi,
1961.   A poetic essay about the problems of the Arab
woman.

1508   Rossi, Ettore.   "Una scrittrice araba cattolica Mayy (Marie
Ziyadah).   Oriente Moderno, 11 (Nov. 1925), 604-13.
An important biobibliographical article on Mayy Ziyadah.

1509   Rushdi, Eugénie.   Les Répudiées.   Paris: Félix Juvens,
1908.   A novel about five women victims of repudiation.
The author, wife of Rashid Pasha, drew from her personal observations.

1510   al-Sa'dawi, Nawal.   al-Bahithah 'an al-hubb.   Cairo: al-
Hay'ah al-misriyah al-'ammah lil-kitab, 1974.   The life
of a woman doctor, drawn partly from the author's experience but written in a much more revolutionary tone
than her Mudhakkirat tabibah.

1511   _____.   Mudhakkirat tabibah.   Cairo: Dar al-ma'arif,
1965.   The memoirs of a woman doctor partially in-
spired by the author's own reminiscences.

1512   Salih, 'Abd al-Muhsin.   Zawjat muftaris.   Cairo: Dar al-
hilal, 1970.

1513   Salim, Ahmad Fu'ad.   "Woman and Sex in the Works of Ten
Egyptian Artists" (in Arabic).   al-Hilal, April 1971, 96-
119.

1514   Samirah, Bint al-Jazirah al-'arabiyah.   Dhikrayat dami'a.
Alexandria: Mu'assasat al-matba'ah al-hadithah, 1962.

1515   Sannu', Ya'qub.   al-Darratan.   In Najm, Muhammad Yusuf.
al-Masrah al-'arabi.   Beirut: Dar al-thaqafah, 1963;
173-88.   A play about rival co-wives showing how
polygamy ruins family happiness.   Performed in the

119   Literary Works

early 1870's, its main interest lies in its having been
censured by Khedive Isma'il.

1516   Sha'rawi, H. "Woman's Poetry and Current News" (in Ara-
       bic). Shi'r, 25 (Winter 1963), 104-08. About poetess
       Jalilah Rida.

1516a al-Sharuni, Yusuf, ed. Laylah al-thaniyah ba'da al-alf.
       Cairo: al-Hay'ah al-misriyah al-'ammah lil-kitab,
       1975. Selections of works by modern women novelists
       in Egypt.

1517   Sidki, J. "Le Sexe faible." La Revue du Caire, 249
       (1961), 355-69. The revenge of a repudiated wife.

1518   Taymur, Ahmad. Tarikh al-usrah al-taymuriyah. Cairo:
       Dar al-ta'lif, 1948. Includes a bibliographical notice
       on 'A'ishah al-Taymuriyah, 85-89.

1519   Taymur, Mahmud. "Victime du divorce." La Revue du
       Caire, 158 (March 1963), 203-31; 159 (April 1953),
       305-30. The victim happens to be a wealthy man
       ruined by a scheming young wife and her relatives.

1520   Thabit, Muhammad. Banat jiwa'. Cairo: Dar al-fikr al-
       'arabi, 1950.

1521   _____. Dunya al-jins al-latif. Cairo: Lajnat al-ta'lif
       wa-al-tarjamah, 1947.

1522   'Uthman, Ahmad. Thawrah fi al-harim. Cairo: n.p.,
       1961. A rather weak novel about harem life.

1523   Vaucher-Zananiri, Nelly. Vierges d'Orient. Paris:
       Jouve & Cie., 1922. A novel which is also a social
       study of the young Egyptian women of the 1920's.

1524   Wadi, Taha 'Imran. Surat al-mar'ah fi al-riwayah al-
       mu'asirah. Cairo: Markaz kitab al-sharq al-awsat,
       1973. The image of woman in the contemporary novel.

1525   Wiet, Gaston. "Les Trois Contes de l'amour et de la
       mort." La Revue du Caire, 29 (April 1941), 607-10.
       A review of the book of Out-el-Kouloub [see entry
       1501].

1526   Yeghen, Foulad. Une Vie de musulmane. Cairo, n.p.,
       n.d. Book dedicated to Huda Sha'rawi.

1527   Yusuf, Ahmad. al-Mar'ah al-misriyah. Cairo: Dar al-
       ma'arif, 1932.

1528   Yusuf, Nicola. "The Poetess Fluri 'Abd al-Malik" (in

Arabic). al-Adib, 4 (1970), 2-5.

1529   al-Zayyat, Latifah. al-Bab al-maftuhah. Cairo: al-Makta-
        bah al-anjlu-al-misriyah, 1960. Novel about the revolt
        of a young girl against established norms and her at-
        tempts to express herself.

1530   Ziyadah, Mayy. 'A'ishah Taymur. Beirut: Mu'assasat
        Nova, 1975. The biography of a major Egyptian poetess.

1531   Zuhayr, Su'ad. I'tirafat imra'ah mustarjilah. Cairo:
        Mu'assasat ruz al-yusuf, 1961.

(9) THE WORKING WOMAN

1532   'Abd al-Fattah, Kamilyah. Fi sikulujiyat al-mar'ah al-
        'amilah. Cairo: Maktabat al-qahirah al-hadith, 1972.

1533   'Abd al-Mun'im, Amirah. "The First Time Jewelry Is
        Made by a Woman for Women" (in Arabic). al-Ahram,
        Dec. 26, 1975, 16. About jewelry designer 'Azzah
        Fahmy, from Cairo.

1534   'Abduh, Ibrahim. Ruz al-yusuf. Cairo: Mu'assasat sijil
        al-'arab, 1961. A biography of actress and journalist
        Ruz al-Yusuf.

1535   Abu al-'Ainain, Hasan. "Woman as Police Officer: How
        Her Preparation Takes Place in Cairo" (in Arabic).
        al-Ahram, May 23, 1975, 5.

1536   Aflatun, Inji. "Equal Work But ... Discrimination" (in
        Arabic). al-Masa', Jan. 5, 1959.

1537   _____. "Four Thousand Teachers Present Their Claims"
        (in Arabic). al-Misri, Feb. 1, 1951.

1538   _____. "The Health Under-Secretary Answers to the
        Nurses' Demands" (in Arabic). al-Misri, Feb. 2,
        1951.

1539   _____. "How the Working Woman Can Assume Her
        Double Responsibility, at Work and at Home" (in Ara-
        bic). al-Masa', Nov. 29, 1958.

1540   _____. "The Minister of Social Affairs Declares the
        New Labor Law Guarantees Equality Between Sexes"
        (in Arabic). al-Misri, Feb. 14, 1951.

1541   _____. "The Nurses Issue a Rousing Call" (in Arabic).
        al-Misri, Jan. 30, 1951.

1542   _____ . "Sixteen Thousand Female Workers Deprived of
        the Same Rights Granted to Men" (in Arabic). al-
        Misri, Jan. 31, 1951.

1543   _____ . "Woman's Role in Production" (in Arabic). al-
        Masa´, Oct. 29, 1958.

1544   Ahmad, A. T. al-Mar´ah, kifahuha wa-'amaluha. Cairo:
        Dar al-jamahir, 1964. A study of the woman worker
        by a leftist journalist.

1545   'Ali Imam, 'Atiyah. Mudhakkirat 'amil fi biga' al-akhirat.
        Cairo: n.p., 1926.

1546   "Arrêté du 31 Décembre 1933 (14 Ramadan 1352) relatif
        aux industries saisonnières dans lesquelles les femmes
        peuvent être employées la nuit. " Journal Officiel
        Egyptien, 7 (Jan. 22, 1934), 5; Bureau International du
        Travail, Série Législative, 1933 Eg. 3B.

1547   Badran, Hoda. "Arab Women in National Development. "
        Paper delivered at the Seminar on Arab Women in Na-
        tional Development, Cairo, September 24-30, 1972.

1548   Bakir, Amal. "Women in Movies: The Number of Female
        Assistants at the Film Institute Now Reaches Nine" (in
        Arabic). al-Ahram, Jan. 18, 1974, 8.

1549   Bakr, 'Abd al-Rahman. al-Mar´ah al-'amilah fi al-
        jumhuriyah al-'arabiyah al-muttahidah. Cairo: Dar
        al-qawmiyah lil-tiba'ah wa-al-nashr, 1963.

1550   al-Bana, Rajab. "At the Same Time: One Step Forward,
        One Step Backward" (in Arabic). al-Ahram, July 9,
        1974, p. 5, col. 3. About barring women from some
        public functions such as judgeships.

1551   _____ . "Muhammad Hasan Hanim at the Door of the
        Supreme Administrative Court" (in Arabic). al-Ahram,
        April 1, 1974, p. 3, col. 4. A plea to change the law
        which bars women from judiciary positions.

1552   al-Bindari, 'Abd al-Wahhab. al-Zawjah al-'amilah wa-al-
        huquq al-zawjiyah. Cairo: al-Matba'ah al-'alamiyah,
        1969.

1553   al-Bindari, Jalil. Raqisat Misr. Cairo: Matabi' akhbar
        al-yaum, 1951. An informative little book on the most
        famous Egyptian belly dancers.

1554   Bint al-Shati´. "What We Have Encountered" (in Arabic).
        al-Hilal, May, 1946, 327-32. The obstacles faced by
        the educated Arab woman.

1555   al-Bisi, Sana´. "She ... " (in Arabic). al-Ahram, March
       28, 1976, p. 13, col. 1. About the working wife and
       the housewife.

1556   _____. "She ... " (in Arabic). al-Ahram, March 7,
       1976, p. 9, col. 1. What types of jobs can the Egyp-
       tian woman perform.

1557   _____. "She Amidst Memories" (in Arabic). al-Ahram,
       May 21, 1976, p. 7, col. 1. About working and non-
       working women.

1558   Clarke, Joan. Labor Law and Practice in the United Arab
       Republic (Egypt). Washington, D.C.: U.S. Department
       of Labor, Bureau of Labor Statistics, 1965. Includes
       texts of labor laws protecting women.

1559   "The Conference of Women's Organizations in Alexandria
       Asking for Two-Month Pregnancy Leave" (in Arabic).
       al-Ahram, July 1, 1976, p. 14, col. 1.

1560   "A Conference to Increase the Productivity of the Working
       Woman" (in Arabic). al-Ahram, Oct. 11, 1976, p. 6,
       col. 2.

1561   "Egypt: Jobs for the Girls. " The Economist, April 18,
       1972, 44. Providing women with jobs may curtail popu-
       lation increase.

1562   "An Egyptian Scholar Cures Sterility in America" (in Ara-
       bic). Akhbar al-Yaum, Aug. 24, 1975, p. 11, col. 1.
       Article on Dr. Khairiyah 'Imran.

1563   "The Egyptian Woman and the Bakery Industry" (in Arabic).
       al-Ahram, July 11, 1976, p. 12, col. 1. A new test
       to train girls in industrial bakeries.

1564   "The Egyptian Woman as Postal Carrier" (in Arabic). al-
       Ahram, Sept. 23, 1976, p. 5, col. 5.

1565   "An Egyptian Works as a Professor at New York University"
       (in Arabic). Akhir Sa'ah, 2178 (July 21, 1976), 34.
       About Dr. Mona Mikhail, professor of Arabic language
       and literature.

1566   "Employing Women in Bakeries in Assyut" (in Arabic). al-
       Ahram, July 16, 1976, p. 8, col. 6.

1567   "An Explanation of This Suggestion is Requested" (in Ara-
       bic). al-Ahram, Oct. 5, 1976, p. 11, col. 6.

1568   "The First Egyptian Doctor to Open a Clinic in America"
       (in Arabic). al-Ahram, June 29, 1975, 7. About

Dr. Fawqiyah Farid.

1569 Garzouzi, Eva. "The Demographic Aspects of Women's Em-
ployment in the United Arab Republic. " International
Union for the Scientific Study of Population. General
Conference. London, 1969, vol. I, 1614-19.

1570 "Girl Traffic Wardens Slow Auto Traffic. " Christian Science Monitor, Sept. 30, 1972, p. 8, col. 4 (Mid-
western ed.).

1571 "Girls Working in Bakeries" (in Arabic). al-Ahram, June
15, 1976, p. 16, col. 1.

1572 al-Haffar, Salma. Nisa´ mutafawwiqat. Beirut: Dar al-
'ilm lil-malayin, 1961. Biographies of illustrious women, the only contemporary Arab figure being Umm
Kulthum, 240-56.

1573 Hasan, Muhammad. "Two Exemplary Young Women" (in
Arabic). Akhir Sa'ah, 2157 (Feb. 25, 1976). About
Dr. Nancy 'Abd al-'Aziz Sulayman, professor of medicine at 'Ain Shams University and Dr. Layla Lutfi Abu
al-Nasir, professor of medicine at Cairo University.

1574 Heykal, Ayten. "Some Managerial Problems of Female
Employment in the U.A.R. " Unpublished M.A. thesis,
American University in Cairo, 1971.

1575 High Council for Service Coordination. Social Study of
Working Women in the Factories of Alexandria. Alexandria, 1961.

1576 Ibrahim, 'Adil. "Agricultural Engineer Among Peasants"
(in Arabic). al-Ahram, Sept. 14, 1976, p. 5, col. 2.

1577 "Implementation of the Working Plan of the National Committee of Women for the New Year" (in Arabic). al-
Ahram, Jan. 16, 1976, p. 5, col. 3.

1577a Jamal al-Din, M. "Umm Kulthum in Baghdad" (in Arabic).
al-Adib, 6 (July 1975), 42-52.

1578 Killean, Carolyn G. "The Language of Women Television
Announcers in Cairo. " Paper delivered at the Tenth
Annual Meeting of the Middle East Studies Association,
Los Angeles, November 10-13, 1976.

1579 Kuhnke, Laverne J. "The 'Doctoress' on a Donkey: Women
Health Officers in Nineteenth Century Egypt. " Clio
Medica, 3 (1974), 193-205.

1580 "The Lady-Manager" (in Arabic). al-Ahram, Feb. 7, 1976,

p. 4. About women in high managerial positions.

1581   "Law Project to Give the Working Woman a Three-Year
        Leave to Take Care of Her Children" (in Arabic). al-
        Ahram, Feb. 22, 1974, p. 2, col. 5.

1582   Loi no. 80 du 10 Juillet 1933 (17 Rabi' Awwal 1352) sur
        l'emploi des femmes dans l'industrie et le commerce.
        Journal Officiel Egyptien, July 17, 1933, no. 65, p. 2;
        Bureau International du Travail, Série Législative,
        1933, Eg. 2.

1583   Londynski, Dr. Rapport sur la prostitution en Egypte. N.p.:
        N.p., 1876.

1584   al-Mahdi, 'Abd al-'Alim. "Until We Establish Playgrounds
        for Rabbit Races" (in Arabic). al-Ahram, May 31,
        1976, p. 5, col. 4. A sarcastic article against a law
        project which would give working mothers leaves of ab-
        sence at half pay to raise their newborn children.

1585   Mahkamat al-qada´ al-idari. Majlis al-dawlah. Mudhakki-
        rah bi-difa' al-sayyidah Sizah Hanim Nabarawi 'an al-
        ittihad al-nisa´i fi qadiyat al-ustadhah 'A´ishah Ratib
        didda Wizarat al-'Adl. Cairo: Maktabat al-'alamiyah,
        1949. A cause célèbre: 'A´ishah Ratib, a former
        Minister of Social Affairs, was prevented from becom-
        ing a magistrate although she graduated first in her law
        class.

1586   Mansur, Anis. "Let Us Help All Women to Make Better
        Men" (in Arabic). Akhir Sa'ah, 2121 (June 18, 1975).
        Mansur sees a conflict between the job held by a woman
        outside her home and the education of her children.

1587   _____ . "The Problems of the Working Woman" (in Ara-
        bic). al-Ahram, May 13, 1976, p. 14, col. 8.

1588   "Maternity Leaves for Working Women Should be Granted
        Only Three Times in a Lifetime" (in Arabic). al-
        Ahram, June 23, 1976, p. 1, col. 7.

1589   Mikhail, Mona. "The Professional Egyptian Women."
        Paper presented at the Conference on Development in
        the Arab World, New York, October 1-3, 1976.

1590   "Mohsna Taoufik actrice égyptienne." Férida, 1 (May 1975),
        42.

1591   Mukhtar, Bahirah. "A Six-Year Leave for Working Mothers;
        The Opinions of Working Mothers" (in Arabic). al-
        Ahram, May 20, 1976, p. 3, col. 1.

1592   _____. "My Wife Is In Politics" (in Arabic). al-Ahram, Dec. 22, 1974, p. 3, col. 4.

1593   _____. "One Million Female Voters Is Not Enough. Shame on the Abstaining Workers" (in Arabic). al-Ahram, Dec. 4, 1974, p. 3, col. 7.

1594   Musa, Nabawiyah. al-Mar´ah wa-al-'amal. Alexandria: al-Matba'ah al-wataniyah, 1920. One of the first Egyptian career women proves that women can hold jobs and are not less intelligent than men.

1595   Mu´tamar Shu´un al-mar´ah al-'amilah. 1st, Cairo, 1963. Mu´tamar Shu´un al-mar´ah al-'amilah. 23-27 nufimbir sanah 1963. Cairo: Wizarat al-shu´un al-ijtima'iyah. al-Lajnah al-da´imah li-shu´un al-mar´ah, 1963. The proceedings of the First Conference on the Working Woman held in Cairo from November 23 to 27, 1963. Includes numerous statistics and tables.

1596   Nabarawi, Ceza. "A propos du droit au mariage des institutrices. " L'Egyptienne, 161 (Jan. 1940), 2-3.

1597   _____. "L'Activité d'une grande dame égyptienne. " L'Egyptienne, 144 (May 1938), 12-22. About archeologist Hatidjeh Fouad and her discoveries in Morocco.

1598   _____. "Deux Poids et deux mesures. " L'Egyptienne. April, 1925, 1-3. C. Nabarawi expresses her surprise at not having been invited as a member of the press to attend the inauguration of the Parliament.

1599   Nachaat, Rahma. "Pages d'un journal. " La République Algérienne, May 12, 1951. The memories of an Egyptian nurse during the 1948 Arab-Israeli war.

1600   Nicole, G. La Prostitution en Egypte. Paris: J. B. Baillière et fils, 1879.

1601   "An Open Letter to All the Female Employees of the Ministry of Awqaf" (in Arabic). al-Ahram, Dec. 3, 1974, p. 8, col. 3.

1602   Perlmann, M. "Memoirs of Rose Fatima al-Yusuf. " Middle Eastern Affairs, 1 (1956), 20-27.

1603   "Project to Free the Working Woman Full-Time or Part-Time, To Take Care of Her Children and Strengthen the Family" (in Arabic). al-Ahram, April 15, 1974, p. 4, col. 8.

1604   "Reasons Accounting for Absenteeism Among Women" (in Arabic). al-Ahram, May 3, 1976, p. 16, col. 1.

1605   "The Role of the Egyptian Woman in Building and Develop-
        ment" (in Arabic). al-Ahram, June 29, 1976, p. 14,
        col. 2.

1606   Sa'ad, Muhib al-Din Muhammad. al-Mar'ah al-'amilah fi
        tashri'at al-'amal wa-ta'minat al-ijtima'i. Cairo:
        Wizarat al-'amal, 1971.

1607   al-Siba'i, Madhat. "Ahmad Rami Talks for the First Time
        About Umm Kulthum" (in Arabic). Sabah al-khayr,
        Jan. 29, 1976, 22-28.

1608   "Suggestions and Explanations of the Central Office of Or-
        ganization and Management" (in Arabic). al-Ahram,
        March 27, 1976, p. 6, col. 4. Working women should
        get two days off per week and special means of trans-
        portation.

1609   Taha-Hussein, Claude. "Notre Aïda Alam." La Revue du
        Caire, 74 (Jan. 1945), 181-90. A short biographical
        article on the first Egyptian woman pianist, who died
        prematurely in 1944.

1610   al-Tahawi, Lamis. "Eight Female Employees Only in Port-
        Said" (in Arabic). al-Ahram, Jan. 9, 1974, p. 3, col.
        8.

1611   "Une Technicienne égyptienne termine à Berlin-Ouest son
        stage de perfectionnement dans le domaine de la TV."
        Le Progrès Egyptien, Dec. 27, 1975.

1612   Tucker, Judith. "Egyptian Women in the Task Force. An
        Historical Survey." Merip Reports, no. 50, 3-9, 26.

1613   al-Tuni, Hasan. "Women Rule the Meat Market" (in Ara-
        bic). al-Ahram, Dec. 24, 1974, p. 3, col. 4. About
        the occupations of the many women working at the meat
        market.

1614   "Umm Kulthum: Living Example for the Arab Woman" (in
        Arabic). al-Mar'ah, 10 (Oct. 5, 1968).

1615   United Arab Republic. Maslahat al-Isti'lamat. Women in
        the U.A.R. Cairo, 1962. A book consisting mostly
        of pictures of women engaged in various activities and
        stating that women in the U.A.R. are equal to men and
        play a great role in the industrial sector.

1616   'Uthman, Mirfat. "The Woman as Director" (in Arabic).
        al-Ahram, Sept. 17, 1976, p. 7, col. 1.

1617   "What Would Happen If Most of the Workers Were on Ma-
        ternity Leave?" (in Arabic). al-Ahram, Feb. 16, 1976,

p. 9, col. 1. About the current discussion to increase
benefits of working women and their possible consequences.

1618 "Why Did This Manager Succeed?" (in Arabic). al-Ahram,
Oct. 29, 1976, p. 7, col. 1.

1619 "The Working Wife Has the Right to Complain When Her
Husband Forbids Her to Travel Abroad" (in Arabic).
al-Ahram, July 10, 1974, p. 1, col. 6.

1620 "The Working Woman in Figures" (in Arabic). al-Ahram,
June 4, 1976, p. 7, col. 1.

1621 "The Working Woman Occupies a Better Position Among the
Members of Her Family" (in Arabic). al-Ahram, May
13, 1974, p. 12, col. 2.

1622 Workshop on the Role and Participation of Women in Community Development Programs in the Arab World. Sirs-
al-Layyan: Arab States Fundamental Education Center,
1959.

1623 al-Yusuf, Fatimah. Dhikriyat. Cairo: Maktabat Ruz al-
Yusuf, 1976. The memoirs of journalist and actress
Ruz al-Yusuf, with an introduction by her son, Ihsan
'Abd al-Quddus.

1624 Zaghlul, Anwar. "The First Meeting Between 'Abd al-
Nasir and Umm Kulthum" (in Arabic). Sabah al-Khayr,
Jan. 29, 1976, 29-33.

(10) FEMINISM AND POLITICS

General

1625 A.H.H. "Le Mouvement féministe en Egypte." L'Egyptienne, Oct. 1926, 30-37.

1626 'Abd al-Fatah. "The Emancipation of the Egyptian Woman"
(in Arabic). al-Hilal, June 1919.

1627 'Abd al-Khaliq, Fatmah. "She Was a Man!" (in Arabic).
al-Akhbar, Sept. 22, 1975. The obituary of Doria
Shafiq.

1628 'Abd al-Rahman, 'A'ishah (Bint al-Shati'). "The Feminist
Renaissance: History, Review and Critic" (in Arabic).
Kitab, Jan. 1951, 115-123. A muslim woman and a
scholar defending women's rights within an Islamic
framework.

1629 _____. "We ... Egyptian Women" (in Arabic). al-
Ahram, March 12, 1950. Critique of Aflatun's book.

1630 Aflatun, Inji. "The Direct Cause of Her Misery Is Inequal-
ity Between Man and Woman" (in Arabic). al-Misri,
April 4, 1950.

1631 _____. "March 16, Day of Heroism in the History of
the Egyptian Woman" (in Arabic). al-Misri, March
1951.

1632 _____. Nahnu al-nisa´ al-misriyat. Cairo: Matba'at
al-sa'adah bi Misr, 1949. The author states all the
grievances of the Egyptian woman and gives statistical
data and many excerpts from the daily press [see entries
1812-16].

1633 _____. "November 13 and the Awakening of the Egyptian
Woman" (in Arabic). al-Misri, n.d.

1634 _____. "The Political Rights of Women. An International Inquiry" (in Arabic). al-Misri, 1950.

1635 _____. Thamanun malayin imra´ah ma'ana. Cairo:
Matba'at Misr, 1948.

1636 Ahsan, Radiyah. Mawlid al-harakah al-nisa´iyah. Cairo:
al-Ittihad al-ishtiraki al-'arabi. Dar matba' al-sha'b,
n.d.

1636a Ali, Parveen Shaukat. Status of Women in the Muslim
World. Lahore: Aziz Publishers, 1975. A study of
feminist movements in Turkey, Egypt, Iran and Pakistan.

1637 "Alliance des deux partis féministes." La Bourse Egyptienne,
March 30, 1949. A tentative agreement between the National Feminist Party and the Bint al-Nil party.

1638 Amin, 'Ali. "An Idea!" (in Arabic). al-Ahram, Sept. 21,
1975. The obituary of Doria Shafiq.

1639 Arab Republic of Egypt. Ministry of Information. State
Information Service. Egyptian Women: A Long March
from the Veil to Modern Times, Cairo, 1975. Includes
a brief outline of feminism in Egypt.

1640 _____. _____. _____. The Egyptian Woman During the October War. Cairo, 1974. Gives the names
of various women's organizations and details on their
activities.

1641 _____. _____. _____. La Femme egyptienne du

Voile au 6 Octobre 1973. A shorter version of the
English booklet, Egyptian Women: A Long March from
the Veil to Modern Times.

1642   Arafah, Bahijah. The Social Activities of the Egyptian
Feminist Union. Cairo: Elias' Modern Press, 1973.
A slim book which gives an outline of the history of
the Egyptian Feminist Union, includes a bibliography.

1643   'Arif, Muhammad. Kitab ghairat al-rijal, mahakk siyanat
al-nisa.͗ Cairo: Matba'at al-adab wa-al-mu´ayyid,
1317 (i. e. , 1900).

1644   Arnet, Mary Flounders. "Qasim Amin and the Beginnings
of the Feminist Movement in Egypt. " Unpublished
Ph. D. dissertation, Dropsie College for Hebrew and
Cognate Learning, 1965. A short biography of Qasim
Amin along with the translation of two of his books:
al-Mar´ah al-jadidah and Kalimat.

1645   al-Ashmawi, 'Abd al-Qadir. "Le Parti féministe au travail. " La Patrie, Feb. 27, 1947. A protest against
the law project of Fikri Abaza depriving illiterate men
of the right to vote. Recommends instead the promotion of education and supports the project of Alluba
Pasha granting the vote to literate women as a first
step towards women obtaining all political rights.

1646   _____. "Le Parti féministe au travail. " La Patrie,
April 17, 1947. About a law project of 'Ali Zaki al-
'Urabi, former minister and president of the Senate,
stating that the Egyptian constitution granted the vote
to all, men and women, illiterate or not.

1647   'Atiyah, Jamilah. "The Conference of Eastern Women" (in
Arabic). al-Misriyah, Nov. 15, 1938, 4.

1648   _____. "The Feminist Union" (in Arabic). al-Misriyah,
3 (March 15, 1937), 25-27.

1649   _____. "A Study of the Feminist Union" (in Arabic).
al-Misriyah, July 1, 1938, 6.

1650   Ayrout, Henry. "Féminism en Egypte; Faisons le point. "
En Terre d'Islam, 17 (1936), 324-29.

1651   Badr, Siham. Frauenbildung und Frauenbewegung in
Ägypten. Wuppertal: Ratigen; Düsseldorf: Henn,
1968.

1652   "Bint al-Nil From Shadow to Light Again" (in Arabic).
Akhir Sa'ah, 2135 (Sept. 24, 1975).

1653   Bohdanowicz, Arslan.   "The Feminist Movement in Egypt."
        The Islamic Review, 8 (Aug. 1951), 24-33.

1654   "Le Bonheur de la femme réside en son foyer déclare le
        parti féministe du Caire." La Réforme, Aug. 15, 1944.

1655   "A Brief Talk With the Head of the Feminist Party" (in
        Arabic). al-Misri Afandi, 443 (1945), 23.

1656   al-Bulaqi, Muhammad Ahmad Hasanayn.   al-Jalis al-anis fi
        al-tahdhir 'amma fi tahrir al-mar'ah min al-talbis.
        Cairo: Matba'at al-ma'arif al-ahliyah, 1899.

1657   C. Z. K.   "First 'Suffragettes' in the Orient: Egypt's Wom-
        en's Party." The Palestine Post, March 1944.

1658   Civis.   "Féminisme et institutions musulmanes." Rayon
        d'Egypte, 28 (July 10, 1938).

1659   Cohen, Benoit.   "Le Féminisme en action." Le Film, 2
        (March 1947), 4-5, 61.   The correspondant of France-
        Illustration takes a brief look at Egyptian feminism.

1660   "Conférence de presse de Madame Fatma Nimet Rached."
        Le Messager, Jan. 25, 1951.   Fatma Ni'mat Rashid
        was the founder of the Women's National Party.

1661   "Considerazioni d'un qadi sulle domande dell'Associazione
        femminile egiziana." Oriente Moderno, 6 (June 1926),
        340-42.   Abstract of the article of an anonymous qadi
        published in al-Ahram of May 12, and 18, 1926.   The
        qadi thinks that proper application of religious law
        would suffice to prevent the abuses denounced by the
        Feminist Union.

1662   Contu, G.   "Le Donne comuniste e il movimento democra-
        tico femminile in Egitto fino al 1965." Oriente
        Moderno, 5-6 (May-June 1975), 237-47.

1663   "Cours de sciences domestiques et ménagères au Parti
        Féministe." La Bourse Egyptienne, Feb. 20, 1951.

1664   "La Création du Parti féministe est prématurée, dit le
        ministre des affaires sociales." La Bourse Egyptienne,
        May 1, 1944.

1665   "Déja! Démissions au Parti féministe égyptien." Le
        Progrès Egyptien, July 8, 1944.   Resignation of Hikmat
        Abu Zaid and six other members denouncing the lack
        of culture, moderation and insight of the National Fem-
        inist Party.

1666   Dhakirat faqidat al-'urubah Hadrit sahibat al-'isma al-sayyi-

dah al-jalilah Huda Hanim Sha'rawi. Cairo: Fann al-
tiba'ah, n.d. Collection of poems and speeches read in
memory of H. Sha'rawi at the Feminist Union on January 30, 1948. Includes press excerpts about H.
Sha'rawi.

1667   "Le Droit de vote pour la femme. " La Bourse Egyptienne,
March 27, 1947. Results of an inquiry of Fatmah N.
Rashid. The majority of the personalities she inter-
viewed expressed their approval of woman's suffrage.

1668   E.R. "Deliberazioni del Comitato dell'Unione femminile
egiziana dopo il Congresso di Roma. " Oriente Moderno,
6 (Nov. 1923), 379. About the meeting held on June 28,
1923, at the Egyptian University asking equal rights to
education and fixation of a minimal age of 16 for marriage.

1669   _____. "Echi del Congresso femminile internazionale di
Roma. " Oriente Moderno, 6 (Nov. 1923), 378-79. Includes the translation in Italian of a letter addressed by
Shaykh 'Abd al-'Aziz Shawish to H. Sha'rawi, accusing
her of giving bad publicity to Islam.

1670   _____. "L'Unione femminile egiziana chiede al Governo
l'abolizione della poligamia. Polemiche e contrasti. "
Oriente Moderno, 9 (Sept. 1935), 476-78. Includes text
of a letter of Ceza Nabarawi to Prime Minister Tawfiq
Nasim Pasha.

1671   "The Egyptian Woman and Nationalist Goals" (in Arabic).
al-Misri, Aug. 13, 1945. About the note of the Feminist Party to British Ambassador Killearn.

1672   "Egyptian Women Found a Party" (in Arabic). al-Ithnain,
Jan. 30, 1944. About the foundation of the National
Feminist Party.

1673   "Encouragements to the Women of Aswan to Join the Feminist Organization of the Governorate" (in Arabic). al-
Ahram, March 16, 1976, p. 14, col. 1.

1674   "Enrollment of Men in the Feminist Party" (in Arabic). al-
Usbu'iyah, July 11, 1945.

1675   "Exemplary Cases" (in Arabic). al-Ithnain, June 1, 1944.
The National Feminist Party and several lawyers recom-
mend the boycott of luxury goods.

1676   Fahmi, Mahir Hasan. Qasim Amin. Cairo: al-Mu'assasah
al-misriyah al-'ammah lil-ta'lif wa-al-tarjamah wa-al-
tiba'ah wa-al nashr, 1963.

1677   Fakhr al-Din, Fu´ad Muhammad. al-mushkilah al-nisa´iyah.
       Cairo: Maktabah wa-matba'at <u>Mustafa al-Babi al-Halabi</u>,
       1956.

1678   Fakhri, Muhammad. <u>Tahrir al-mar´ah wa-al-sufur</u>. Cairo:
       Maktabat al-hilal, <u>1920.</u>

1679   Farid, Amani. al-Mar´ah al-misriyah wa-al-barlaman.
       Cairo: Matba'at al-tawakkul, 1947. A plea in favor of
       women's political rights. Includes the opinion of seve-
       ral Egyptian personalities.

1680   Fawwaz, Zaynab. <u>al-Rasa´il al-zaynabiyah</u>. Cairo:
       Matba'at al-mutawassitah, n.d. A series of essays
       dealing with woman's rights, the education of women
       and like matters; especially in reference to conditions
       in Egypt.

1681   "Feminist Movement in Egypt. " <u>The Islamic Review</u>, 8
       (1958), 14-16.

1682   "The Feminist Movement in Egypt" (in Arabic). <u>al-Mustami'</u>
       <u>al-'arabi</u>, 10 (1949), 14. About the Bint al-Nil party
       founded by Doria Shafiq.

1683   "Les Femmes revendiquent les droits politiques. " <u>La</u>
       <u>Bourse Egyptienne</u>, Nov. 13, 1950. Text of a letter
       sent to the Prime Minister by four feminist leaders
       asking for equality between men and women.

1684   G.F. "Les Egyptiennes et la politique. " <u>La Bourse</u>
       <u>Egyptienne</u>. March 16, 1944. About the creation of
       <u>National Feminist</u> Party.

1685   G.S. "Les Revendications de la femme. " <u>Le Progrès</u>
       <u>Egyptien</u>, May 13, 1945. About a lecture given by
       Ibrahim 'Abd al-Qadir al-Mazini.

1686   Gallad, Lita. "Je vous invite.... " <u>Journal d'Egypte</u>,
       Sept. 22, 1975. An obituary of Doria Shafiq which
       raises the possibility of suicide.

1687   Habib, Tawfiq. "Qasim Amin" (in Arabic). <u>al-Hilal</u>, 36
       (1908), 460.

1688   _____. "Qasim Amin and the Egyptian Woman" (in Ara-
       bic). <u>al-Hilal</u>, 36 (May 1908), 945-59.

1689   Hard, Anne. "Madame Hoda Charaoui, a Modern Woman
       of Egypt. " <u>The Woman Citizen</u>, Sept. 1927, 10-12, 33.

1690   Harry, Myriam. <u>Les Derniers Harems</u>. Paris: Ernest
       Flammarion, <u>1933.</u> A reportage from Egypt with

interviews with Huda Sha'rawi and Ceza Nabarawi.

1691   Haykal, Muhammad Husayn. "After Qasim Amin" (in Arabic). al-Hilal, 1934, 28-31.

1692   _____. "Revendications ou émancipation?" L'Egyptienne, June 1925, 140-42. Haykal claims that women have to free themselves of their own prejudices and ask for more rights.

1693   "The Head of the Feminist Party Declares ... " (in Arabic). Ruz al-Yusuf, 831 (June 17, 1944), 9.

1694   Husayn, 'Abd Allah. al-Mar'ah al-hadithah wa-kaif nususuha. Cairo: al-Matba'ah al-'asriyah, 1927.

1695   Husayn, Salih. Qibal al-radd 'ala tahrir al-mar'ah. Cairo: n.p., 1898.

1696   Husni, Munirah. Ayyam fi al-jami'ah al-nisa'iyah. Cairo: Matba'at al-miliji, 1956.

1697   'Ibadah, 'Abd al-Fatah. Nahdah al-mar'ah al-misriyah. Cairo: Dar al-hilal, 1919.

1698   Idris, Hawa'. Ana wa al-sharq. Unpublished ms., Cairo, 1973. The memoirs of an active member of the Feminist Union since the 1930's, and the niece of its founder, Huda Sha'rawi.

1699   Idris, Yusuf. "Letter to You, Madam" (in Arabic). al-Ahram, Sept. 24, 1976, p. 9, col. 13. A message to female club members urging them to go out and serve the nation instead of wasting their time in idle talks.

1700   al-Ittihad al-Ishtiraki al-'Arabi. al-Lajnah al-Markaziyah. The Plan of Action of the Woman's General Secretariate (sic). Cairo, 1975.

1701   al-Ittihad al-Nisa'i al-Misri. al-Mar'ah al-'arabiyah wa qadiyat Falastin. Cairo: al-Matba'ah al-amiriyah, 1939.

1702   Izzet, Fatma. "Notre Combat." La République Algérienne, May 12, 1951. Article of an Egyptian feminist in the special issue of an Algerian paper devoted to Egypt.

1703   al-Jam'iyah al-nisa'iyah al-wataniyah fi 'ashar sanawat, 1944-1954. Cairo: al-Maqarr al-ra'isi, 1954. A small brochure outlining the aims of the National Feminist Party and their accomplishments, including a brief biography of its leader, Fatma Ni'mat Rashid.

1704   "J'apprécie l'effort de l'Egyptienne." La Patrie, Dec. 19,
        1946. Declarations of visiting Turkish journalist Nuzhet
        Kerimoglu. She is surprised that women are not in-
        vited to official functions.

1705   al-Junaydi, Muhammad. Rabat al-khudur fi al-hijab wa-al-
        sufur. Cairo: Matba'at Muhammad Matar, n.d.
        Studies in social ills.

1706   Kalil al-Irqani, 'Ali. "An Outline of the History of Egyptian
        Feminist Movements" (in Arabic). al-Thuraya, vol. 2,
        no. 9.

1707   Khaki, Ahmad. Qasim Amin. Cairo: Matba'at 'Isa al-
        Halabi, 1944.

1708   Khalifah, Ijlal. al-Harakah al-nisa´iyah al-hadithah, qissat
        al-mar´ah al-'arabiyah 'ala ard misr. Cairo: al-
        Matba'ah al-'arabiyah al-haditha, 1973.

1709   al-Khatib, Hikmat Sabbagh. Qasim Amin: islah qiwamuhu
        al-mar´ah. Beirut: Bayt al-hikmah, 1970.

1710/1 Khayri, 'Abd al-Majid. al-Daf' al-matin fi al-radd 'ala
        hadrat Qasim Bak Amin. Misr: Matba'ah al-Turqi,
        1899.

1712   Madaman, Zinnie Zaroubie. "The Emerging of the New
        Egyptian Woman as Seen in l'Egyptienne: The Redefini-
        tion of Egyptian Womanhood." Unpublished M.A. thesis,
        American University in Cairo, 1975.

1713   Mahmud, Hafiz. "Les Partis féministes et les hommes."
        La Bourse Egyptienne, March 10, 1949. Translation
        of an article published in Ruz al-Yusuf, against women's
        participation in political life.

1714   "La Mission de la femme égyptienne." La Bourse Egyptienne,
        March 31, 1945. Reportage on the inauguration of the
        headquarters of the National Feminist Party by the Min-
        ister of Social Affairs.

1715   "The Modern Egyptian Girl According to the Secretary of
        the Feminist Union" (in Arabic). al-Ahram, Oct. 21,
        1976, p. 5, col. 5.

1716   "Le Mouvement féministe égyptien; Entretien avec la
        présidente du Bent el Nil et la présidente du parti ri-
        val." Progrès Dimanche, Feb. 20, 1949.

1717   "Movimento femministe egiziano." Oriente Moderno, 9
        (Sept. 1935), 530-31. Mentions several female writers
        and educators.

1718   Mudhakkirah min al-ittihad al-nisa´i ila al-barlaman al-
          misri. Cairo: n. p. , 1949.

1719   al-Mughani, Muhammad Mustafa Manfaluti. "About the New
          National Feminist Party" (in Arabic). al-Sabah, March
          23, 1944, 17.

1720   Muhanna, Majidah. "Five Groups Engaged in Feminist Ac-
          tivities Last Year" (in Arabic). al-Ahram, Dec. 30,
          1974, p. 4, col. 8.

1721   "My Husband ... Qasim Amin: An Interview with Mrs.
          Zaynab Hanum Qasim Amin" (in Arabic). Ruz al-Yusuf,
          April 1943, 10-11. The widow of the champion of fem-
          inism claims that her husband's views have been dis-
          torted and women have gone too far in their emancipa-
          tion.

1722   Nabarawi, Ceza. "Les Egyptiennes vont-elles voter?"
          L'Egyptienne, 145 (June 1938), 2-4. About a proposal
          by 'Abd al-Hamid al-Haqq to modify the 1935 electoral
          law to allow women to vote.

1723   _____. "L'Evolution du féminisme en Egypte. "
          L'Egyptienne, 2 (March 1925), 40-47.

1724   _____. "Le Mouvement féministe en Egypte. "
          L'Egyptienne, 5 (June 1925), 159-63.

1725   Nallino, C. A. "Opera e domande dell'Associazione per
          l'Unione femminile egiziana. " Oriente Moderno, 1926,
          339-42.

1726   Nasif, Majdi al-Din Hifni. Tahrir al-mar´ah fi al-Islam.
          Cairo: Sphinx, 1924. A short history of Muslim wom-
          en with biographies of Malak Hifni Nasif and Huda
          Sha'rawi.

1727   Athar Bahithat al-Badiyah, ed. by Nasif, Majdi al-Din.
          Cairo: al-Mu´assasah al-misriyah al-'ammah lil-
          ta´lif wa-al-tarjamah wa-al-nashr, 1962. The works
          of Malak Hifni Nasif edited by her brother.

1728   Nasif, Malak Hifni. al-Nisa´iyat. Cairo: Matba'at al-jaridah,
          1910. Articles published by the author under the pseud-
          onym of Bahithat al-Badiyah in defense of women's
          rights and feminine education.

1728a   _____. "Rapport sur les moyens de relever la condition
          de la femme musulmane. " In Recueil des Travaux du
          Premier Congrès Egyptien. Alexandria: Muh. A.
          Kalza, 1329-1911. The first list of comprehensive de-
          mands presented by a woman to a representative body.

1729 _____. Über die ägyptische Frauenfrage. Istanbul:
        Buchdruckerei Abajoli, 1926.

1730 "Open Dialogue Between Feminist Organizations and a Dele-
        gation of American Women" (in Arabic). al-Ahram,
        November 20, 1974, p. 10, col. 2.

1731 "Opera e domande dell'Associazione per l'Unione femminile
        egiziana. " Oriente Moderno, June 1926, 339-40.

1732 Osman, Sayed. "Questions impulsives. " La Patrie, March
        13, 1947.   Some members of the National Feminist
        Party answer a few questions.

1733 "Le Parti féministe célèbre l'anniversaire de sa fondation.
        Deux requêtes écrites avec du sang. " La Bourse
        Egyptienne, March 14, 1951.

1734 "Le Parti féministe demande l'entraînement militaire des
        jeunes filles. " La Bourse Egyptienne, Jan. 26, 1951.

1735 "Le Parti féministe égyptien n'est pas dissous déclare sa
        présidente. " Le Journal d'Egypte, July 26, 1944.

1736 "Le Parti féministe fonde un club sportif. " La Bourse
        Egyptienne, May 2, 1944.

1737 "Le Parti féministe national et la lutte contre la vie chère. "
        La Bourse Egyptienne, Feb. 16, 1951.

1738 "Le Parti féministe reçoit les étudiantes. " La Bourse
        Egyptienne, Dec. 22, 1950.

1739 Perlmann, M. "Women and Feminism in Egypt. " Pales-
        tinian Affairs, 4 (March 1949), 36-69.

1740 Phillips, Daisy Griggs.   "The Awakening of Egypt's Woman-
        hood. " The Muslim World, 18 (1929), 402-08.

1741 _____.   "The Growth of the Feminist Movement in
        Egypt. " The Muslim World, 1926, 227-85.

1742 "The Political Rights of Women" (in Arabic). al-Ithnain,
        March 20, 1950.

1743 "The Position of Women ... in the First 1977 Interview of
        Egypt's First Lady" (in Arabic). al-Ahram, Jan. 14,
        1977.

1744 Qanun jam'iyat al-ittihad al-nisa'i al-misri. Cairo: n.p.,
        1950.

1745 Qasim Amin. "L'Emancipation de la femme égyptienne. "

Revue de l'Islam, 1899, 157-58, 173-75.

1746   . "L'Emancipation de la femme en Egypte. " Revue Tunisienne, 1900, 147-52. Translation by Eusèbe Vassel of an article which had been published by the Imperial and Asiatic Quarterly Review.

1747   . "La Femme nouvelle. " Le Lotus, 2 (May 1901), 88-93.

1748   . Fi al-mar´ah. Cairo: Dar al-kutub al-misriyah, 1927. The best articles of Qasim Amin published in al-Siyasah al-Usbu'iyah and other pieces.

1749   . al-Mar´ah al-jadidah. Cairo: Matba'at al-ma'arif, 1901. See entries 1249, 1749a.

1749a al-Mar´ah al-jadidah, trans. by Krachkovskii, Ignatii Iulianovich. Leningrad: n. p. , 1931. The first Western translation of Qasim Amin's book [see entry 1749] with an introduction by the translator.

1750   . Tahrir al-mar´ah. Cairo: Maktabah al-sharqiyah, 1899. The first work of Qasim Amin in defense of women which caused an uproar in Egypt and abroad.

1751   "Quand ces dames ne sont pas d'accord. " Le Journal d'Egypte, Feb. 20, 1950. Fatma N. Rashid protests against the declaration of Doria Shafiq that the National Feminist Party had agreed to be absorbed by the Bint al-Nil.

1752   Ragai, Doria (Shafiq). "Egyptian Feminism. " Middle Eastern Affairs, 3 (Aug. 1952), 233-38. A very broad article by the founder of the Bint al-Nil Association.

1753   . La Femme nouvelle en Egypte. Cairo: Schindler, 1944. The first book of Shafiq to expound her theories and offer a few suggestions on improving the condition of Egyptian women.

1754   . al-Kitab al-abiyad li-huquq al-mar´ah al-siyasiyah. Cairo: al-Matba'ah al-sharqiyah, 1953?

1755   . al-Mar´ah al-misriyah min al-fara'unah ila al-yaum. Cairo: Matba'at Misr, 1955.

1756   . "Les Revendications politiques de la femme égyptienne. " La Bourse Egyptienne, April 28, 1949.

1757   , and Ibrahim 'Abduh. Tatawwur al-nahdah al-nisa´iyah fi Misr. Cairo: Maktabat al-tawwakul, 1945.

1758   al-Ramli, Su'ad. Kifah al-mar´ah. Cairo: Dar al-tiba'ah
        al-hadithah, 1948.

1759   Rapport de l'Union Féministe, 1928-1933. Cairo: Paul
        Barbery Press, 1933.

1760   Rashid, Fatma Ni'mat. "A propos de féminisme." La
        Bourse Egyptienne, June 4, 1944.

1761   _____. "Adequate Conditions for Women" (in Arabic).
        al-Hawadith, July 25, 1945.

1762   _____. "Le But réel du Parti Féministe National." Le
        Messager, Dec. 7, 1950.

1763   _____. "Coup d'oeil sur le féminisme égyptien." Revue
        de la Radio, April 24, 1948, 6-7.

1764   _____. "La Femme et les principes humanitaires du
        programme du Parti Féministe National." Le Messager,
        Jan. 18, 1951.

1765   _____. "La Femme et sa mission." Le Messager,
        Jan. 4, 1951.

1766   _____. "Femmes égyptiennes et arabes modernes."
        Revue de la Radio, July 9, 1948, 6-7.

1767   _____. "Les Femmes égyptiennes fêtent l'anniversaire
        du 13 novembre." Le Messager, Nov. 16, 1950.
        Enumerates the various attempts at reforming the voting
        system to grant suffrage to women.

1768   _____. "Les Femmes et le mouvement national; Une
        Interview exclusive de Mme Safia Saad Zaghloul." Le
        Progrès Egyptien, Nov. 13, 1944. Mrs. Zaghlul
        reminisces about the 1919 manifestations organized by
        the Ladies' Wafd.

1769   _____. "Une Histoire comme les autres." La Patrie,
        May 1, 1947. The author explains why she is a femi-
        nist.

1770   _____. "If Women Were to Become Military Gover-
        nors..." (in Arabic). al-Hawadith, July 18, 1945.

1771   _____. "al-Isma" (in French). La Patrie, Dec. 17,
        1935. About the 'ismah clause which every Muslim
        bride could have included in her marriage contract but
        which is seldom used.

1772   _____. "Le Jour des mères au Parti Féministe National,
        preuve entre mille de sa double mission civique et

humanitaire. " Le Messager, Dec. 24, 1950.

1773 _____. "Le Mouvement féministe égyptien. " La Bourse Egyptienne, Feb. 2, 1949.

1774 _____. "Les Partis féministes et les femmes. " La Bourse Egyptienne, March 16, 1949. An answer to the article of H. Mahmud which had appeared in La Bourse Egyptienne on March 10, 1949. The author justifies women's involvement in politics.

1775 _____. "Le Vote des femmes. " La Bourse Egyptienne, May 27, 1944. An answer to an article on women's suffrage which had appeared two days earlier in the same paper.

1776 "A Recommendation from the General Conference of Women Organizations Calling for Women to Hold Judgeships and High Positions in the Public Sector and the Civil Service" (in Arabic). al-Ahram, July 6, 1976, p. 1, col. 4.

1777 Rossi, Ettore. "Discussioni e polemiche in Egitto sull'uguaglianza tra l'uomo e la donna. " Oriente Moderno, 6 (1930), 284-85.

1778 _____. "L'Unione femminile egiziana ed il Congresso dell'Alleanza femminile internazionale a Roma. " Oriente Moderno, 6 (Nov. 15, 1923), 376-78. Huda Sha'rawi founded the Feminist Union just before she attended the Congress of the International Women's Alliance in Rome in 1923.

1779 Rushdi, Inji. "An Examination of the Activities of Female Deputies" (in Arabic). al-Ahram, Feb. 20, 1976, p. 6.

1780 _____. "The Feminist Organization is Going to Have Its Own Character in the Future" (in Arabic). al-Ahram, July 3, 1974, p. 5, col. 2.

1781 Sa'id, Fatimah. "Hawa' Without Home" (in Arabic). Akhir Sa'ah 2131 (Aug. 27, 1975). The tribulations of feminist Hawa' Idriss, niece of H. Sha'rawi.

1782 Sayf al-Nasr, 'Aliyah. "An Outlook for the Future, A Call to Go Back to the Harem Age" (in Arabic). al-Ahram, March 17, 1976, p. 4, col. 1. Opinions of some Egyptian thinkers to give women greater responsibilities.

1783 Seton, Grace Thompson. A Woman Tender Foot in Egypt. London: Bodley Head, 1923.

1784 _____. "The Women Leaders of Modern Egypt. "

American Review of Reviews, Oct. 1922, 380-86. A
short presentation of a few prominent Egyptian ladies,
mostly members of the Ladies Wafd, with their picture
published for the first time.

1785   al-Shaf'i, Kamil. Tatawwur al-mar´ah. Cairo: Dar al-
       kitab al-'arabi, 1952.

1786   al-Shahidi, 'Ali Ahmad. Amrina lillah, aw al-mar´ah wa-
       halatuha. Cairo: Matba'at al-tamaddun, 1903. Al-
       though the author denounces the abuses perpetrated
       against women throughout history, he is in favor of the
       veil and recommends only a very limited education for
       girls.

1787   Sha'rawi, Huda. "Appel aux représentants de la nation
       égyptienne." L'Egyptienne, 158 (Sept.-Oct. 1939), 9-
       10. H. Sha'rawi expresses her opposition to martial
       law and cautions against the entrance of Egypt into the
       war alongside Great Britain.

1788   _____. "La Coopération entre les femmes d'Orient et
       d'Occident." L'Egyptienne, 157 (July-Aug. 1939), 14-16.
       Text of the speech delivered by the author to the Peace
       Meeting of the International Alliance of Women for
       Peace and Suffrage on July 12, 1939.

1789   _____. Daur al-mar´ah fi al-nahdah al-sharqiyah.
       Cairo: Matba'at Misr, 1935.

1790   _____. "L'Emancipation de la femme." Journal Tech-
       nique du Commerce, Sept. 1926, 170-71.

1791   _____. "L'Evolution du féminisme en Egypte." La Voix
       des Humbles, Dec. 1, 1934.

1792   _____. "The Feminine Renaissance" (in Arabic). In
       al-Hilal, al-Kitab al-dhahabi, Cairo: al-Hilal, 1946;
       28-31.

1793   _____. "The First Results of the Conference on the
       Palestinian Question" (in Arabic). al-Misriyah, 15/16
       (Feb. 1, 1939).

1794   _____. "Kassem Amine, promoteur du mouvement
       féministe en Egypte." L'Egyptienne, 155 (May 1939),
       6-9. Translation of a speech given by the author on
       the Egyptian radio network.

1795   _____. "Lettre ouverte à Mr. Neville Chamberlain à
       l'occasion de la publication du Livre Blanc." L'Egypti-
       enne, 156 (June 1939), 2-3.

1796   . al-Salam al-'alami wa-nasib al-mar´ah fi
              tahqiqih. Cairo: Matba'at Misr, 1938.

1797 Sidki, Bahijat Rashid. The Egyptian Feminist Union, Now
          the Hoda Sha'rawi Association. Cairo: Anglo-Egyptian
          Bookshop, 1973. A history of the Feminist Union
          written on the occasion of its 50th anniversary.

1798 Suleiman, Michael W. "Changing Attitudes Toward Women
          in Egypt: The Role of Fiction in Women's Magazines."
          Paper delivered at the Eighth Annual Meeting of the
          Middle East Studies Association, Boston, November 6-
          9, 1974.

1799 Tal'at Harb. Fasl al-khitab fi al-mar´ah wa-al-hijab.
          Misr: Matba'at al-taraqqi, 1901. A virulent pamphlet
          against Qasim Amin's Tahrir al-mar´ah [entry 1750].

1800   . Tarbiyat al-mar´ah wa-al-hijab. Cairo:
              Matba'at al-taraqqi, 1900. The second book of the au-
              thor in his polemic with Qasim Amin.

1801 Taqrir jam'iyat al-ittihad al-nisa´i. Cairo: n.p., 1951.

1802 "Ten Recommendations at the Conference of Women's Or-
          ganizations to Remedy the Problems of Women in
          Cairo" (in Arabic). al-Ahram, July 6, 1976, p. 7,
          col. 1.

1803 "Texte des demandes à Son Excellence le Président du Con-
          seil des Ministres et Son Excellence le Ministre de la
          Justice." L'Egyptienne, 16 (May 1926), 105-08.

1804 Thabit, Munirah. "La Femme égyptienne et le Livre Blanc
          britannique." L'Egyptienne, 156 (June 1939), 4-8. A
          lucid analysis of the White Book on Palestine and an
          appeal to Egyptian women to oppose it.

1805 Thompson, Anna Y. "The Woman Question in Egypt." The
          Muslim World, 3 (July 1914), 266-72.

1806 "L'Unione femminile egiziana ed il Congresso dell'Alleanza
          femminile internazionale a Roma." Oriento Moderno,
          6 (Nov. 1923), 376-78. Includes the French text of the
          speech of H. Sha'rawi to the Congress of the Interna-
          tional Women's Alliance.

1807 Vacca, Virginia. "L'Unione femminile egiziana domanda al
          Presidente del Consiglio numerose riformi sociali."
          Oriente Moderno, 5 (May 1936), 295-96.

1808 Veccia-Vaglieri, L. "Movimento femminista egiziano."
          Oriente Moderno, 9 (1936), 530-31.

1809   "La Vérité sur le parti féministe égyptien telle que nous la
        dit Mme Fatma Nimet Rached. " Le Progrès Egyptien,
        July 29, 1944.

1810   "Le Vote des femmes. " La Bourse Egyptienne, March 25,
        1944. The vote having just being denied Egyptian wom-
        en, Ceza Nabarawi had expressed the opinion that it
        should have been granted at least to literate women,
        but the author of the article thinks women should not
        vote at all for the sake of domestic peace.

1811   Wali al-Din Yakan. al-Saha´if al-sud. Beirut: Bayt al-
        hikmah, 1966. The author was a strong supporter of
        Qasim Amin. This anthology of his work includes al-
        Mar´ah, pp. 47-53 and Huwwa wa-hiya, a chapter of
        his novel by the same name, pp. 54-60.

1812   "We ... Egyptian Women" (in Arabic). al-Balagh, May 5,
        1950. Critique of Aflatun's book, Nahnu ... al-nisa´
        al-misriyat [entry 1632].

1813   "We ... Egyptian Women" (in Arabic). al-Misri, Jan. 22,
        1950. See entry 1812.

1814   "We ... Egyptian Women" (in Arabic). al-Nida´, Feb. 20,
        1950. See entry 1812.

1815   "We ... Egyptian Women" (in Arabic). al-Ummah, May 11,
        1950. See entry 1812.

1816   Weghorn, E. "La Femme égyptienne et le problème de
        l'égalité des droits. " Die Neue Saar, June 10, 1949.

1817   "What Happened During the Meeting of the Colonel and al-
        Sadat with the Feminist Leaders in Cairo?" (in Arabic).
        al-Bayt, 10, 1974.

1818   "What the President of the Feminist Party Has to Say" (in
        Arabic). al-Hawadith, July 2, 1944, 12.

1819   "The Women's Conference in Berlin ... Disappointed Those
        Who Attacked Egypt" (in Arabic). al-Akhbar, Nov. 17,
        1975.

1820   "The Women's Organization Supports Feminists in the Elec-
        tions of the People's Assembly" (in Arabic). Akhir
        Sa'ah, 2179 (July 28, 1976), p. 8.

1821   Ziyadah, Mayy. Bahithat al-Badiyah: bahth intiqadi.
        Cairo: Matba'at al-muqtataf, 1920. Mayy Ziyadah
        reminisces about her departed friend and analyzes her
        works.

1822   . Ghayat al-hayah. Cairo: al-Muqtataf, 1921.
Text of lecture given on April 29, 1921, at the Egyptian
University to members of the association Misr al-fata´.

1823   . "Il risveglio della donna in Egitto negli ultimi
cento anni. " Oriente Moderno, 5 (May 1929), 236-48.
A condensed text of two lectures given at the American
University in Cairo in 1928 on woman's condition in
Egypt since Muhammad 'Ali.

1824   . al-Saha´if. Cairo: al-Salafiyah, 1924. Includes articles previously published in al-Nahdah al-
nisa´iyah, a Cairo newspaper and al-Mar´ah al-jadidah,
a Beirut newspaper.

Jihan al-Sadat

1825   "The Egyptian Woman Is Still Demanding Equality and
Rights" (in Arabic). al-Ahram, June 23, 1975, 5.
Text of an interview granted by Mrs. al-Sadat to ABC
TV network after she had attended the Mexico Con-
ference on Women.

1826   "Egypt's First Lady. " Christian Science Monitor, Dec. 18,
1974, p. 5, col. 1.

1827   Field, Peter. "Jehan Sadat: Working to Improve Women's
Position. " The Times, Nov. 5, 1975.

1828   "A Great Welcome for Jihan al-Sadat in Japan" (in Arabic).
al-Ahram, Oct. 27, 1976, 8.

1829   Hasan, Zaynab. "A Medal for the Peace Lady" (in Arabic).
al-Musawwar, Oct. 24, 1975, 30-31.

1830   "In an American TV Interview, Jihan al-Sadat Calls for
Complete Rights for Women All Over the World" (in
Arabic). al-Ahram, April 19, 1976, p. 6, col. 8.

1831   al-Ittihad al-Ishtiraki al-'Arabi. al-Lajnah al-Markaziyah.
Misr: al-Hayah wa-al-amal min kalimat umm al-abtal,
Jihan al-Sadat. Cairo, 1974. Text of the speeches of
Mrs. al-Sadat during the year 1973-74.

1832   .   .   . Cairo, 1975. Text of
the speeches of Mrs. al-Sadat during the year 1974-75.

1833   "Jihan al-Sadat Declared on Mothers Day: Society Must
Provide Stability for Mothers" (in Arabic). al-Ahram,
March 22, 1976, p. 6, col. 6.

1834   "Jihan al-Sadat Gives a Lecture in Germany About the

Egyptian Woman" (in Arabic). al-Ahram, March 31,
1976, p. 3, col. 3.

1835   "Jihan al-Sadat: Our Hope and Our Work for Peace" (in
        Arabic). Akhir Sa'ah, 2121 (June 18, 1975). The ad-
        dress of Mrs. al-Sadat delivered at the International
        Women's Conference in Mexico.

1836   "Mrs. al-Sadat Speaks on the American Television" (in
        Arabic). Hawwa', 979 (June 28, 1975).

1837   "My Husband Anwar al-Sadat" (in Arabic). Ruz al-Yusuf,
        Dec. 15, 1975, 11-16.

1838   Rushdi, Inji. "Before Jihan al-Sadat Became the First
        President of a Free Parliament in Egypt" (in Arabic).
        al-Ahram, Dec. 5, 1975, p. 4.

1839   _____. "Jihan al-Sadat and Historical Days" (in Arabic).
        al-Ahram, Oct. 4, 1975, 4. Mrs. al-Sadat talks about
        her husband during the 1973 War. She expresses her
        intention to publish her memoirs.

1840   _____. "Jihan al-Sadat: They Wanted to Trap Her for
        the Sake of Mrs. Rabin" (in Arabic). al-Ahram, June
        29, 1975, p. 3.

1841   al-Sa'ati, 'Abla. "Jihan al-Sadat at the Conference of Wom-
        en and Struggle: We Do Not Want War But a Just
        Peace" (in Arabic). al-Ahram, Nov. 18, 1974, p. 6,
        col. 4.

1842   al-Sa'id, Aminah. "Jihan al-Sadat at the Podium of the
        Mexican Conference" (in Arabic). al-Musawwar, July
        4, 1975, 6-8.

1843   al-Sha'ir, Husayn. "An Invitation From the First Lady of
        Egypt to All Egyptian Women for the New Year" (in
        Arabic). al-Ahram, Jan. 2, 1976, p. 5, col. 1. Mrs.
        al-Sadat asks Egyptian women to help solve social
        problems.

1843a Winkel, Annegret. Jehan El Sadat: First Lady und
        Frauenrechtlerin am Nil. Koblenz: Gorres-Verlag,
        1976.

V

IRAQ

1844   'Abbas, 'Abd al-Jabar. "Love and Woman in the Poetry of
        al-Sayyab" (in Arabic). al-Adab, Feb. 1966, 5-7, 78-
        79.

1845   al-Alusi, Gamal Husayn. "The Effects of Certain Analytic,
        Psychological, Social and Sex Factors in the Prediction
        of Success in the Faculty of Engineering" (in Arabic).
        Unpublished M.A. thesis, Department of Psychology and
        Education, Baghdad University, 1972.

1846   Amin, Amin Muhammad. "Traffic Policewomen in the
        Streets of Baghdad" (in Arabic). al-Ahram, Nov. 26,
        1974, p. 8, col. 4.

1847   Anderson, James N. D. "A Draft Code of Personal Law
        for Iraq." Bulletin of the School of Oriental Studies, 1
        (1953), 43-60.

1848   _____. "A Law of Personal Status for Iraq." Interna-
        tional & Comparative Law Quarterly, Oct. 1960, 542-
        563. Summary, commentary and criticism of the 1959
        Iraqi Code of Personal Status.

1849   al-'Ani, Muhammad Shafiq. Ahkam al-ahwal al-shakhisiyah
        fi al-'Iraq. Cairo.

1850   al-'Ani, Shuja' Muslim. al-Mar'ah fi al-qisah al-'iraqiyah.
        Baghdad: Wizarat al-a'lam, 1972.

1851   Baali, F. "Educational Aspirations Among College Girls
        in Iraq." Sociological & Social Research 4 (July 1967),
        485-93. Aspiration toward higher education is corre-
        lated with family status, the education of the parents
        and the authority of the father.

1852   El-Bustani, Afifa Ismail. "Problems Facing a Selected
        Group of Iraqi Women." Unpublished Ph.D. disserta-
        tion, Columbia University, 1956.

145

1853   Butti, Rufa´il. "La donna irachena moderna." Oriente
        Moderno, 4-6 (April–June 1948), 108-12.

1854   Corti Ghannam, L. "L'emancipazione della donna nell'Iraq."
        Oriente Moderno, 6 (1953), 297.

1855   al-Darbandi, 'Abd al-Rahman Sulayman. Dirasat 'an al-
        mar´ah al-'iraqiyah al-mu'asirah. Baghdad: Matabi'
        dar al-'asri, 1968.

1856   al-Daylami, Nazihah Jawdat. Namudhaj min mashakil al-
        mar´ah al-'arabiyah. Tunis: Kitab al-ba'th, 1958.

1857   Drower, Ethel Stefana (Stevens), Lady. "Woman and Taboo
        in Iraq." Iraq, 5 (1938), 105-17. Lady Drower
        studied the Arab world all her life and spent 16 years
        in Iraq.

1858   Elder, J. "Family Life in Shia Islam." Moslem World,
        18 (1929), 250-55.

1859   Fakhoury, Haifa. "Women and Professions in Iraq: A Dy-
        namic Change." Paper delivered at the Conference on
        Development in the Arab World, New York, October 1-
        3, 1976.

1860   Faraj Allah, Bahiyah. "al-'Iraq" (in Arabic). al-Katib al-
        misri, 2 (April 1946), 481-85. About feminism and
        education in Iraq.

1861   Fattouhi, Bahija. "Iraq's Women Turn from Aba and Veil."
        Lands East, 2 (Jan. 1957), 10-12.

1862   Fernea, Elizabeth W. Guests of the Sheikh. Garden City,
        N.Y.: Doubleday Anchor Book, 1969. Lively descrip-
        tion of feminine conditions in Southern Iraq.

1863   al-Hamdani, Muwaffak, and Abu-Laban, Baha. "Game In-
        volvement and Sex-Role Socialization in Arab Children."
        International Journal of Comparative Sociology, 12
        (1971), 182-191. Results of a study conducted in 1967
        in a lower-class neighborhood in Baghdad.

1864   Hansen, Henny Harald. Daughters of Allah: Among Moslem
        Women in Kurdistan. London: G. Allen & Unwin,
        1960.

1865   _____. The Kurdish Woman's Life: Field Research in
        a Muslim Society, Iraq. Copenhagen: Nationalmuseet,
        1961. (Nationalmuseets Skrifter, Etnografisk raekke,
        7.) This anthropological study includes an extensive
        bibliography.

1866 al-Hilli, Muhammad 'Ali Hasan. Mashakil al-zawaj wa-al-talaq. Mosul, n.p., 1961.

1867 Husayn, Ja'far. Ta'lim al-mar'ah. Baghdad: al-Sha'b, 1930.

1868 'Imarah, Lumay'ah 'Abbas. Yusammunahu al-hubb. Beirut: Dar al-'awdah, 1972.

1869 "Iraq: Woman Branch Out to New Careers." Christian Science Monitor, Dec. 7, 1971, p. 11, col. 1.

1870 "The Iraqi Feminist Organization Is Calling for an End to Legal Differences Between Sexes" (in Arabic). al-Ahram, Oct. 2, 1976, p. 14, col. 1.

1871 "The Iraqi Woman and Childbirth" (in Arabic). al-Ahram, Sept. 15, 1976, p. 12, col. 1.

1872 Izzidien, Yousif. "The Emancipation of Iraqi Women: Women and Their Influence on Iraqi Life and Poetry." Bulletin of the College of Arts & Science, Baghdad University, 1 (1959), 33-41.

1873 Jam'iyat al-Khadamat al-Diniyah wa-al-Ijtima'iyah fi al-Iraq. Kayfa 'alajna mushkilat al-bigha.' Baghdad: Sharikat al-tijarah wa-al-tiba'ah, 1952.

1874 al-Kassir, Maliha Awni. Family Planning in Iraq. Baghdad, n.d.

1875 _____. "The Iraqi Family: Stability and Change." Unpublished M.A. thesis, University of California at Berkeley, 1956.

1876 al-Kassir, Maliha. The Origin of the Family (in Arabic). Baghdad: n.p., 1964.

1877 _____. Women's Status in Modern Iraq (in Arabic). Baghdad: al-Tadamon Press, 1965.

1878 Khulusi, A. "'Atika, a Modern Poetess." Journal of the Royal Asiatic Society, no. 3-4 (1950), 149-57.

1879 Linant de Bellefonds, L. "Le Code du statut personnel irakien du 30 décembre 1959." Studia Islamica, 13 (1960), 79-135.

1880 al-Mala'ikah, Nazik. Diwan Nazik al-Mala'ikah. 2 vols. Beirut: Dar al-'udah, 1971. The complete edition of the work of a major Iraqi poetess.

1881 Maskuni, Yusuf Ya'qub. Min 'abqariyat nisa' al-qarn al-tasi' 'ashar. Baghdad: n.p. , 1947.

1882   Nahas, M. Kamel. "Married Life in Iraq. " In Nels Ander-
       son, ed. , Studies in the Family. Tubingen: J. C. B.
       Mohr, 1956; 183-210. Includes the results of a ques-
       tionnaire answered by 924 people.

1883   Qadry, H. T. "Problems of Women Teachers in Iraq. "
       Unpublished Ph. D. dissertation, Stanford University,
       1957.

1884   al-Qazzar, Ayad. "Female Higher Education in Iraq. "
       Paper delivered at the 10th Middle East Studies Associ-
       ation meeting, Los Angeles, 1976.

1885   al-Rashid, 'Abd al-'Aziz. Tahdhir al-muslimin 'an ittiba'
       ghayr sabil al-mu´minin. Baghdad, n. p. , 1911.

1886   al-Shakarshi, Shibzinan. The Application of International
       Laws to Protect Working Women in Iraq (in Arabic).
       Baghdad: n. p. , n. d.

1887   al-Shaykh Dawud, Sabihah. Awwal al-tariq ila al-nahdah al-
       niswatiyah fi al-'Iraq. Baghdad: Matabi' al-rabitah,
       1958. The author, who had a remarkable personality,
       was the first Iraqi woman admitted to the Baghdad Law
       School.

1888   Tekerli, Fu'ad. "al-Tannur. " al-Adab, April 1973. Short
       story about a crime of honor.

1889   'Umarah, Lami'ah 'Abbas. 'Iraqiyah. The love poetry of
       an Iraqi woman.

1890   al-Umari, S. "Participation of Women in Community Life
       in Iraq. " International Women's News, 50 (June 1956),
       535-36.

1891   Westphal-Hellbush, Sigrid. "Transvestiten bein arabischen
       stämmen. " Sociologus, 2 (1956), 126-27. Bibliographi-
       cal article on an unusual Iraqi woman poet who dresses
       as a man.

1892   al-Yusbaki, Salamani. "Problems of University Education
       for Women" (in Arabic). Unpublished M.A. thesis,
       Baghdad University, 1971.

VI

JORDAN

1893   Anderson, J. N. D. "Recent Developments in Shari'ah
        Law, VIII. " Muslim World, 42 (July 1952), 190-206.
        An analysis of the Jordanian law of family rights of
        August 15, 1951.

1894   Hirabayashi, Gordon K. and May Ishaq. "Social Change in
        Jordan: A Quantitative Approach in a Non-Census Area."
        American Journal of Sociology, 1 (1958), 36-40. Re-
        sults of interviews conducted with 100 housewives in
        Amman in 1955.

1895   Lunt, J. D. "Love in the Desert. " Blackwood's Magazine,
        278 (Oct. 1955), 333-339. Description of a Bedouin
        marriage.

1896   Lutfiyya, A. M. "The Family. " In A. M. Lutfiyya and
        C. W. Churchill, eds. , Readings in Arab Middle
        Eastern Societies and Cultures. The Hague: Mouton;
        New York: Humanities Press, 1970; 505-525. A study
        of family life in the village of Baytin.

1897   Musallam, Abeebeh. "Nursing in Jordan: Jordanian
        Nurses are Improving Nursing Care of Their People,
        Educating Their Country Women and Building a Profes-
        sion. " American Journal of Nursing, 58 (Sept. 1958),
        1249-1251.

1898   al-Nabulsi, Shakir. Fadwa Tuqan wa-al-shi'r al-'urduni al-
        mu'asir. Cairo: al-Dar al-qawmi lil-tiba'ah wa-al-
        nashr, 1966.

1898a   "Queen Alia of Jordan Dies in Copter Crash. " New York
        Times, Feb. 10, 1977, p. 7. Includes a short bio-
        graphical notice of a modernized queen.

1899   Rizk, Hanna. "National Fertility Sample Survey for Jor-
        dan, 1972: The Study and Some Findings. " Population
        Bulletin of the United Nations Economic and Social Of-
        fice in Beirut, 5 (July 1973), 14-31.

149

1900   Vacca, Virginia. "Le associazioni femminili chiedono il
          voto per le donne. " Oriente Moderno, 1 (1960), 13.
          Excerpt from the paper Filastin on suffrage demands
          from feminist organizations.

VII

KUWAIT

1901 'Abd al-Rahman, Sa'd. Dirasat awda' wa-ittijahat al-mar´ah al-kuwaytiyah. Kuwait: Matabi' dar al-siyasah, 1971.

1902 al-Bura' i, Najib. "How to Keep Your Husband: Don't Put All Your Eggs in the Same Basket." Majallat al-Kuwayt, 246 (Sept. 1, 1973), 44-45.

1903 Calverley, Eleanor J. "Beauty for Ashes." Moslem World, 10 (1920), 391-401. Religious attitudes of women in the Persian Gulf area where the author practiced medicine.

1904 _____. My Arabian Days and Nights. New York: Crowell, 1958. The memoirs of a doctor who spent twenty years in Kuwait; her observations on women, social life and customs.

1905 Chelhod, J. "Notes sur le mariage chez les arabes au Kuwait." Journal de la Société des Africanistes, 26 (1956), 255-62.

1905a Commission in Charge of Women's Affairs, Council of Planning. A Report on Women's Status in Kuwait. Kuwait, 1975. An assessment of the present situation of Kuwaiti women in regard to family, education, work and politics.

1906 "Employment of Women at Night in Kuwait" (in Arabic). al-Ahram, Jan. 27, 1976, p. 14, col. 1.

1906a "A Hit With the Misses: Inside the University College for Women." Kuwaiti Digest, 2 (April-June 1977), 22-24.

1907 Husayn, 'Abd Allah Ghulum, and 'Izzat Sayyid Isma'il. al-Zawaj fi al-Kuwayt. Kuwait: Matba'at Hukumat al-Kuwayt, 1967?

1908 al-Kayyal, Suhayr. "The Kuwaiti Girl Says: 'Comprehension, Sharing and Simplicity Are the Common Bases of

a Happy Marriage' " (in Arabic).   Hawwa´, Jan. 26,
1975.

1908a Kotb, Isaac.   Social and Academic Adjustment of University
       Women of the Arab Gulf States.   Kuwait, 1975.   The
       author is professor of sociology at Kuwait University
       where he conducted a survey of its women students.

1909   Mejido, Manuel.   "Kuwait: Oil Millions Bring Little
       Change. " Atlas-World Press Review, March 1975, 36-
       37.   Education and independence remain male preroga-
       tives.

1910   Sa'ad al-Din, F.   "Lecture On the Status of the Working
       Woman in the State of Kuwait" (in Arabic).   Journal of
       the Gulf and Arabian Peninsula Studies, 11 (July 1977),
       209-212.

1911   Stuers, Cora Vreede-de.   "Girl Students in Kuwait. "
       Bijdragen Tot De Taal-, Land-En Volkenkunde, 1 (1974),
       110-131.

1912   al-Sultan, Najat.   "The Kuwaiti Professional Women. "
       Paper delivered at the Conference on Development in
       the Arab World, New York, October 1-3, 1976.

1913   Tantawi, M.   "The Women of Kuwait" (in Arabic).   al-
       'Arabi, 151 (July 1971), 84-91.

1914   "Women From Kuwait" (in Arabic).   Hawwa´, Jan. 26,
       1975, 76-77.   Interviews of Kuwaiti students and career
       girls by an Egyptian journalist.

VIII

LEBANON

1915 Abu Khadra, Rihab. "Recent Changes in Lebanese Moslem
      Marriage Shown by Changes in Marriage Contracts."
      Unpublished M.A. thesis, Department of Sociology and
      Anthropology, American University of Beirut, 1959.
      The changes indicate a trend toward increased secular-
      ism.

1916 Accad-Sursock, R. "La Femme libanaise: de la tradition
      à la modernité." Travaux et Jours, 52 (July-Sept.
      1974), 17-38.

1917 Alamuddin, Rima. Spring to Summer. Beirut: Khayats,
      1963. The author draws from her experiences as a
      student at the American University in Beirut.

1918 _____. The Sun Is Silent. London: Hodder & Stoughton,
      1964. The short stories of a young Lebanese who died
      in 1963, age 22.

1919 Alouche, R. "La Femme libanaise et le travail." Travaux
      et Jours, 52 (July-Sept. 1974), 61-70.

1920 "Arab Women Today: The Old Ways Are Changing." Daily
      Star, Aug. 30, 1970, 8.

1921 Ayoub, Millicent Robinson. "Endogamous Marriage in a
      Middle Eastern Village." Unpublished Ph.D. disserta-
      tion, Radcliffe College, 1957. Research conducted in
      a Druze community.

1922 _____. "Parallel Cousin Marriage and Endogamy: A
      Study in Sociometry." South Western Journal of Anthro-
      pology, 15 (1959), 266-275. Study of a Druze commu-
      nity.

1923 Bagros, Sylvia. "Lorsqu'une française épouse un libanais:
      étude de cas." Travaux et Jours, 52 (July-Sept. 1974),
      39-60.

1924   Ba'labakki, Layla. al-Alihah al-mansukhah. Beirut:
       Matabi' dar majallat shi'r, 1960.

1925   . Je vis! Paris: Editions du Seuil, 1961. The
       author caused quite a stir with her first book because
       of the feelings of revolt against tradition she expressed.
       This is the translation of her Ana ahya.

1926   . Nahnu bila aqni'ah. Beirut: Cénacle Libanais,
       1959. A lecture given to the Cénacle Libanais.

1927   . "Nous sans masques, ou la jeunesse arabe
       dévoilée." Orient, 11 (1959), 145-163. A translation
       of item 1926.

1928   . Safinat hanan ila al-qamar. Beirut: al-Maktab
       al-tijari lil-tiba'ah wa-al-tauzi' wa-al-nashr, 1964. A
       gathering of short stories.

1929   Bayham, Muhammad Jamil. al-mar´ah fi al-ta´rikh wa-al-
       shara´i'. Beirut: n.p., 1921. A history of the Arab
       woman up to modern times, including Lebanese emi-
       grants to North and South Americas. Mention is made
       of new feminist ideas in Lebanon and abroad.

1930   Chamoun, Mounir. "Les Femmes dans la société libanaise:
       couples." Travaux et Jours, 52 (July-Sept. 1974), 5-14.

1931   . "Image de la mère et sexualité au Liban."
       Travaux et Jours, 44 (July-Sept. 1972), 107-14.

1932   . "Problèmes de la famille au Liban." Travaux
       et Jours, 25 (1967), 13-40.

1933   Chemali, Béchara. "Mariage et noce au Liban." Anthropos,
       10-11 (1915), 913-41.

1934   . "Moeurs et usages au Liban: l'éducation."
       Anthropos, 12-13 (1917), 625-40.

1935   . "Naissance et premier âge au Liban." Anthro-
       pos, 5 (1910), 734-47, 1072-86.

1936   Chidiac, M. "Travail des femmes et des enfants." Mé-
       langes Proche-Orientaux d'Economie Politique. Annales
       de la Faculté de Droit de Beyrouth, 1956, 79-127.

1937   Des Villettes, Jacqueline. La Vie des femmes dans un
       village maronite libanais, Ain el-Kharoube. Tunis:
       Bascone & Muscat, 1964.

1938   Dupré la Tour, Augustin. "Leila Baalbaki: 'Je vis.'"
       Travaux et Jours, 2 (July-Sept. 1961), 91-94.

1939   "An Examination of the Attitudes of Young Lebanese Wom-
        en. " Middle East Forum, 40 (June 1964), 16-17. Re-
        sults of the interviewing of 200 middle-class women by
        a Beirut newspaper.

1940   Farsoun, Samih K. 'Family Structure and Society in
        Modern Lebanon. " In Louise E. Sweet, ed. , Peoples
        and Cultures of the Middle East, Garden City, N.Y. :
        Natural History Press, 1970; Vol. 2, 257-307.

1941   _____. "The Family Structure of the Urban Middle
        Class of a Modernizing Society: Lebanon. " Unpublished
        Ph. D. dissertation, University of Connecticut, 1971.

1942   "From the Lebanese Press. " Middle East Forum, April
        1962, 13-15.

1943   Fuller, A. H. "The World of Kin. " In A. M. Lutfiyya
        and C. W. Churchill, eds. , Readings in Arab Middle
        Eastern Societies and Cultures. The Hague: Mouton;
        New York: Humanities Press, 1970; 526-534.

1944   Germanos-Ghazaly, L. "La Femme et la terre. " Travaux
        et Jours, 56-67 (July-Dec. 1975), 75-94.

1945   Ghurayyib, Mishal Sallam. al-Zawaj al-madani. Beirut:
        n. p. , 1965. The civil marriage in Lebanon.

1946   Haddad, Anees Adib. "The Effects of Generation, Religion,
        and Sex on the Relationship of Family Vertical Solidarity
        and Mental Health in Lebanon. " Unpublished Ph. D. dis-
        sertation, University of California at Los Angeles, 1971.

1947   Hajjaj, Abdul-Wadud. "Divorce in Lebanon. " Daily Star
        Supplement, Aug. 22, 1971, 9.

1948   Harfouche, Jamal Karam. Infant Health in Lebanon: Cus-
        toms and Taboos. Beirut: Khayats, 1965. The re-
        sults of an inquiry led by a woman physician who inter-
        viewed 379 mothers.

1949   _____. Social Structures of Low-Income Families in
        Lebanon. Beirut: Khayats, 1965.

1950   Hasan, Muhammad Kamil. Sutur ma'a al-'azimat. Beirut:
        Dar al-buhuth al-'ilmiyah, 1969.

1951   Hashim Madi, Labibah. Qulub al-rijal. Cairo: Matba'at
        Fatiya al-nil, 1940.

1952   _____. Shirin fatat al-sharq. Cairo, n. p. , n. d.

1953   Ibrahim, Imili Faris. Adibat lubnaniyat. Beirut: Dar alrayhani, 1961. A critical study of 16 Lebanese female writers, including Zaynab Fawwaz and Julia Tuma.

1954   . al-Harakah al-nisa´iyah fi Lubnan. Beirut: Dar al-thaqafah, 1966. A history of feminism in Lebanon, including statistical information.

1955 "It Just Isn't Fare!" Christian Science Monitor, Jan. 27, 1971, p. 10, col. 4.

1956 Jabr, Jamil. Mayy Ziyadah fi hayatiha wa-adabiha. Beirut: al-Matba'ah al-katulikiyah, 1960.

1957 Jalbi, Niqula Yusuf. Mashakil al-hayah bayna al-shabab wa al-fatah. Beirut: n.p., 1924.

1958 Joly, Gertrude. "The Woman of the Lebanon." Journal of the Royal Central Asian Society, April-July 1951, 177-84.

1959 Joseph, Suad. "Urban Poor Women in Lebanon: Does Poverty Have Public and Private Domains?" Paper delivered at the Middle East Studies Association Ninth Annual Meeting, Louisville, Nov. 19-21, 1975. Men and women are both oppressed in this system and neither participate in the public domain as it is conventionally defined.

1960 Khalaf, Samir. Prostitution in a Changing Society: A Sociological Survey of Legal Prostitution in Beirut. Beirut: Khayats, 1965.

1961   , and E. Shwayri. "Family Associations in Lebanon." Journal of Comparative Family Studies, 2 (1971), 235-250.

1962 Kher, Amy. Remous à Bab-Touma. Cairo: La Semaine Egyptienne, 1940. This novel describes the fight of a modern Lebanese woman against the prejudices of people around her.

1963 Lahoud, Aline. "In Search of the 'Lebanese Woman.'" Middle East Forum, 36 (Jan. 1960), 18-21. There is no stereotype of the Lebanese woman according to this journalist.

1964 McCabe, Justine. "The Status of Aging Lebanese Women: A Thematic Apperception Study." Paper delivered at the 10th Annual Meeting of the Middle East Studies Association, Los Angeles, November 10-13, 1976.

1965/6 Mazas, P. "La Semaine sociale de Beyrouth." En Terre d'Islam, 23 (1948), 109-114. An informative article on

Lebanese feminists.

1967 al-Mu´ayyad, Mukhtar ibn Ahmad. Fasl al-khitab. Beirut:
      al-Matba'ah al-adabiyah, 1901.

1968 Nahhas, Jaklin. Sayyidat al-a'mal wa-al-mujtama'. Beirut:
      Matba'at al-thawrah, 1972. Biographies of working
      women in Lebanon.

1969 Nallino, Maria. "Discussione per la concessione alla donna
      libanesa della parità cogli uomini nel godimento dei
      diritti politici." Oriente Moderno, 1-3 (Jan.-March
      1951), 132.

1970 Oulié, Marthe. "Femmes du Liban et de Syrie." Le
      Monde Colonial Illustré, 195 (Sept. 1939), 210-11.
      Lebanese and Syrian women are participating more and
      more in the life of their countries and crave national
      independence.

1971 Prothro, Edwin Terry. Child Rearing in the Lebanon.
      Cambridge, Mass.: Harvard University Press, 1961.
      (Harvard Middle East Monograph Series, No. 8.)

1972 "Il quinto congresso dell'Unione femminile araba a Beirut."
      Oriente Moderno, 6 (June 1934), 280-81.

1973 al-Riyashi, Iskandar. al-Ayyam al-lubnaniyah. Beirut:
      Sharikat al-tab' wa-al-nashr al-lubnaniyah, 1956?

1974 Rosenfeld, H. "On Determinants of Status of Arab Village
      Women." Man, May 1960, 66-70. Shows how some
      Lebanese women renounce their lawful inheritance rights
      to secure family protection.

1975 al-Rusafi, Ma'aruf. "La Répudiée." Bulletin des Etudes
      Arabes, 24 (Sept.-Oct. 1945), 149. Translation of a
      short poem by A. Lentin.

1976 Sabri, Marie Aziz. "Beirut College for Women and Ten of
      Its Distinguished Pioneering Alumnae." Unpublished
      Ph.D. dissertation, Columbia University, 1965.

1977 _____. Pioneering Profiles: Beirut College for Women.
      Beirut: Khayats, 1967.

1978 Sa'd, Faruq. Baqat min hada´iq Mayy. Beirut: Zuhir
      Ba'labaki, 1973. A biography of Mayy Ziyadah.

1979 Safi, M. "Mariage au nord du Liban." Anthropos, 12-13
      (1917-1918), 134-43.

1980 Sa'idi, 'Abd al-Razzaq. "al-Qara´in fi al-qanunayn al-lubnani wa-al-tunisi. " al-Qada´ wal-tashri', 10 (1966), 21-37.

1981   Sakakini, Widad. Mayy Ziyadah fi hayatiha wa-athariha. Cairo: Dar al-ma'arif, 1969.

1982   Sbaity, Fatima. "Job Opportunities for American University of Beirut Women Graduates and Their Impact on National Development. " Unpublished MA thesis, American University in Beirut, 1970.

1983   Shararah, 'Abd al Latif. Mayy Ziyadah, 1882-1941. Beirut: Dar Sadr, 1965.

1984   Shararah, Yula Puliti. L'Image de la femme dans la presse féminine au Liban. Beirut: Centre de Recherches, Institut des Sciences Sociales, Université Libanaise, 1974. Research for this monograph was conducted in 1971.

1985   al-Shinnawi, Kamil. Alladhina ahabbu Mayy. Cairo: Dar al-ma'arif, 1972.

1986   Sukkarieh, Bassimah Elias. "Divorce Factors Among the Greek Orthodox in Beirut. " Unpublished MA thesis, American University in Beirut, 1960. Social changes since 1933 as reflected by divorce decrees.

1987   Sweet, Louise E. "The Women of 'Ain al-Dayr. " Anthropological Quarterly, 3 (July 1967), 167-83. 'Ain al-Dayr is a Druze village.

1988   Tannous, Afif I. "Social Change in an Arab Village. " American Sociological Review, 1941, 651-62. Mentions how the girls of Bishmizzeen in Northern Lebanon started to work at the silk factory.

1989   Tarcici, A. L'Education actuelle de la jeune fille musulmane au Liban. Vitry sur Seine: Librairie Mariale, 1941.

1990   Tawile, M. "La Femme libanaise au travail. " Action Proche-Orient, 21 (Sept. 1963), 39-43.

1991   Tomeh, Adia K. "Birth Order and Dependence Patterns of College Students in Lebanon. " Journal of Marriage and the Family, 2 (1972), 361-374.

1992   _____. "The Impact of Reference Groups on the Educational and Occupational Aspirations of Women College Students. " Journal of Marriage and the Family, 1 (1968), 102-110.

1993 Vacca, Virginia. "Libro di una musulmana druza contro il
      velo delle donne. " Oriente Moderno, 10 (1928), 497.
      About Nazirah Zayn al-Din's al-Sufur wa-al-hijab.

1994/5 Van Dusen, Roxann A. "Urbanization and Women in a Sub-
      urb of Beirut. " Paper delivered at the Middle East
      Studies Association Meeting, Milwaukee, November 8-
      10, 1973 (revised 1974). "The newcomers, as outsid-
      ers in the community, find themselves free from many
      of the constraints which membership and participation
      in community activities impose. "

1996 Vexivière, J. , and M. Gillet. "Un Manifeste féministe
      musulman. " En Terre d'Islam, July 1928, 172-189.
      Includes a translation of an article by Lammens in al-
      Mashriq of May 1928, pp. 366ff. , reviewing the book
      of Nazirah Zayn al-Din, al-Sufur wa-al-hijab, and at-
      tributing parts of it to her father.

1997 Wigle, Laurel D. "Economic and Political Activities of
      Village Women in Lebanon. " Paper delivered at the
      annual meeting of the American Anthropological Asso-
      ciation, Mexico City, 1974.

1998 Williams, Herbert H. , and Judith R. Williams. "The Ex-
      tended Family as a Vehicle of Culture Change. " Hu-
      man Organization, 1 (Spring 1965), 59-64. A study of
      the village of Hauch.

1999 Yaukey, David. Fertility Differences in a Modernizing
      Country: A Survey of Lebanese Couples. Princeton,
      N. J. : Princeton University Press, 1961. A sociologi-
      cal inquiry conducted with 900 women.

2000 _____. "Some Immediate Determinants of Fertility Dif-
      ferences in Lebanon. " Marriage and Family Living,
      25 (Feb. 1963), 27-34.

2001 Zayn al-Din, Nazirah. al-Fatat wa-al-shuyukh. Beirut:
      n. p. , 1929.

2002 _____. al-Sufur wa-al-hijab. Beirut: Matba'ah Kuzma,
      1928. This book raised much attention because it was
      one of the first books written by a woman to uphold
      the feminist cause.

2003 Ziyadah, Mayy. "Amia--Souvenirs du Liban. " L'Egypti-
      enne, 36 (March-April 1928), 21-24. In this short
      story, elopement is the only way a young Christian
      woman can marry a man of her own choosing.

IX

LIBYA

(1) GENERAL

2004 'Abd Allah, Iman. "The Place of Woman" (in Arabic). al-Mar´ah al-Jadidah, 8 (Oct. 15, 1970), 23, 28.

2005 'Abd al-Latif, 'Ali. "Four Young Women and a Lot of Ideas" (in Arabic). Libiya al-hadithah, 11 (Nov. 5, 1968), 46-47.

2006 "About the Topic, 'Who Is Responsible?' " (in Arabic). Majallat al-mar´ah, 4 (April 10, 1965), 20-21.

2007 Ahmad, Najat. "The Crisis of Shared Responsibility" (in Arabic). al-Mar´ah, 10 (Oct. 1967), 30, 39.

2008 al-'Alim, 'Umar Lutfi. "Needle-Pricking" (in Arabic). al-Mar´ah, 1 (Jan. 2, 1969), 9.

2009 Amin, Su'ad. "Should Woman Stay Home?" (in Arabic). al-Mar´ah, 7 (July 1967), 36.

2010 'Amir, Sana'. "The End of the Road" (in Arabic). al-Mar´ah, 12 (Dec. 1967), 22.

2011 _____. "Struggle With Reality" (in Arabic). al-Mar´ah, 12 (Dec. 5, 1966), 78.

2012 "The Arab Woman From the Time of the Harem to the Time of Pleasure" (in Arabic). Risalat al-Jam'iyah, 5 (1968).

2013 "Aspirations To a Better Future for Our Young Libyan Girl" (in Arabic). Libiya al-Hadithah, 41 (June 3, 1969), 48-49.

2014 al-'Awiti, Nadra. "A Citizen From al-Arish" (in Arabic). al-Mar´ah, 8 (Aug. 1967), 24-25.

2015 al-Awjili, Amihah. "The Young Muslim Woman" (in Arabic).

Risalat al-Jam'iyah, 1968.

2016   Barudi, 'Abd al-Hadi. "So That the Caravan Arrives Safe-
       ly" (in Arabic). al-Mar´ah, 10 (Oct. 1967), 31.

2017   Bayuni, Fawziyah 'Isa. "The Struggle of Woman and Evolu-
       tion" (in Arabic). al-Mar´ah, 10 (Oct. 5, 1966), 13.

2018   Buargub, 'Abd al-Latif. "The Efforts of a Libyan Woman
       Abroad" (in Arabic). al-Mar´ah, 5 (May 1967), 30-31.

2019   C. N. "Our Women Between Two Eras" (in Arabic).
       Majallat al-mar´ah, 5 (May 10, 1965), 6-7.

2020   "The Danger Which Threatens Man" (in Arabic). Libiya
       al-hadithah, 12 (Nov. 12, 1968), 44-47. This danger
       happens to be ... woman.

2021   "Diary of An Unmarried Young Woman" (in Arabic). al-
       Mar´ah, 8 (Aug. 1967), 42; 10 (Oct. 1967), 9; 12 (Dec.
       1967), 64.

2022   "Encounter With Her" (in Arabic). al-Mar´ah, 5 (May
       1967), 6-7. An interview with 'Aidah Talib.

2023   "Encounter With Her" (in Arabic). al-Mar´ah, 10 (Oct.
       1967), 6-7. An interview with Mariam Kanuni.

2024   "Encounter With Her" (in Arabic). al-Mar´ah, 8 (Aug.
       1967), 6-7. An interview with Latifah al-Arnuwati.

2025   "Encounter With Her" (in Arabic). al-Mar´ah, 3 (March
       1967), 6-7. An interview with Hamidah al-Barrani.

2026   Fikry, Mona. "La Femme et les conflits de valeur en
       Libye." Revue de l'Occident Musulman et de la Médi-
       terranée, 18 (1974), 93-110.

2027   "Four Reasons for the Problems of the Separation of the
       Sexes" (in Arabic). Jil wa-risalah, 3 (July 1967), 16-
       17, 31.

2028   "From the Archives of the Broadcast 'Lights on Society'"
       (in Arabic). al-Mar´ah, 12 (Dec. 1967), 13.

2029   al-Ghudhban, Muhammad. "Social Issues" (in Arabic).
       al-Mar´ah, 1 (Jan. 2, 1969), 66. About purchasing
       habits of Libyan women.

2030   "Hello!" (in Arabic). al-Mar´ah al-jadidah, 3 (April 1970),
       43.

2031   'Izzat, Sulayman Mudhaffar. "Woman and Society" (in

Arabic). al-Mar'ah, 12 (Dec. 1967), 32-33, 37.

2032 al-Jahmi, Khadijah. "A Meeting With Her" (in Arabic). al-Mar'ah, 10 (Oct. 5, 1966), 6-7, 15.

2033 _____. "Problems" (in Arabic). al-Mar'ah, 2 (Feb. 1967), 60-61; 3 (March 1967), 56-57; 4 (April 1967), 56-57; 5 (May 1967), 35-36; 8 (Aug. 1967), 54-55; 10 (Oct. 1967), 60-61; 12 (Dec. 1967), 94-95.

2034 _____. "Problems" (in Arabic). al-Mar'ah, 4 (April 5, 1968); 6 (June 5, 1968); 10 (Oct. 5, 1968); 11 (Nov. 5, 1968).

2035 _____. "Woman Between Yesterday and Today" (in Arabic). al-Mar'ah, 3 (March 1967), 46; 10 (Oct. 1967), 36-37, 59.

2036 _____. "Word and Text" (in Arabic). al-Mar'ah, 1 (Jan. 2, 1969), 44.

2037 Jalidi, 'Abd al-Hamid. "A Project Worthy of Consideration" (in Arabic). Libiya al-hadithah, 15 (March 25, 1967), 58-59. About the project of the Ministry of Labor and Social Affairs to set up a women's club.

2038 al-Kabti, Nadiah. "Don't Be Ashamed, Be Sociable" (in Arabic). al-Mar'ah, 10 (Oct. 5, 1966), 27.

2039 _____. "The Emancipated Young Woman and the New Society" (in Arabic). al-Mar'ah, 3 (March 1967), 9.

2040 Karim, Faraj M. "Woman Has An Important Role in Life" (in Arabic). al-Mar'ah, 4 (April 5, 1968).

2041 "Letter From a Bachelor" (in Arabic). al-Mar'ah, 11 (Nov. 5, 1968).

2042 "Letter From a Reader" (in Arabic). Libiya al-hadithah, 12 (Feb. 10, 1967), 52-53.

2043 "Libya: Growing Interest for the Future of Woman" (in Arabic). Libiya al-hadithah, 15 (March 25, 1968).

2044 Mead, Richard, and George Allan. "The Women of Libya." Middle East International, July 1973, 18-20.

2045 Mu'ammar, 'Ali Yahya. al-Fatah al-libiyah wa-mushakil al-hayah. Beirut: Dar al-fath lil-tiba'ah wa-al-nashr, 1970.

2046 al-Muntasir, 'Abd al-Hamid Mukhtar. "The Cultural Center of the Libyan Woman" (in Arabic). Libiya al-hadithah, 16 (March 1965), 38-39.

2047   Mustafa, Khalifah Husayn.   "Woman ... and the Horse of
       Clay" (in Arabic).   al-Usbu' al-thaqafi, 80 (Dec. 21,
       1973), 15.

2048   al-Na'as, Mardhiyah.   "As I Wish" (in Arabic).   al-Mar´ah,
       2 (Feb. 1967), 58; 3 (March 1967), 30-31; 8 (Aug. 1967),
       14; 12 (Dec. 1967), 29, 37.

2049   _____.   "Dialogue Is Our Method" (in Arabic).   al-
       Wahdah al-'arabiyah, 22 (Jan. 1, 1973), 44.

2050   _____.   "A Few Words About the Situation" (in Arabic).
       al-Mar´ah, 9 (Sept. 5, 1968).

2051   _____.   "The Freedom of Woman" (in Arabic).   Libiya
       al-hadithah, 3 (Sept. 25, 1966), 32-33.

2052   _____.   "From Woman to Man" (in Arabic).   al-Mar´ah,
       2 (Feb. 1967), 20; 3 (March 1967), 38-39; 4 (April
       1967), 33, 39; 8 (Aug. 1967), 22, 25; 10 (Oct. 1967),
       56-57; 12 (Dec. 1967), 36-37.

2053   _____.   "The Harvest of Two Years" (in Arabic).   al-
       Mar´ah, 12 (Dec. 5, 1968), 8-13.

2054   _____.   "Letter From a Reader Discussing Woman's
       Mission" (in Arabic).   Libiya al-hadithah, 4 (Oct. 10,
       1967), 50-51.

2055   _____.   "Pity For the Men" (in Arabic).   Libiya al-
       hadithah, 12 (Feb. 10, 1967), 52.

2056   _____.   "Woman and the Young Writers" (in Arabic).
       Libiya al-hadithah, 1 (Aug. 25, 1967), 62-63.

2057   al-Najjar, In'am.   "The Letter" (in Arabic).   al-Mar´ah,
       5 (March 6, 1969), 30-35.

2058   Nardh´mi, Na'imah.   "Question and Answer" (in Arabic).
       al-Mar´ah, 12 (Dec. 5, 1966), 72-73.

2059   "Open Letter of a Young Libyan to the Minister of Commu-
       nications" (in Arabic).   Libiya al-hadithah, 42 (June 10,
       1969), 37-38.

2060   "Opinions of Men, Opinions of Women" (in Arabic).   al-
       Mar´ah, 5 (March 6, 1969), 21.   Various opinions on
       the miniskirt.

2061   "Our Women and the Experience of Western Civilization" (in
       Arabic).   Majallat al-mar´ah, 4 (April 1965), 18-19.

2062   "Our Young Libyan Woman As I Have Seen Her This Week"
        (in Arabic). Libiya al-hadithah, 40 (May 27, 1969), 40.

2063   al-Qaba'ili, Lutfiyah.   "A Letter to My Arab Sister in
        Egypt" (in Arabic), al-Bayt, 10 (Aug. 5, 1973), 14-15.

2064   _____. "Pride" (in Arabic). al-Mar'ah al-jadidah, 7
        (March 1970), 42-43.

2065   _____. "With Our Girls Coming Back From Uncle Sam's
        Country" (in Arabic). al-Mar'ah al-jadidah, 1 (Jan. 5,
        1973), 14-17.

2066   al-Qabsi, Hayfa.   "Woman Yesterday, Today, Tomorrow"
        (in Arabic). Libiya al-hadithah, 20 (June 11, 1968), 49.

2067   al-Qazla, Haniyah.   "The Giant Steps of Woman in Libya"
        (in Arabic). al-Mar'ah, 10 (Oct. 5, 1968).

2068   "The Real Differences Between Man and Woman" (in Arabic).
        al-Mar'ah, 12 (Dec. 1967), 18-19, 27.

2069   "Le Rôle de la femme libyenne dans notre société moderne."
        Réalités Libyennes, 1 (Jan.-Feb. 1969), 16-17.

2070   "The Role of Woman in Modern Life Must be Revised" (in
        Arabic). al-Mar'ah, 4 (April 5, 1968).

2071   "The Role of Women in Development" (in Arabic). Majallat
        al-mar'ah, (July 15, 1970), 22-26.

2072   Saduk, Sharifah.   "How Long Is This Din Going to Last?"
        (in Arabic). al-Mar'ah, 12 (Dec. 1967), 55.

2073   Sallafi, Jadhibiyah.   "The Libyan Girl Today" (in Arabic).
        Libiya al-hadithat, 20 (Jan. 7, 1969), 37.

2074   "Sincere Talk from Woman to Woman" (in Arabic). al-
        Mar'ah, 1 (Jan. 2, 1969), 35-36.

2075   "The Social Mission of the Libyan Woman" (in Arabic).
        Libiya al-hadithah, 19 (Dec. 31, 1968), 34-35, 38.

2076   Souriau, C. "La Société féminine en Libye." Revue de
        l'Occident Musulman et de la Méditerranée, 6 (1969),
        127-155.

2077   Sulayman, Layla.   "Letters Between Traditionalists and
        Modernists" (in Arabic). al-usbu' al-thaqafi, 40 (March
        16, 1973), 19.

2078   _____. "My Foot Is in a Cast" (in Arabic). al-Usbu'
        al-thaqafi, 47 (May 4, 1973), 19.

2079 _____. "O You, Women From Khalij ... " (in Arabic).
      al-Usbu' al-thaqafi, 55 (June 29, 1973), 19.

2080 _____. "Pictures From the Beach" (in Arabic). al-Usbu'
      al-thaqafi, 58 (July 20, 1973), 19.

2081 _____. "Please" (in Arabic). al-Usbu' al-thaqafi, 57
      (July 13, 1973), 19.

2082 _____. "A Society Full of Love" (in Arabic). al-Usbu'
      al-thaqafi, 65 (Sept. 4, 1973), 19.

2083 _____. "When Will the Siege End?" (in Arabic). al-
      Usbu' al-thaqafi, 77 (Nov. 30, 1973), 19; 78 (Dec. 7,
      1973), 19.

2084 Tajuri, Fawziyah. "Woman and Society" (in Arabic). al-
      Mar'ah, 12 (Dec. 5, 1966), 49.

2085 "Three Questions Answered by Our Readers" (in Arabic).
      al-Bayt, 19 (Dec. 20, 1973), 4-13.

2086 al-Tira, Fatmah. "Woman and National Awakening" (in
      Arabic). al-Mar'ah, 10 (Oct. 5, 1966), 40.

2087 "To the Next Time" (in Arabic). al-Mar'ah, 1 (Jan. 2,
      1969), 67.

2088 al-Tumi, al-Tahir. "Appeal to All the Girls of My Coun-
      try" (in Arabic). Libiya al-hadithah, 30 (March 18,
      1969), 40.

2089 Turkhan, Najat. "Meeting With Him" (in Arabic). al-
      Mar'ah, 5 (March 1969), 16-17. Interview with Mr.
      Mansur Kikhia, head of the Libyan Scout Movement, on
      women.

2090 Umm Ghadab. "Aspirations Towards a Better Future for
      the Young Libiyan Woman" (in Arabic). Libya al-hadi-
      that, 39 (May 20, 1969), 37; 40 (May 27, 1969), 44-45;
      42 (June 10, 1969), 48.

2091 Umm Inticar. "Letters to My Daughter" (in Arabic). al-
      Mar'ah, 2 (Feb. 1967), 30-31; 3 (March 1967), 18-19;
      8 (Aug. 1967), 28-29; 10 (Oct. 1967), 54-55.

2092 'Uthman, Hasan Mas'ud. "Everything About Woman" (in
      Arabic). al-Mar'ah, 2 (Feb. 1967), 28-31; 4 (April
      1967), 48; 5 (May 1967), 46-47; 7 (July 1967), 54; 8
      (Aug. 1967), 36-37; 10 (Oct. 1967), 50.

2093 _____. "Trip of a Journalist to Europe: It is Forbidden
      to Marry Her Cousin" (in Arabic). al-Mar'ah, 7

(April 3, 1969), 12-13.

2094   "What Arab Youth Thinks About Love, Sex, Co-education, Mar-
       riage, Contraception, Culture and Teaching" (in Arabic).
       al-Bayt, 5 (May 20, 1973), 4-6.

2095   "Woman" (in Arabic). Libiya al-hadithah, 13 (Feb. 25,
       1968). About feminist associations, theater and fashion
       in Libya.

2096   "Woman and the Mentality of Fathers in Our Society" (in
       Arabic). al-Mar´ah, 10 (Oct. 1967), 66.

2097   "Woman: Conflict of Two Generations, Who Is Right?" (in
       Arabic). Jil wa-risalah, 1 (July 1968).

2098   "Women Get Equal Rights." Christian Science Monitor,
       May 9, 1970, p. 13, col. 5.

2099   "Wrong Interpretations of Female Emancipation" (in Arabic).
       al-Mar´ah, 5 (May 10, 1965), 18-19.

2100   "The Young Libyan Girl" (in Arabic). Libiya al-hadithah, 8
       (Oct. 15, 1968), 40-43.

(2) ISLAM

2101   'Abd al-Hadi, Fatmah. "Liberation of the Arab Woman
       Through Islam" (in Arabic). al-Mar´ah, 5 (May 10,
       1965), 12-13.

2102   Badr, Ayyad. "The Realistic Point of View of Islam About
       Woman" (in Arabic). al-Mar´ah, 8 (Aug. 1967), 16-17.

2103   "Fatwas According to the Shari' " (in Arabic). al-Hadi al-
       Islami, 4 (March 1968). Fatwas against the misconduct
       of married women.

2104   al-Jahmi, Khadijah. "Woman in Islam" (in Arabic). al-
       Mar´ah, 2 (Feb. 10, 1965), 8-9.

2105   Shahin, 'Abd al-Hamid. "Woman Between Religion and
       Work" (in Arabic). al-Wahdah al-'arabiyah, 28 (July
       1, 1973), 56-58; 29 (Aug. 1, 1973), 56-57.

2106   "The Sheikh of the Islamic University Talks About the Great
       Imam, the Efforts of the University and the Muslim
       Woman" (in Arabic). Libiya al-hadithah, 21 (June 19,
       1968), 10-11.

2107   'Umarah, Mahmud Muhammad. "Islam Establishes the

Basis for a Happy Home" (in Arabic). <u>al-Mar´ah</u>, 10 (Oct. 5, 1966), 14-15.

2108   'Woman in the Qur´an" (in Arabic). <u>al-Bayt</u>, 14 (Oc   5, 1973), 8-9. A review of al-'Aqqad's book.

(3) THE RURAL WOMAN

2109   'Abd al-Latif, 'Ali. "Eleven Young Women at the Service of the Rural Woman" (in Arabic). <u>Libiya al-hadithah</u>, 28 (Aug. 6, 1968), 32-33.

2110   'Abd al-Qadir, Khadijah. <u>al-Mar´ah fi al-rif fi Libiya.</u> Beirut: Matabi' al-ahram, 1961.

2111   al-'Awiti, Nadra. "Days in the South" (in Arabic). <u>al-Mar´ah al-jadidah</u>, 8 (April 15, 1970), 4-9.

2112   _____ . "The Rural Center of Home Economics" (in Arabic). <u>al-Bayt</u>, 3 (Feb. 20, 1973), 8-11.

2113   "An Event at Wadi Ka'am" (in Arabic). <u>Libiya al-hadithah</u>, 15 (March 25, 1968). About female rural social workers.

2114   Gazlah, Hamidah. "Remarks on the Woman of Southern Libya" (in Arabic). <u>al-Mar´ah</u>, 12 (Dec. 1967), 14-15.

2115   al-Huni, Ahmad Habib. "With the Southern Woman" (in Arabic). <u>al-Mar´ah</u>, 3 (March 10, 1965), 4-7.

2116   Mason, John. "Sex and Symbol in a Libyan Oasis." Unpublished ms., n.d. [author teaching anthropology at American University in Cairo in early 1970's].

2117   "Woman and Life in the Countryside" (in Arabic). <u>al-Mar´ah</u>, 10 (Oct. 1967), 10-14.

(4) THE FAMILY

2118   Abdelkafi, Mohamed. <u>Les Mariages en Tripolitaine.</u> Tripoli: Libyan Publishing House, 1964.

2119   Abodaya, M. "Changing Marriage Patterns in Cyrenaican Towns." Ph.D. dissertation in progress, University of Manchester, Dept. of Social Anthropology.

2120   "The Accomplishments of the Revolution and the Family" (in Arabic). <u>al-Bayt</u>, 12 (Sept. 6, 1973), 6-10.

2121   'Aribi, Sadiqah.   "Without Experience" (in Arabic).   al-
            Mar´ah, 5 (March 6, 1969), 14-15. About the refusal
            to marry a "modern" girl.

2122   al-'Awiti, Nadra.   "The Drama of Repudiation in Libyan So-
            ciety" (in Arabic).   al-Mar´ah, 1 (Jan. 2, 1969), 38-41.

2123   _____. "Family Remembrances" (in Arabic).   al-Mar´ah,
            al-jadidah, 3 (April 1970), 50; 7 (March 1970), 53.

2124   al-'Azabi, Sa'id 'Ali.   "Opinions on Conjugal Life" (in Ara-
            bic). al-Mar´ah, 6 (June 5, 1968).

2125   Basagna, R. , and Ali Sayad.   "La Pratique matrimoniale
            aux At-Yanni. " Libyca, 19 (1971), 199-216.

2126   Bugrine, 'Abd al-Razzak.   "Opinions--Setting-Up of the
            Higher Committee for Family Protection" (in Arabic).
            al-Mar´ah, 10 (Oct. 1967), 18-19.

2127   Farid, Zaynab Ahmad.   "Opinion About Marriage Problems"
            (in Arabic). al-Mar´ah, May 10, 1965, 8.

2128   Gabelli, O.   "Usanze nuziali in Tripolitania. " Rivista
            Tripolitana, 2 (1925-1926), 295-306, 351-362.

2129   Ghudban, Muhammad.   "Is Marriage a Problem?" (in Ara-
            bic). al-Idha'ah al-libiyah, 9 (May 30, 1967), 35.

2130   "If We Want to Reform Ourselves, We Must Start By the
            Family" (in Arabic).   al-Mar´ah al-jadidah, 17 (Sept.
            1, 1970), 28-30.

2131   "Image" (in Arabic). al-Mar´ah, 11 (Nov. 5, 1968).
            Article against the forced marriage of girls.

2132   Lollini, C.   "Del matrimonio precoce in Libia. " Libia, 1
            (1955), 73-75.

2133   Madani, Nasir.   "The Importance of Family in Society" (in
            Arabic). al-Mar´ah, 2 (Feb. 1967), 24-25; 3 (March
            1967), 8, 51.

2134   "Marriage and the High Price of Dowry" (in Arabic).   al-
            Mar´ah, 4 (April 1967), 10.

2135   "The Ministry of Labor, Social Affairs, Family and Child"
            (in Arabic). al-Mar´ah al-jadidah, 8 (Oct. 15, 1970),
            40-41.

2136   Muhammad, Nabilah.   "A Very High Dowry" (in Arabic).
            al-Mar´ah, 2 (Feb. 10, 1965), 36.

2137   Munah. "The Libyan Family Between Stagnation and Mobil-
       ity" (in Arabic). al-Mar´ah, 3 (March 10, 1965), 34-
       35.

2138   Muraji, Isma´il. "About the Project of Higher Council for
       the Protection of Family" (in Arabic). al-Mar´ah, 12
       (Dec. 1967), 62-63.

2139   Mustafa, Salwah Muhammad. "The Problem of Marriage to
       Foreigners" (in Arabic). al-Mar´ah, 3 (March 10,
       1965), 18-21.

2140   al-Na´as, Mardhiyah. "The Woman" (in Arabic). Libiya
       al-hadithah, 15 (March 25, 1967), 62-63.

2141   Najm, Kawthar. "With Four Daughters in a Happy Home"
       (in Arabic). al-Mar´ah, 10 (Oct. 5, 1966), 11-12; 12
       (Dec. 5, 1966), 40-41.

2142   "The Necessity of Comprehension Between Spouses" (in
       Arabic). al-Mar´ah, 12 (Dec. 1967), 24-25.

2143   al-Qaba´li, Lutfiyah. "Family Situations, Remembrances"
       (in Arabic). al-Mar´ah al-jadidah, 17 (Sept. 1, 1970),
       38-39; 21 (Nov. 15, 1970), 15.

2144   "Repercussions of the Positive Effect of the Decisions of
       the Revolution Felt by the Libyan Family" (in Arabic).
       al-Mar´ah al-jadidah, 17 (Sept. 1, 1970), 8-9.

2145   "The Right Place of Woman Is the House" (in Arabic).
       Libiya al-hadithah, 14 (Feb. 1965), 44-45.

2146   Shalak, Siddiq Ahmad. "Opinion on Marriage" (in Arabic).
       al-Mar´ah, 3 (March 1967), 31-33.

2147   Sharif, Hayat. "Talk About the Family" (in Arabic). al-
       Mar´ah, 10 (Oct. 1967), 20.

2148   Sulayman, Layla. "One Hundred and One Ways to a Happy
       Married Life" (in Arabic). al-Usbu' al-thaqafi, 39
       (Sept. 9, 1973), 19.

2149   "Talks on the Family" (in Arabic). al-Mar´ah, 8 (Aug. 5,
       1968), 9 (Sept. 5, 1968).

2150   "The Targui Woman and the Problem of the Higher Cost of
       Dowries" (in Arabic). al-Mar´ah, 11 (Nov. 5, 1968).

2151   al-Tir, Mustafa 'Umar. "Property and Marriage Proposal"
       (in Arabic). al-Ruwwad, March 1968, 76-81.

2152   'Uthman, Hasan Mas'ud. "Imagination and Reality" (in

Arabic). al-Mar´ah, 7 (July 1967), 22-23.

2153   al-Zantani, 'Abd al-Hamid al-Sayyid. "Talks to the Fam-
        ily" (in Arabic). al-Mar´ah, 5 (March 6, 1969), 50-51;
        7 (April 3, 1969), 24, 29; 9 (May 1, 1969), 24-25.

2154   Zaqzuq, Hamid 'Ali. "The Exemplary Mother" (in Arabic).
        al-Mar´ah, 3 (March 1967), 12-14; 4 (April 1967), 26-
        27, 32.

2155   _____. "The Exemplary Wife" (in Arabic). al-Mar´ah,
        7 (July 1967), 42-43.

(5) EDUCATION, SPORTS AND SCOUTING

2156   'Abd al-Fattah, 'Afaf. "What Occupies the Mind of Second-
        ary School Girls?" (in Arabic). al-Mar´ah al-jadidah,
        1 (Jan. 5, 1973), 8-11.

2157   'Abd al-Latif, 'Ali, and al-Tahir al-Rahibi. "The Normal
        School of Female Teachers, or the Citadel Forbidden
        to Men" (in Arabic). Libiya al-hadithah, 12 (Nov. 12,
        1968), 36-39.

2158   "About the Girl Scouts Jamboree" (in Arabic). al-Mar´ah,
        10 (Oct. 5, 1966), 8-10.

2159   'Aqil, al-Hadi. "The First Class Graduates This Year
        From the Girls Religious Institute" (in Arabic). al-
        Balagh, 180 (June 18, 1972), 3.

2160   al-'Awiti, Nadra. "The Nuns' Sewing School" (in Arabic).
        al-Mar´ah, 14 (July 17, 1969), 16-17.

2161   _____. "A Very Frank Dialogue With a Libyan Young
        Lady, Graduated in Muslim Law" (in Arabic). al-
        Wahdah al-'Arabiyah, 27 (June 1, 1973), 48-49, 51.

2162   al-Baruniyah, Za'imah. "Promising Results" (in Arabic).
        al-Mar´ah, 7 (July 5, 1968). The progress of literacy
        programs among Libyan women.

2163   "Celebration of a New Promotion of Nurses" (in Arabic).
        Libiya al-hadithah, 30 (Aug. 20, 1968), 5.

2164   "The Education of the Libyan Young Women" (in Arabic).
        Libiya al-hadithah, 1 (Aug. 25, 1967), 23-30.

2165   "Encounter With Her" (in Arabic). al-Mar´ah, 11 (Nov. 5,
        1968). Interview with a Libyan medicine student in
        Cairo.

2166   "Encounter With Her" (in Arabic). al-Mar´ah, 9 (Sept. 5,
        1968). Interview with a graduate of adult courses.

2167   "Encounter With Her" (in Arabic). al-Mar´ah, 6 (June 5,
        1968). Interview with the head of the Sabha Normal
        School of Female Teachers.

2168   "Encounter With Three Girls From the Arab Commission of
        Girl Scouts" (in Arabic). Jil wa-risalah, 11 (May 1968).
        The opinions of three Girl Scouts, a Kuwaiti, an Al-
        gerian and a Libyan, about the veil and work for women.

2169   "Fifty Questions Asked to the First Female Libyan Student
        Who Studies Military Medicine" (in Arabic). al-Bayt,
        18 (Dec. 5, 1973), 34-35.

2170   "Formation Centers of Home Economic Teachers" (in Ara-
        bic). Libiya al-hadithah, 33 (April 8, 1969), 30-33.

2171   Hasan, I'tidal. "A Serious Meeting with 850 Young Girls"
        (in Arabic). al-Bayt, 9 (July 20, 1973), 4-9.

2172   "The Home for Young Girls" (in Arabic). al-Mar´ah, 10
        (Oct. 1967), 34.

2173   "Interview for the Woman's Corner" (in Arabic). Jil wa-
        risalah, 9 (March 1968). Interview with one of the
        first Girl Scout leaders.

2174   al-Kuni, Ibrahim. "Sabhah Witnesses a Unique Sport Festi-
        val ... Women Participate as Spectators and Perform-
        ers" (in Arabic). Libiya al-hadithah, 38 (May 13, 1969),
        32-33. Reportage about the first mixed sport festival
        in Libya.

2175   "The Libyan Woman at the Next Meeting of the Arab
        Games" (in Arabic). al-Mar´ah, 4 (April 5, 1968).

2176   al-Na'as, Mardhiyah. "Two Ways of Seeing" (in Arabic).
        al-Mar´ah al-jadidah, 3 (April 1970), 16-17; 7 (March
        1970), 56-57; 21 (Nov. 15, 1970), 30-31. About mili-
        tary training for girls.

2177   al-Najjar, 'Abd al-Mun'im Qasin. "The Feeling of Shame"
        (in Arabic). Jil wa-risalah, 12 (June 1968). An inter-
        view with the head of the Normal School of Female
        Teachers.

2178   "Open Talk Between Man and Woman" (in Arabic). Libiya
        al-hadithah, 21 (June 18, 1968), 38-41. This article
        recommends that the last years of schooling be coedu-
        cational in order for women to help build society.

2179   "Our Daughters and Teaching" (in Arabic).   al-Mar'ah al-
        jadidah, 21 (Nov. 15, 1970), 3.

2180   "Our Daughters and Teaching" (in Arabic).   al-Mar'ah, 5
        (May 10, 1965), 8.

2181   "Pioneers of Female Education" (in Arabic).   al-Mar'ah, 2
        (Feb. 10, 1965), 10-11.

2182   al-Qaba'ili, Lutfiyah.   "The Girl Along With the Boy in
        Sport Competition" (in Arabic).   al-Mar'ah, 6 (March
        20, 1969), 8-9.

2183   _____. "With the Wives of the Researchers" (in Arabic).
        al-Bayt, 13 (Sept. 20, 1973), 12-19. A report on the
        wives of Libyan students in Europe and the U.S.

2184   Shalak, Siddiq.   "The Importance of Woman's Role in the
        Education of Children" (in Arabic).   al-Mar'ah, 2
        (Feb. 1967), 50-51.

2185   _____. "Teaching and the Formation of a Useful Fe-
        male Citizen" (in Arabic).   al-Mar'ah, 4 (April 1967),
        32.

2186   Sukkari, 'Abd al-Fattah.   "The Mother and the Education of
        Children" (in Arabic).   al-Mar'ah, 3 (March 1967), 39-
        41, 51; 4 (April 1967), 28-30; 5 (May 1967), 41-43.

2187   al-Sukni, 'Ali Bashir.   "Female Students Demand Mixity in
        Teaching" (in Arabic).   Libiya al-hadithah, 39 (May 20,
        1969), 33-34.

2188   _____. "The Girl Pupils of the Ha'iti School" (in Ara-
        bic). Libiya al-hadithah, 20 (Jan. 7, 1969), 30-36.

2189   "A Teaching Problem" (in Arabic).   Libiya al-hadithah, 15
        (March 25, 1968). This article deplores the lack of
        paternal encouragement to girls' education.

2190   "Three Young Girls ... " (in Arabic).   Libiya al-hadithah,
        14 (Nov. 26, 1968), 41. About the girl scouts.

2191   Umm Ghadah.   "Letter of a Young Lady to a Person in
        Authority, the Minister of Education and Instruction"
        (in Arabic).   Libiya al-hadithah, 41 (June 3, 1969),
        22-23.

2192   _____. "Open Letter to Two Gentlemen, the Minister
        of Information and Culture and the Minister of Youth
        and Sport" (in Arabic).   Libiya al-hadithah, 39 (May
        20, 1969), 50-51.

2193   Wajih, Ibrahim.   "The Young Lady of Today Between Home
        and School" (in Arabic).   al-Ida'ah al-libiyah, 18 (Nov.
        1964), 22-23.

2194   "Woman Demands That More Fields of Knowledge Be Opened
        to Her" (in Arabic).   al-Mar´ah al-jadidah, 8 (April 15,
        1970), 3.

2195   Wuhibah, Siddiq.   "Jil wa-risalah Meets the Pioneers of
        Arab Girl-Scouts" (in Arabic).   Jil wa-risalah, 6 (Nov.
        1967), 4-8.

2196   Yunis, Muhammad.   "The Center for Home Economics
        Teachers in Sabha: A New Experience for the Young
        Libyan Girl in the South" (in Arabic).   Libiya al-
        hadithah, 39 (May 20, 1969), 34-36.

(6) THE WORKING WOMAN

2197   'Abd al-Fattah, 'Afaf.   "The Salary of the Wife" (in Arabic).
        al-Bayt, 13 (Sept. 20, 1973), 20.

2198   al-'Awami, Raj'ah.   "Brief Encounter" (in Arabic).   al-
        Mar´ah, 5 (March 6, 1969), 4.   Interview with the
        first Libyan female agronomic engineer from Cairo
        University.

2199   al-'Awiti, Nadra.   "Success of a Project for Children Pre-
        sented by the Working Women Association" (in Arabic).
        al-Mar´ah al-jadidah, 17 (Sept. 1, 1970), 32-33.

2200   _____.   "The Working Woman Association" (in Arabic).
        al-Mar´ah, 5 (May-June 1967), 20-21.

2201   "Encounter With the Announcer 'A´ishah al-Dilawi" (in Ara-
        bic).   al-Idha'ah, 19 (Nov. 1, 1968).

2202   "Encounter With the Great Writer Za'ima al-Baruni" (in
        Arabic).   al-Mar´ah, 2 (Feb. 10, 1965), 4-6.

2203   "Feminine News" (in Arabic).   al-Mar´ah, 7 (July 5, 1968).
        The role of woman in Libyan broadcasting.

2204   Gazlah, Hamidah.   "For a Better Future for the Working
        Woman and Her Children" (in Arabic).   al-Mar´ah, 7
        (July 1967), 13, 19.

2205   "The Libyan Woman Enters the Professions. " The Libyan
        Review, 9-10 (Sept. -Oct. 1967), 24-29.

2206   al-Mihi, Fawziyah.   "Embarrassing Question" (in Arabic).

al-Mar´ah, 8 (Aug. 5, 1968).

2207   N.A.   "The Libyan Woman Enters the Professional World"
       (in Arabic). al-Wahdah al-'arabiyah, 27 (June 1, 1973),
       54-55.

2208   "The Nursing Career" (in Arabic). al-Mar´ah, 1 (Jan. 2,
       1969), 62-63.

2209   "Our Young Libyan Woman Conquers the Field of Technol-
       ogy" (in Arabic). al-Mar´ah, 10 (May 15, 1969), 6-11.

2210   al-Qaba´ili, Lutfiyah. "Woman and Work" (in Arabic). al-
       Bayt, 18 (Dec. 5, 1973), 4-10.

2211   "The Rights of the Working Woman to Maternity Benefits"
       (in Arabic). al-Balagh, 135 (March 5, 1972), 5.

2212   al-Tumi, al-Tahir. "What Is the Role of the Nurse in So-
       ciety?" (in Arabic). Libiya al-hadithah, 14 (Nov. 26,
       1968), 36-38.

2213   Turkhan, Layla. "Under the Sunlights" (in Arabic). al-
       Mar´ah, 9 (May 1, 1969), 10-11. About the first fe-
       male announcer on Libyan TV.

2214   'Uraybi, Siddiqah. "The Negative Attitude of the Libyan
       Young Woman and Labor Camps" (in Arabic). Libiya
       al-hadithah, 25 (July 16, 1968), 50.

2215   "Voluntary Work: The Young Libyan Woman Experiences
       Labor Camps for the First Time" (in Arabic). Libiya
       al-hadithah, 27 (July 30, 1968), 8-9.

2216   "Woman and the Field of Information" (in Arabic). al-
       Mar´ah, 5 (May 1967), 14-17.

2217   "The Working Woman" (in Arabic). al-Mar´ah, 8 (Aug.
       1967), 44-45.

(7) FEMINISM AND POLITICS

2218   "Akhbar al-yaum Publishes an Article About Layla Sulayman
       and Calls Her a Libyan Huda Sha'rawi" (in Arabic).
       al-Usbu' al-thaqafi, 47 (May 4, 1973), 16.

2219   "The Association of the Feminist Movement in Dirna" (in
       Arabic). al-Mar´ah, 2 (Feb. 1967), 38-41.

2220   al-'Awiti, Nadra. "Feminine Endeavors in 1968" (in Ara-
       bic). al-Mar´ah, 1 (Jan. 2, 1969), 10-13.

2221 _____. "Four Feminine Associations on a Trip to
     Cairo" (in Arabic). al-Mar'ah al-jadidah, 18 (Oct. 1,
     1970), 14-15; 21 (Nov. 15, 1970), 22-25.

2222 al-Baruniyah, Za'imah. "The Libyan Woman and Her Sa-
     cred Struggle" (in Arabic). Libiya al-hadithah, 18
     (Dec. 24, 1968), 50-51. About feminine resistance to
     the Italian occupation of Libya.

2223 Bashir, Su'ad. "al-Bayt Spends a Whole Day Among the
     Girls of the Popular Resistance in One of the Tripoli
     Camps" (in Arabic). al-Bayt, 12 (Sept. 5, 1973), 24-
     29.

2224 "Encounter With Her" (in Arabic). al-Mar'ah, 5 (May
     1968). Interview with the head of the Association of
     Libyan Women.

2225 "Encounter With Her" (in Arabic). al-Mar'ah, 4 (April 5,
     1968). Interview with the head of the Dirna feminist
     association, al-Nahdah.

2226 "Encounter With the President" (in Arabic). al-Mar'ah, 6
     (June 5, 1968).

2227 "The First Woman Honored by the State" (in Arabic). Jil
     wa-risalah, 8 (May 1969), 37.

2228 "From Morocco" (in Arabic). Libiya al-hadithah, 27 (July
     30, 1968), 49. About the trip to Morocco of the head
     of the Libyan Women's Liberation Committee.

2229 Ghasin, Tuhf. "The Role of the Arab Woman and Her
     Preparation for the Coming Struggle" (in Arabic). al-
     Mar'ah, 8 (Aug. 1967), 53.

2230 Ghudban, Muhammad. "Social Reflections" (in Arabic). al-
     Mar'ah, 7 (July 1967), 59.

2231 Habib, Henry. "The Social and Political Role of Libyan
     Women." Paper delivered at the 10th annual meeting
     of the Middle East Studies Association, Los Angeles,
     November 10-13, 1976.

2232 "An Image of Feminist Struggle in Our Country" (in Arabic).
     al-Mar'ah, 7 (July 1967), 8-10.

2233 al-Jahmi, Khadijah. "My Grandmother and World Politics"
     (in Arabic). al-Mar'ah al-jadidah, 3 (March 1970), 17;
     7 (April 1970), 11.

2234 "The Libyan Woman and Revolution" (in Arabic). al-
     Hawadith, Jan. 1970, 84-85.

2235   "The Libyan Woman to the African Women's Congress" (in
        Arabic). al-Mar´ah, 9 (Sept. 5, 1968).

2236   al-Na'as, Mardhiyah. "Revolutionary Ideas" (in Arabic).
        al-Mar´ah al-jadidah, 7 (March 1970), 36-37.

2237   _____. "What Is the Secret Behind This Campaign?" (in
        Arabic). Libiya al-hadithah, 5 (Oct. 25, 1967), 32.
        About a campaign against feminism.

2238   al-Na´ili, Salah. "Interview With Members of the Arab
        Women's Association" (in Arabic). al-Balagh, 186
        (July 2, 1972), 10.

2239   "A New Experience for the Libyan Young Woman" (in Ara-
        bic). Libiya al-hadithah, 22 (June 25, 1966), 26.
        About the first feminist colloquium in Algiers.

2240   "The Organization al-Nahdah in Front of Its Responsibilities"
        (in Arabic). al-Mar´ah, 9 (Sept. 5, 1968). About
        courses organized by a feminist organization in Tripoli.

2241   al-Qaba´ili, Lutfiyah. "A Dialogue With the New Woman
        Association in Binghazi" (in Arabic). al-Wahdah al-
        'arabiyah, 22 (Jan. 1, 1973), 42-43.

2242   _____. "Lights On the Meetings of the Women's General
        Union" (in Arabic). al-Bayt, 2 (Feb. 5, 1973), 16-17.

2243   _____. "Our Revolution in Four Years and ... Women"
        (in Arabic). al-Wahdah al-'arabiyah, 30 (Sept. 1, 1973),
        59-61.

2244   _____. "The Women's Union Discusses Its Next Role"
        (in Arabic). al-Bayt, 3 (Feb. 20, 1973), 4-7.

2245   al-Qabsi, Fatimah. "What You Do Not Know About the
        Feminist Association al-Nahdah" (in Arabic). al-Mar´ah,
        10 (Oct. 5, 1968).

2246   Samiyah. "Have Our Feminist Organizations Accomplished
        Something for Women?" (in Arabic). al-Mar´ah, 12
        (Dec. 1967), 16, 31.

2247   al-Shalli, Khadijah. "Message of the Feminist Association"
        (in Arabic). Libiya al-hadithah, 19 (June 4, 1968), 50.

2248   "A Trip With Three Pioneers" (in Arabic). Libiya al-
        hadithah, 17 (April 25, 1968). About the activities of
        feminist organizations.

2249   "Two Weeks in Morocco" (in Arabic). al-Mar´ah, 8 (Aug.
        5, 1968); 9 (Sept. 5, 1968); 10 (Oct. 5, 1968); 11 (Nov.

5, 1968). A delegation of Libyan feminists visits Morocco.

2250   "Woman After the Speech of the President" (in Arabic). al-
Mar'ah, 9 (Sept. 5, 1968).

2251   "Woman and Her Role in the Struggle for Liberation" (in
Arabic). al-Mar'ah, 7 (July 1967), 24-25.

2252   "Woman and Political Action" (in Arabic). al-Mar'ah al-
jadidah, 3 (April 1970), 3.

2253   "Woman and the Battle for Honor" (in Arabic). al-Mar'ah,
7 (July 1967), 28-30.

2254   "Woman Has Followed the Revolution From the Beginning"
(in Arabic). al-Mar'ah al-jadidah, 17 (Sept. 1, 1970),
4-7.

2255   "Woman in the Speech of the President" (in Arabic). al-
Mar'ah, 12 (Dec. 1967), 3. About the speech of
President Bourguiba to a Libyan delegation.

2256   "Woman: What Have Our Feminist Associations Done?" (in
Arabic). Libiya al-hadithah, 14 (March 10, 1968).

2257   Zihiri, Qasim. "Seventy Years Later: Woman's Liberation According to Qasim Amin and Tawfiq al-Hakim"
(in Arabic). Da'wat al-haqq, 7 (June 1970), 74-77.

2258   "Alger: la famille maghrébine à l'étude. " El-Moudjahid,
        May 9, 1968.

2259   Bernheim, Nicole. "Les Femmes du Maghreb sur la rude
        voie de l'indépendance. " Le Monde, Jan. 3, 4, 5, 6,
        7, 1969; also in Revue de Presse, 131 (Jan. 1969), 21-
        22.

2260/1 _____. "Révolution féminine au Maghreb. " Jeune
        Afrique, 545 (July 15, 1971), 55-59.

2262   Borrmans, Maurice. Documents sur la famille au Maghreb
        de 1940 à nos jours. 2 vols. and suppl. Paris:
        Université de Paris, Faculté des Lettres et Sciences
        Humaines, 1968.

2263   _____. "La Famille et le droit positif maghrébin. "
        Revue Algérienne des Sciences Juridiques, Economiques
        et Politiques, 1974, 29-56.

2264   _____. "Statut personnel et famille au Maghreb de 1940
        à nos jours. " Thèse, Université de Paris, Faculté des
        Lettres et des Sciences Humaines. Rome, 1969-1970.

2265   Buttin, P. "Le Malaise nord-africain. " Contacts en
        Terres d'Afrique, 1940, 26-30.

2266   Charnay, J. P. "De la grande maison au couple moderne:
        interférences entre droit, psychologie et économie dans
        l'évolution de la famille maghrébine. " Revue Algérienne
        des Sciences Juridiques, Economiques et Politiques, 53
        (1974), 57-83.

2267   Chelli, Mounira. "Les Maghrébines en dehors de la cité. "
        Jeune Afrique, 327 (April 1967), 50-51.

2268   _____. "Mariage sans horizon. " Jeune Afrique, 314
        (Jan. 15, 1967), 68-69.

178

2269   Desanti, D. "Une Enquête sur la femme africaine." Jeune
       Afrique, 188/189 (1964), 29-31.

2270   "Deux Femmes du Maghreb devant l'Islam." Croissance
       des Jeunes Nations, 118 (Dec. 1971), 8-9.

2271   Dieterlen, G., and Z. Ligers. "Contribution à l'étude des
       bijoux touareg." Journal de la Société des Africanistes,
       42 (1972), 29-53.

2272   Douedar, Maryse. "Libération du mariage." Revue Algé-
       rienne des Sciences Juridiques, Economiques & Politi-
       tiques, 53 (1974), 133-147.

2273   "Les Etudiantes maghrébines à Paris." Ferida, 1 (May
       1975), 11-13.

2274   "Evolution des relations d'autorité dans la famille maghré-
       bine." Bulletin d'Information--Fédération Internationale
       des Ecoles, de Parents et d'éducateurs, 6 (Jan. 1967),
       1-54.

2275   "Femmes rurales: colloque maghrébin." L'Action, April
       6, 1968.

2276   Fico, Carmela. "La donna musulmana dell'Africa settentri-
       onale." In Secundo Congresso di Studi Coloniali, Naples,
       1934, Atti, Florence, 1934; vol. 4, 155-164. The Ber-
       ber woman is seen as a depository of the past.

2277   Fontaine, C. "De la femme objet à la femme sujet, évo-
       lution de la condition féminine en Afrique du Nord."
       Revue de Psychologie des Peuples, 3 (1963), 273-82.

2278   "Le Ghetto de la femme immigrée." Jeune Afrique, 745
       (April 18, 1975), 55. The problems of the Maghreb
       woman in France.

2279   Hamet, Ismaël. "Les Musulmanes du Nord de l'Afrique."
       Revue du Monde Musulman, 23 (1913), 280-95. Gives
       some statistics on polygamy.

2280/1 Jouin, Jeanne. "Iconographie de la mariée citadine dans
       l'Islam nord-africain." Revue des Etudes Islamiques,
       4 (1931), 313-39. An important record of remarkable
       costumes no longer worn; includes 23 plates with cap-
       tions.

2282   Lame-Desprées, V. "Evolution de la Musulmane en Afri-
       que du Nord." Le Monde Colonial Illustré, 38 (Oct.
       1926), 230-31; 39 (Nov. 1926), 236-40; 40 (Dec. 1926),
       273.

2283   .   . En Terre d'Islam, May 1928, 103-
110; June 1928, 140-144; July 1928, 190-195.

2284   Lapham, R. "Population Policies in the Maghrib." Middle
East Journal, 1 (1972), 1-10.

2285   Leclerc, Adrien. De la condition de la femme musulmane
dans nos possessions du nord de l'Afrique. Besançon:
Dodivers, 1907.

2286   Le Coeur, Charles. Notes sur les moussems de femmes.
N. p.: M. Ajiste, 1946.

2287   Lemaire, Charles. Africaines; contribution à l'histoire de
la femme en Afrique. Brussels: Ch. Bulens, 1897.

2288   Letellier, G. "L'évolution de la famille musulmane en
Afrique du Nord." IBLA, 1939, 109-115.

2289   Le Tourneau, Roger. "L'Evolution de la famille musulmane
en Afrique du Nord." La France Méditerranéenne et
Africaine, 3 (1938), 5.

2290   Lucas, F. "La femme musulmane: enquête dans le nord-
africain." En Terre d'Islam, 47 (1931), 186-193.

2291   Malley, François. "Les couples franco-musulmans,
ombres et lumières." Croissance des Jeunes Nations,
122 (April 1972), 19-26.

2292   Marçais, Philippe. "Réflexions sur la structure de la vie
familiale chez les indigènes de l'Afrique du Nord." In
Mémorial André Passet. Paris: Maisonneuve, 1957;
69-82.

2293   Marchand, H. "Considérations sur les mariages franco-
musulmans." Annales Juridiques, Politiques, Economiques et Sociales, 3-4 (1955).

2294   . "Les Mariages mixtes franco-musulmans."
Compte-rendus de l'Académie des Sciences Coloniales,
12 (1952), 351-59.

2295   Marie Andrée du Sacré-Coeur. "Propos sur le vêtement en
Afrique." Rythmes du Monde, 1946, 66-67.

2296   Martenson, Mona. "La Planification familiale au Maghreb,
enquête nationale concernant les connaissances, les
attitudes et les pratiques." Bulletin Economique et
Social du Maroc, 112-113 (1969), 197-210.

2297   Mercier, Ernest. La Condition de la femme musulmane
dans l'Afrique septentrionale. Algiers: Typographie

Adolphe Jourdan, 1895.

2298   Meylan, M.   Les mariages mixtes en Afrique du Nord.
        Paris: Recueils Sirey, 1934.

2299   Michel, A.   "Planification traditionnelle et planification
        moderniste dans les familles maghrébines." Confluent,
        41 (May 1964), 423-35.

2300   Milliot, L.   Etude sur la condition de la femme au Maghreb,
        (Maroc, Algérie, Tunisie). Paris: J. Rousset, 1909.

2301   "Les Mutations actuelles de la famille au Maghreb:
        troisième Séminaire de sociologie, Décembre 1966."
        Revue Tunisiennes de Sciences Sociales, 11 (Oct. 1967),
        7-128.

2302   "Polygamie et promotion de la femme." Cahiers Nord-
        Africains--ESNA 62 (Dec. 1957), 1-23.

2303   "Premier Congrès de l'Union des femmes maghrébines."
        Perspectives Maghrébines, 1 (Oct. 1970), 60.

2304   Probst-Biraben, J. H.   "Prêtresses d'amour berbères et
        intentions de fécondité agricole." Revue Anthropologique
        45 (1935), 257-64. The author sees in the prostitution
        of the azriat and thidjal (free Berber women widowed
        or divorced) the persistence of an old agrarian and
        phallic cult once practiced from Morocco to Syria.

2305   "Promotion de la femme à travers quelques textes maghré-
        bins." Faiza, 58 (July 1967), 2-3.

2306   "La Régulation des naissances au Maghreb." Maghreb, 25
        (1968), 9-13.

2307   Roberds, Frances E.   "Moslem Women of North Africa."
        Moslem World, (1937), 362-369.

2308   Roussier, J.   "La Femme dans la société islamique: droit
        malikite maghrébin." Recueils de la Société Jean Rodin,
        2 (1959), 223-236.

2309   Safwad, Osman.   "Contradiction entre situation de fait et
        situation de droit concernant la femme dans les pays
        arabes." Revue Algérienne des Sciences Juridiques,
        Economiques et Politiques, 53 (1974), 113-14.

2310   Thiercelin, Raquel, and Christiane Souriau.   "La Condition
        des femmes dans la tradition, la modernité, la révo-
        lution; Etude comparative du Mexique et du Maghreb."
        Paper delivered at the Trigésimo Congreso Internacional
        de Ciencias Humanas en Asia y Africa del Norte,

Mexico, Aug. 3-8, 1976.

2311 Tsourikoff, Zénaide. L'Enseignement des filles en Afrique du Nord. Paris: Pedone, 1935.

2312 Valriant, Jane. "Musulmanes du Maghreb." Le Monde Colonial Illustré, 179 (May 1938), 86.

2313 Vaucher-Zananiri, N. "L'Emancipation de la femme au Maghreb." Preuves-Information, 405 (July 7, 1964).

XI

MOROCCO

(1) GENERAL

2314 Abu 'Abd Allah. "Religiosity of the Muslim Woman" (in Arabic). Da'wat al-haqq, 1 (Nov. 1964), 21-22.

2315 'A'isha, Princess Lalla. "La Promotion de la femme marocaine." Toumliline, 2 (1958), 151-54.

2316 Albarracín de Martinez Ruiz, Joaquina. Vestidos y adorno de la mujer musulmana de Yebala (Marruecos). Madrid: Consejo Superior de Investigaciones Científicas, 1964.

2317 Assadullah, Raid. "La Condition de la femme musulmane en Afghanistan. Etude de droit comparé: Afghan, Marocain, Tunisien, Syrien." Ph.D. dissertation, Université de Paris I, 1971.

2318 Balbachír, Muhammad. "The Condition of the Muslim Womam in Fes in Ancient Times and at the Beginning of the 20th Century" (in Arabic). al-'Alam al-thaqafi, 171 (Dec. 1, 1972), 5.

2319 Bekhoucha, Mohamed. Savoir-vivre: la vie sociale et religieuse des marocains, folklore. Casablanca: n.p., 1943.

2320 Belghiti, Malika; Najat Chraibi; and Tanou Adib. "La Ségrégation des garçons et des filles à la campagne." Bulletin Economique et Social du Maroc, 120-121 (Jan. - June 1972), 81-144.

2321 Bernheim, Nicole. "Les Femmes du Maghreb sur la rude voie de l'indépendance. I. Le Maroc entre la djellaba et le bikini." Le Monde, Jan. 3, 1969, 1, 5.

2322 "Beyond the Veil." New York Times, Nov. 11, 1957, 32-36. Focuses on Princess Aisha.

183

2323   Binkiran, Latifah.   "Time Is Money Too, My Sister" (in
          Arabic).   al-Ittihad al-watani, 19 (Sept. 6, 1973), 2.

2324   Boubakeur, H.   "La Musulmane nord-africaine d'aujourd'hui."
          Synthèses, Dec. 1951, 26-33; also in: Rythmes du
          Monde, 5 (1950), 25-33; and Ecrits de Paris, Dec.
          1953, 48-55.

2325   Bugéja, Marie.   Enigme musulmane, lettres à une bretonne.
          Tangiers: Editions Internationales, 1938.

2326   Buttin, Paul.   "Ombres et lumière sur le Maroc. II. La
          Promotion féminine." Confluent, 22 (June 1922), 466-
          75.   An informative article about the very low per-
          centage of educated Moroccan women and their efforts
          to set up cooperatives and day care centers.

2327   "Colloque sur les problèmes de l'émancipation de la femme
          marocaine" (in Arabic).   al-Kifah al-watani, 18-19
          (June 1967), 18-22.

2328   Crabbe, Paul, and Jean Wolf.   "Superficie, population, re-
          ligion: la marocaine d'aujourd'hui entre le passé et
          l'avenir." Le Maroc, 11-12 (Nov. -Dec. 1966), 26-33.

2329   Denison, S. M.   "A Moorish Woman's Life." Muslim
          World, 11 (1921), 24-28.   Principally a description of
          childhood in Fez.

2330   De Robert, René.   "Chance du Maroc." Confluent, 45-46
          (Nov. -Dec. 1964), 979-84.

2331   Donath, Doris.   L'Evolution de la femme israélite à Fès.
          Aix-en-Provence: La Pensée Universitaire, 1962.

2332   Dwyer, Daisy.   "Moroccan Women in a Traditional Urban
          Setting: An Analysis of Their Conflict Behaviors."
          Unpublished Ph.D. dissertation, Yale University, 1973.

2333   Essafi, Tahar.   La Marocaine (Etude sociologique).   n.p.,
          n.p., 1935.   By a Tunisian lawyer who had taught in
          Morocco.   He contributed several articles in favor of
          feminine emancipation to L'Egyptienne.

2334   "La Femme marocaine." Révolution Africaine, 197 (Nov.
          18, 1966), 8-13.

2335   Fernea, Elizabeth Warnock.   A Street in Marrakech: A
          Personnal Encounter with the Lives of Moroccan Wom-
          en.   Garden City, N.Y.: Doubleday, 1975.

2336   Francisi, A.   "Marocco: l'emancipazione della donna in
          une intervista della principessa 'Aisha." Oriente

185   General

Moderno, 7-9 (1965), 777.

2337 Goichon, Amélie M. "La Femme dans la moyenne bourgeoisie fasiya. " Revue des Etudes Islamiques, 3 (1929),
1-74.

2338 Gonzales Gimeno, Maria de las Mercedes. Antropología de
la mujer berber en Marruecos. Madrid: Consejo Superior de Investigaciones Científicas. Instituto Bernar-
dino de Sahagun, 1946 (Trabajos de antropología y etno-
logía, no. 2).

2339 Hakim, Koceïla. "Incitation à la débauche; Nécessité d'un
contrôle et d'une répression sévère. " Aicha, 23-24
(1972), 8-10.

2340 _____. "Répression de la sexualité; Ignorance et hypo-
crisie sociale. " Aicha, 13-14 (Aug. 1971), 31-36.

2341 Hassar, F. "L'Emancipation de la femme. " Confluent, 21
(1958), 210-13.

2342 Herber, J. "La Boucle d'oreille et les 'lobes percés' chez
les Marocains. " Hespéris, 32 (1945), 89-93.

2343 _____. "Les Tatouages de la face chez la Marocaine. "
Hespéris, 33 (1946), 323-51.

2344 _____. "Les Tatouages des bras de la Marocaine. "
Hespéris, 38 (1951), 299-325.

2345 _____. "Les Tatouages du cou, de la poitrine et du
genou chez la Marocaine. " Hespéris, 36 (1949), 333-45.

2346 Joubin, Odette. "L'Intégration des femmes à une société
moderne par la revalorisation; Deux Exemples: la
Tunisie et le Maroc. " Unpublished thesis, Ecole Pratique des Hautes Etudes, Paris, 1965.

2347 Jouin, J. "Chansons de fillettes à Rabat. " Journal de la
Société des Africanistes, 12 (1942), 49-53.

2348 Kaddour ben Ghabrit. "La Femme dans l'Islam. "
Revue de la Cie Paquet, 1939.

2349 Kharras, 'A'ishah. "Look for the Cause!" (in Arabic).
al-Ittihad al-watani, 37 (April 19, 1973), 2.

2350 _____. "Woman, Once Again. " al-Ittihad al-watani, 1
(April 26, 1973), 2.

2351 al-Khatibi, 'Abd al-Kabir. Etudes sociologiques sur le
Maroc. Rabat: Société d'Etudes Economiques, Sociales

et Statistiques, 1971.

2352   Kossowitch, N., and M. F. Benoît. "Contribution à l'étude
       des indigènes du Maroc (Série féminine)." Revue
       Anthropologique, 43 (1933), 318-41.

2353   Lahbabi, Fatimah. "The Situation of the Muslim Woman in
       Modern Society" (in Arabic). al-'Alam al-thaqafi, 130
       (Jan. 28, 1972), 5-8. According to this Moroccan writer,
       Muslim law alone guarantees woman her dignity and rights.

2354   La Mazière, Alice (Kuhn). Le Maroc Secret. Paris:
       Editions Baudinière, 1932.

2355   Legey, Dr. Essai de folklore marocain. Paris: Geuthner,
       1926. About magico-religious practices.

2356   Maher, Vanessa. Women and Property in Morocco: Their
       Changing Relation to the Process of Social Stratification
       in the Middle Atlas. London: Cambridge University
       Press, 1974.

2357   "Les Marocaines dressent leur bilan." Jeune Afrique, 305
       (Nov. 13, 1966).

2358   Meissa, M. S. La Femme musulmane. Casablanca: Edi-
       tions Réunies, 1928.

2359   Mernissi, Fatima. Beyond the Veil: Male-Female Dy-
       namics in a Modern Muslim Society. New York:
       Schenkman, 1975. Moroccan women are starting to in-
       vade male preserves.

2360   _____. "Les Femmes marocaines face aux institutions
       bureaucratiques." Paper delivered at the Conference on
       Urban Systems and Development in North Africa, Hamma-
       met, Tunisia, June 20-30, 1976.

2361   Michaux-Bellaire, E. "Une Histoire de rapt." Archives
       Marocaines, 5 (1905), 436-42.

2362   Mihat, Fadwa. "Where Goes the Moroccan Woman?" (in
       Arabic). al-haqq, 6-7 (June-July 1971), 184.

2363   Morocco. Ministry of Foreign Affairs. Quelques Aspects
       de la vie de la femme marocaine. Rabat, n. d.

2364   N'Ait Attik, Mririda. Songs of Mririda, Courtesan of the
       High Atlas. Translated by Daniel Halpern and Paula
       Paley. Greensboro: Unicorn Press, 1974.

2365   Navarro, Joaquina Albarracin. "El hayk en la zona atlánti-
       ca del Marrueco español." Tamuda, 2 (1954), 309-14.

2366   Oulié, Marthe. "Femmes marocaines." Le Monde Colonial
       Illustré, 86 (Oct. 1930), 248.

2367   Ovilo y Canales, Felipe. La mujer marroqui; estudio so-
       cial. Madrid: M. G. Hernandez, 1881.

2368   Quilici, Jacqueline. La Condition de la femme marocaine
       à travers la presse de 1965 à nos jours. Aix-en-
       Provence: Institut d'Etudes Politiques, 1971.

2369   al-Ramdhani, Faridah. "Women in the Front Guard" (in
       Arabic). Aicha, 25-26 (1972), 16.

2370   Sloughi, P. J. "Les Premiers Pas de la femme marocaine."
       Maroc-Monde, March 30, 1951.

2371   "Souvenirs et soucis de trois jeunes femmes marocaines."
       Confluent, 11 (Jan.-Feb. 1961), 20-31; 12 (March-April
       1961), 133-142.

2372   Uplegger, H. "Djellaba und Litham: Zur Verschleierung
       der arabischen Frau in Marokko." Bustan, 2 (1968),
       22-26.

2373   Vinogradov, Amal Rassam. "French Colonialism as Re-
       flected in the Male-Female Interaction in Morocco."
       Transactions of the New York Academy of Sciences,
       n.s. 36, 2 (Feb. 1974), 192-99.

2374   _____. "Women and Power: the Politics of Domestic
       Interaction in Morocco." In Lois Beck and Nikki Keddie,
       eds. Women in the Muslim World, Harvard University
       Press, under publication.

2375   Wannich, Badia. "Why Hasn't the Moroccan Woman Evolved?
       Is There a Religious Influence?" (in Arabic). Shuruq,
       2 (1965), 10-12, 30.

(2) THE FAMILY

2376   al-Amin, Ahmad. "L'Evolution de la femme et le problème
       du mariage au Maroc." Présence Africaine, 68 (1968),
       32-51.

2377   Baron, Anne-Marie. "Mariages et divorces à Casablanca."
       Hespéris, (3rd & 4th trim.), 419-440.

2378   Belghiti, Malika. "Les Relations féminines et le statut de
       la femme dans la famille rurale, dans trois villages
       de la Tessaout." Bulletin Economique et Social du
       Maroc, 114 (July-Sept. 1969), 1-73.

2379 _____. "Le Statut de la femme dans trois villages de la Tessaout." Lamalif, 45 (Jan.-Feb. 1971), 28-31.

2380 Ben Cheneb, M. "Du mariage entre musulmans et non-musulmans." Archives Marocaines, 15 (1909), 55-79.

2381 Bousser, and Khelladj. "Enquête sur le trousseau choura et le sadag au Maroc." Revue Africaine, 390-391 (1942).

2382 Cazautets, J. "Les Mariages consanguins dans la plaine du Loukkos." Revue de Géographie du Maroc, 8 (1965), 35-40.

2383 Corjon, F. "Le Mariage collectif dans les tribus berbères du Maroc central." Bulletin, BEPM, 119 (1932), 116-21.

2384 Daoud, Zakya. "Les Jeunes Marocains devant le mariage." Jeune Afrique, 206 (Nov. 15, 1964), 28-29.

2385 _____; Jamal al Achgar; and Hazazam Chkounda. "Les Mariages mixtes." Lamalif, 6 (Oct. 1966), 24-35.

2386 Decroux, Paul. "La Forme civile du mariage au Maroc." Revue Marocaine de Droit, 1953, 385-97.

2387 _____. Le Mariage et le divorce en droit international marocain. Casablanca: n.p., 1945.

2388 _____. "Mariages mixtes au Maroc." Revue Marocaine de Droit, 1956, 1-28.

2389 De Lens, A. R. "Un Mariage à Meknès dans la petite bourgeoisie." Revue du Monde Musulman, 35 (1917-18), 31-55.

2390 Garcia-Barriuso, Patrocinio. Proyección interconfesional e internacional del nuevo estatuto personal marroqui. Madrid: n.p., 1961. Provisions of the Moroccan Personal Status Laws concerning mixed marriages.

2391 Graff-Wassink, M. W. "Opinion Survey on Mixed Marriages in Morocco." Journal of Marriage and Family, 29 (1967), 578-89.

2392 Hassar-Zeghari, Latifa. "La Femme marocaine et sa préparation à la vie familiale et professionnelle." Confluent, Sept.-Oct. 1962, 641-68.

2393 Houel, Christian. Maroc: mariage, adultère, prostitution; anthologie. Paris: H. Davagon, 1912.

2394 Ibn Thabit, 'Abd al-Karim. "A Wedding Fête in Morocco"

(in Arabic). al-'Alam al-'arabi, June 1947, 40-41.

2395 el-Jazouli, Nourredine. "Les Causes d'instabilité du mariage; Les Modes de dissolution du mariage en droit marocain." Revue Algérienne des Sciences Juridiques, Economiques et Politiques, 1968, 1117-1125.

2396 Jouin, Jeanne. "Chants et jeux maternels à Rabat." Hespéris, 37 (1950), 137-56.

2397 _____. "Chez les mariées marocaines." Le Monde Colonial Illustré, 101 (Jan. 1932), 7. A well-illustrated article.

2398 Kaci, Houcein. "Les Cérémonies du marriage à Bahlil." Hespéris, 1921, 337-42. Bahlil is a large village of Berber cave-dwellers, south of Fez, where ancient Berber rites still prevailed when the school teacher of the place wrote this article.

2399 Kattani, Idris. "The Traditional Moroccan Family" (in Arabic). al-Ba'th al-'ilmi, 7 (Jan.-April 1966), 127-46.

2400 Kohen, Ahmed. "La Crise du mariage au Maroc." Aicha, 21-22 (1972), 12-13.

2401 Kohen, Jamila. "Mariage mixte et crise du mariage au Maroc." Aicha, Dec. 1971, 13-14.

2402 Lahlou, Abbas. "Etude sur la famille traditionnelle de Fès." Revue de l'Institut de Sociologie (Solvay), 3 (1968), 407-442.

2403 Laoust, E. "Le Mariage chez les Berbères du Maroc." Archives Berbères, 2 (1915), 40-76.

2404 Maher, Vanessa. "Divorce and Property in the Middle Atlas of Morocco." Man, 9 (1974), 103-122.

2405 Marcy, Georges. "Le Mariage en droit coutumier zemmoûr." Revue Algérienne, Tunisienne et Marocaine de Législation et de Jurisprudence, June 1930, 77-92; July 1930, 141-58; Aug.-Sept. 1930, 208-20; Oct. 1930, 221-41.

2406 "A Marriage in Fez." Muslim World, 7 (1917), 233-44.

2407 Masson, D. "Les Influences européennes sur la famille indigène au Maroc." Renseignements Coloniaux, 1938, 36-42.

2408 "Opinions de Marocains sur les problèmes de la famille et de la promotion de la femme." Documents Nord-

Africains, 620 (Sept. 30, 1965), 1-8.

2409   Pascon, Paul, and Mekki Bentahar. "Ce que disent 296
       jeunes ruraux. " Bulletin Economique et Social du
       Maroc, 112-113 (1969), 1-143.   What young peasants
       think about education, work and the family.

2410   Salmon, G. "Les Mariages musulmans à Tanger. " Ar-
       chives Marocaines, 1 (1904), 273-89.

2411   Sbai, Zhor. "Confessions d'une fille-mère. " Aicha, 12
       (March 31, 1971), 23-27.

2412   SCMAT. "Comment vivent les Ménagères musulmanes. "
       Faits et Idées, Nov. 1961, 7-10.

2413   Shams al-Din, Muhammad. "Poverty and the Splitting-Up
       of the Family" (in Arabic). Da'wat al-haqq, 9 (Nov.
       1971), 20-24.

2414   Vinogradov, Amal Rassam. "What Price Women? The
       Evolution of the Status of Women Among the Aith Ndhir
       of the Middle Atlas. " Paper delivered at the 1973
       Middle East Studies Association meeting, Milwaukee,
       November 8-10, 1973.

2415   Wassink, M. W. Graeff. "Opinion Survey on Mixed Mar-
       riages in Morocco. " Journal of Marriage and the
       Family, 1967, 578-88.

2416   Westermarck, Edward. "Cérémonies du mariage au Maroc. "
       Archives Berbères, 2 (1917), 1-35.

2417   _____ . "Marriage Ceremonies in Morocco. " Sociologi-
       cal Review, 5 (1912), 187-201.

2418   _____ . Marriage Ceremonies in Morocco.   London:
       Curzon Press; Totowa, N.J. : Rowman & Littlefield,
       1972.   A reprint of the 1914 edition.

2419   Zuhayri, Qasim. "The Role of Family in Society" (in Ara-
       bic). Da'wat al-haqq, 6-7 (April-May 1966), 39-42.

(3) FERTILITY AND FAMILY PLANNING

2420   Alhilay, T. "Opinions sur la limitation des naissances. "
       Confluent, 50-52 (April-May-June 1965), 315-19.

2421   Brown, G. F. J. "Le Programme de planification familiale
       au Maroc. " Revue Tunisienne de Sciences Sociales,
       17-18 (1969), 283-92.

2422   Brown, G. W. "Moroccan Family Planning Program:
       Progress and Problems. " Demography, 2 (1968), 620-
       26.

2423   "Les Consultations de Da'ouat al-haqq au sujet de la contra-
       ception et de la limitation des naissances. " Confluent,
       50-52 (1965), 320-22.

2424   Delmarès, C. 'Sortilèges pratiques à Mazagan pour pré-
       server les jeunes épousées d'une maternité trop
       précoce. " Revue Anthropologique, 43 (1933), 477-78.

2425   Elamrani, Jamel. "La Planification familiale au Maroc. "
       Revue Tunisienne de Sciences Sociales, 17-18 (1969),
       321-36.

2426   "Enquête d'opinion sur la planification familiale au Maroc,
       1966. " Bulletin Economique et Social du Maroc, 104-
       105 (Jan. -June 1967), 95-149.

2427   "Family Planning. " Aicha, 25-26 (1972), 13-15.

2428   Jouin, J. 'Invocations pour l'enfantement. " Hespéris, 40
       (1953), 343-57.

2429   Khatibi, Abdelkabir. "Etude sociologique du planning
       familial au Maroc. " Le Journal de Médecine du Maroc,
       1967.

2430   Lapham, R. "Modernisation et contraception au Maroc
       central: illustration de l'analyse des données d'une
       enquête C.A. P. " Population, 2 (March 1971), 79-104.

2431   Lesthaeghe, R. "La Fécondité urbaine au Maroc; Quelques
       Notes de recherche. " Bulletin Economique et Social du
       Maroc, 110-111 (1968), 91-99.

2432   "Les Marocains et la planification familiale: enquête
       d'opinion. " Aicha, 9 (April 1971), 7-11.

2433   "Le Plan familial au Maroc. " Population, 27 (1972), 1145-
       47.

2434   Sbai, Zhor. "L'avortement: entre la faiseuse d'ange et la
       gynécologie. " Aicha, 8 (Jan. 30, 1971), 19-22.

(4) SECLUSION OF WOMEN

2435   Celarié, Henriette. Behind Moroccan Walls. New York:
       Macmillan, 1931; reprint: Freeport, N.Y.: Books
       for Library Press, 1970. Translations of short stories

selected from Amours marocaines and La Vie mystéri-
euse des harems.

2436   Dolinger, Jane.   Behind Harem Walls.   London: Alvin Red-
       man, 1960.   A very poor exploitation of the "magic of
       the East" cliches.

2437/8 Machard, Raymonde.   Les Femmes cachées.   Paris:
       Flammarion, 1938.   See chapter, "Dans les harems du
       Maroc. "

2439   Wharton, Edith.   "Harems and Ceremonies. "   The Yale Re-
       view, Oct. 1919, 47-71.   During her sojourn in Moroc-
       co, Mrs. Wharton was invited into the Imperial Harem
       with the wife of Resident General Lyautey.   She met
       the Sultan, his mother, his favorites and children.   On
       her own she visited other harems and describes their
       "melancholic respectability. "

(5) EDUCATION

2440   Counillon.   "Les Ecoles franco-musulmanes de fillettes au
       Maroc. "   Bulletin Economique et Social du Maroc, 1946.

2441   Joubin, O.   "L'Incidence de la scolarisation sur l'intégra-
       tion des femmes musulmanes à une société moderne,
       deux exemples: la Tunisie et le Maroc. "   Unpublished
       dissertation, Paris, 1966.

2442   Ouazzani, Yasmine.   "La Femme et le sport. "   Aicha, 21-
       22 (1972), 31-32.

2443   "Pour une éducation totale; Quelques Réflexions à la lumière
       de la réalite marocaine. "   Confluent, 23-24 (Sept. -Oct.
       1962), 527-560.   The opinions of a group of French and
       Moroccan researchers.

(6) LITERARY WORKS BY OR ABOUT WOMEN

2444   Bonjean, François.   Confidences d'une fille de la nuit.
       Tangiers: Editions Marocaines & Internationales, 1969.
       Reprint of a book originally published in 1939, which
       vividly describes the popular beliefs and customs of
       Fez.

2445   Rhaïs, Elissa.   Le Mariage de Hanifa.   Paris: Plon-
       Nourrit & Cie, 1926.   A good description of Moroccan
       traditional life.

2446 _____. La Riffaine. Paris: E. Flammarion, 1929.

2447 _____. Saada la Marocaine. Paris: Plon, Nourrit &
Cie., 1919. The life of poor Moroccan immigrants in
Algeria during World War I. The book includes an
abundance of details such as the text of popular songs
in dialectal Arabic with their French translation.

2448 Tergoule, Léon de. "Confidences d'une fille de la nuit."
IBLA, 4 (Oct. 1941), 445-56. Laudatory critique of
Bonjean's book.

2449 al-Wazzani, 'Abd al-'Ali. "Necessity for the Feminine Ele-
ment in Our Literary Life" (in Arabic). Da'wat al-haqq,
6-7 (April-May 1965), 43-46.

(7) THE WORKING WOMAN

2450 Alia-Bsis. "Le Chômage féminin: un des grands problèmes
qui se posent au Maroc." Maroc d'Aujourd'hui, 2 (1972),
47-49.

2451 _____. "Conditions de travail en milieu rural: une
étude de l'U.F.M." Aicha, 23-24 (April 1972), 11-14.

2452 Baron, A. M. "La Femme dans le prolétariat marocain."
Masses Ouvrières, 118 (1956), 84-91.

2453 "The Changing Status of Women and the Employment of Wom-
en in Morocco." African Women, 1 (Dec. 1962), 17-20.

2454 Davis, Susan S. " 'Liberated' Women in a Moroccan Village: The Wages of Self-Support." Paper delivered at
the 1975 Middle East Studies Association Meeting,
Louisville, Ky., Nov. 19-22, 1975.

2455 Forget, Nelly. "Attitudes Towards Work by Women in
Morocco." International Social Science Journal, 1
(1962), 92-124.

2456 Herber, J. "Tatoueuses marocaines." Hespéris, 35
(1948), 289-98.

2457 Martenson, Mona. "Attitudes vis-à-vis du travail professionnel de la femme marocaine." Bulletin Economique
et Social du Maroc, 100 (1966), 133-46.

2458 Mesdali, Bennani. "Quelques Considérations sur la prostitution au Maroc." Revue Tunisienne de Sciences Sociales, 11 (Oct. 1967), 79-84.

2459   Nouacer, K. "Evolution et travail professionnel de la
            femme au Maroc. " Revue Internationale des Sciences
            Sociales, 1 (1962), 124-130.

2460   Sabbagh, Entisar. "Women Participation in the Labor
            Force in Morocco. " Paper delivered at the Conference
            on Development in the Arab World, New York, October
            1-3, 1976.

2461   "Some Slave Girls of Morocco. " Muslim World, 26 (1936),
            176-85.

2462   Vinogradov, Amal Rassam. "What Price Autonomy? Wom-
            an and Work in Morocco. " Paper prepared for the
            Conference on Women and Development, sponsored by
            the Center for Research on Women and Higher Education
            and the Professions, Wellesley College, June 2-6, 1976.

2463   "Women and Professions in Morocco. " International Social
            Science Journal, 1 (1962), 92-129.

(8) WOMEN'S CONGRESSES AND FEMINISM

2464   "Une Centaine de foyers féminins créés dans tout le Maroc. "
            La Vie Economique, March 10, 1961.

2465   "One Hundred and Fifty Nine Urban and Mutual Women's
            Clubs in Morocco" (in Arabic). al-Ahram, May 27,
            1974, p. 6, col. 3.

2466   "Pour la promotion de la femme marocaine. " Maroc-Docu-
            ments, 6 (July 1969), 68-89.

2467   "La Promotion féminine. " Maroc, 7 (May 1966), 29-37.

2468   Puigaudau, Odette du. "Femmes célèbres du Maroc. "
            Maroc Tourisme, 59 (1971), 34-41.

2469   Souad X. "Nous voulons l'égalité avec l'homme. " Démo-
            cratie, Feb. 1957.

2470   "L'Union Progressiste des Femmes Marocaines: Unité,
            Force, Enthousiasme. " Casablanca, n. d.

XII

PALESTINE

2471 Arafat, Ibtihaj, and James Gornwell. "The Palestinian Woman in the Labor Force. " Paper delivered at the Conference on Development in the Arab World, New York, Oct. 1-3, 1976.

2472 'Azzam, Samirah. al-Sa'ah wa-al-insan. Beirut: al-Mu'assassah al-ahliyah lil-tiba'ah wa-al-nashr, 1963.

2473 _____. Wa qisas ukhra. Beirut: Dar al-tali'ah, 1960.

2474 Baldensperger, Philip J. "Birth, Marriage and Death Among the Fellahin of Palestine. " Palestine Exploration Fund Quarterly Statement, 1894, 127-144.

2475 Barbot, Michel. "Destins de femmes arabes. " Orient, 31 (1964), 109-128. Gives three excerpts translated from the works of the Syrian Colette al-Khuri and the Palestinian Samira Azzam.

2476 Canaan, T. "Unwritten Laws Affecting the Arab Woman of Palestine. " Journal of the Palestine Oriental Society, 11 (1931), 172-203.

2477 Canova, Giovanni. "Due poetesse: Fadwa Tuqan e Salma 'l-Khadra' al-gayyusi. " Oriente Moderno, 10 (Oct. 1973), 876-893.

2478 Crowfoot, G. E. "Custom and Folktale in Palestine: The Dowry or Bride Price. " Folk-lore, 48 (1937), 28-40.

2479 Farah, Najwa. "Mendelbaum Gate. " New Outlook, 1 (Jan. 1964), 52-57.

2480 Fitch, Florence Mary. The Daughter of Abd Salam. Boston: B. Humphries, 1934. The life of a Palestinian peasant woman.

2481 Ghandur, Muna Ahmad. al-Fida'iat, Umm Ahmad wa-banatha al-thalathah fi al-ma'arakah. Beirut: Matba'at

195

al-wafa´, 1969.

2482   Ginat, Joseph. "A Rural Arab Community in Israel: Mar-
       riage Patterns and Woman's Status. " Unpublished Ph. D.
       dissertation, University of Utah, 1975.

2483   Grandqvist, Hilma. Birth and Childhood Among the Arabs.
       Helsinki: Soderstrom & Co. , 1950.

2484   _____ . Marriage Conditions in a Palestinian Village.
       2 vols. Helsinki: Societas Scientiarum Fennica, 1931-
       1935.

2485   Hijazi, 'Arafat. al-Fida´iyat wa-al-fida´iyun. Amman?
       1968.

2486   Jafarey, S. A. , et al. "Use of Medical, Para-Medical
       Personnel and Traditional Midwives in the Palestine
       Family Planning Program. " Demography, 5 (1968),
       666-679.

2487   Jamil al-Sarraj, Nadirah. "In Remembrance of Samirah
       'Azzam on the Fifth Anniversary [of Her Death]" (in
       Arabic). Shu´un Filastiniyah, 14 (Oct. 1972); 69-82.

2488   Jouin, Jeanne. "Le Costume féminin dans l'Islam syro-
       palestinien. " Revue des Etudes Islamiques, 4 (1934),
       481-505. A detailed article which includes many illus-
       trations.

2489   al-Khadra´, Salma. 'Arraf al-riyah [unpublished; author
       plans to publish in late 1970's].

2490   _____ . al-'Awdah min al-nab' al-halim. Beirut: Dar
       al-Adab, 1960.

2491   _____ . 'Ushshaq fi al-manfa´ [unpublished; author plans
       to publish in late 1970's]. Items 2489-91 are nonfiction
       prose by a Palestinian woman poet.

2492   Khalid, Laila. My People Shall Live: The Autobiography
       of a Revolutionary. London: Hodder & Stoughton,
       1973. A militant since the age of 14, Laila Khalid
       participated in the hijacking of two planes.

2493   Layish, Aharon. "Women and Succession in the Muslim
       Family in Israel. " Asian and African Studies, 1973.

2494   _____ . "Shari'ah and Custom in the Muslim Family in
       Israel" (in Hebrew). Hamizrah Hehadash, 4 (1974),
       377-409.

2495   Lev, Ilana. "Profile of an Arab Authoress: Najwa Farau. "

New Outlook, 1 (Jan. 1964), 51-52.

2496   Makhloul, Najawa.   "The Women Question in Third World
       Development: Examples From the Palestinian Case."
       Paper delivered at the Conference on Development in
       the Arab World, New York, October 1-3, 1976.

2497   Marx, Emanuel.   "Marriage Patterns Among the Negev
       Beduin" (in Hebrew).   Hamizrah Hehadash, 4 (1963),
       395-409.

2498   Mogannam, Matiel E. T.   The Arab Woman and the Pales-
       tine Problem.   Westport, Conn.: Hyperion Press,
       1975.   Reprint of a book originally published in 1937,
       written by a member of the Palestinian National Defense
       Party.

2499   Muhsam, H. V.   "Fertility of Polygamous Marriages."
       Population Studies, 10 (July 1956), 3-16.   The results
       of a study conducted among the Bedouin of the Negev
       desert.

2500   Nasif, Munirah.   "Madame Fatma Nimet Rachid reçoit la
       délégation féminine palestinienne."   La Réforme, Jan.
       9, 1946.   Article from an Egyptian paper which in-
       cludes the declaration of Palestinian Khairia al-Fara
       about the Palestinian Arabs having no university of their
       own.   Miss al-Fara complains that women are admitted
       to secondary schools only, and still wear veils in the
       countryside.

2501   Ode-Vasileva, K. V.   "Les Coutumes relatives à l'accouche-
       ment et le traitement du nouveau-né chez les Arabes du
       nord de la Palestine."   Sovetskaya Etnografiya, 3
       (1963), 93-97.

2502   "Palestinian Arab Women and the Vote."   Middle East Re-
       view, 2 (Winter 1976/77), 52-54.   Excerpted from
       "Exercise in Democracy," an article by Augustine Zy-
       cher, Jerusalem Post Weekly, May 4, 1976.

2503   "Palestinian Women Honor Huda Sha'rawi" (in Arabic).   al-
       Ahram, Dec. 17, 1974, p. 8, col. 1.

2504   "A Picture of the Fighting Palestinian Woman in the Moun-
       tain District of Lebanon" (in Arabic).   al-Ahram, Oct.
       10, 1976, p. 5, col. 2.

2505   Rosenfeld, H.   "An Analysis of Marriage and Marriage Sta-
       tistics for a Muslim and Christian Arab Village."   In-
       ternational Archives of Ethnology, 1 (1957), 32-62.

2506/7 Rosenfeld, Henry.   "Change, Barriers to Change, and

Contradictions in the Arab Village Family. " American
Anthropologist, 4 (Aug. 1968), 732-752. Also in New
Outlook, 2 (Fall 1970), 28-44.

2508   . "Social Factors in the Explanation of the In-
creased Rate of Patrilineal Endogamy in the Arab Village in Israel. " Paper delivered at the Mediterranean
Social Anthropological and Sociological Conference, Ni-
cosia, Cyprus, Sept. 7-12, 1970.

2509   Samed, Amal. "The Proletarization of Palestinian Women
in Israel. " Merip Reports, 50 (Aug. 1976), 10-15, 26.

2510   Sirhan, B. "The Traditional Aspect of the Palestinian Woman in Lebanon and Her Participation in the Revolution:
A Preliminary Study" (in Arabic). Shu´un Filastiniyah,
6 (Jan. 1972), 142-155.

2511   "Social Values Changing. " Christian Science Monitor, May
2, 1972, p. 4, col. 1.

2512   "The Status of the Arab Woman in Israel. " Middle East
Review, 2 (Winter 1976/77), 55-57.

2513   Tubi, Asma. 'Abir wa-majd. Beirut: Matba'at Qalfat,
1966. Biographies of Palestinian women, mostly contemporary, prominent in art, literature and social
service.

2514   Tuqan, Fadwa. al-Layl wa al-fursan. Beirut: Dar al-
adab, 1969. The poems of a major Palestinian poetess
in praise of Palestinian resistance.

2515   . "Pages From My Diary" (in Arabic). al-Tariq,
29:2, Feb. 1970. F. Tuqan, who was born in Nablus
in 1920, has been the witness of many traumatic events.

2516   Watad, Muhammad. "The War of the Generations in the
Arab Village. " New Outlook, 1964, 29-33, 50.

2517   Weighert, Gideon. "Women Want Freedom. " New Outlook,
5 (June 1964), 60-62.

2518   Weir, S. , and Widad Kawar. "Costumes and Wedding Customs in Bayt Dajan. " Palestine Exploration Quarterly,
107 (1975), 39-52.

2519   Wingate, R. O. "Moslem Women in Palestine and Syria. "
World Dominion, 1934, 177-185.

2520   Yaghi, Hashim, and 'Abd al-Rahman Yaghi, eds. Sh'ir
Fadwa Tuqan, Amman. n.p., 1970. The poems of
the poet Tuqan with an analysis of her work and political evolution.

XIII

SAUDI ARABIA

2521 Bint al-Jazirah, Samirah. Yaqzat al-fatat al-'arabiyah al-
      sa'udiyah. Beirut: Maktab Tijari, 1963.

2522 "Education of Women in Saudi Arabia. " Moslem World, 46
      (1956), 366-367.

2523 Nallino, C. A. "Il velo delle donne e i Wahhabiti. "
      Oriente Moderno, 6 (1926), 338-339.

2524 Reintjens, Hortense. Die soziale Stellung der Frau bei den
      nordarabischen Beduinen. Bonn: Selbsverlag des
      Orientalischen Seminars der Universität, 1975.

2525 Saudi Arabia. Wizarat al-I'lam. Education for Girls.
      Riyad, 1963.

2526 _____ . _____ . Ta'lim al-fatah. Riyad, 1963?

2527 "The Saudi Woman Is Represented in the Arab League by
      Two Women" (in Arabic). al-Ahram, Aug. 7, 1976,
      p. 5, col. 8.

2528 "Six Universities for Girls in Saudi Arabia" (in Arabic).
      al-Ahram, Sept. 17, 1976, p. 7, col. 5.

2529 'Soraya Altorki, First Woman Ph. D. Explains Her Position."
      The Christian Science Monitor, Sept. 23, 1974, p. 10,
      col. 5.

2530 Sterba, James P. "For Arab Princess, Education Is Taste
      of Forbidden Fruit. " The New York Times, Oct. 17,
      1976, 1, 27. Princess Rima of Saudi Arabia is start-
      ing work on her B.S. in psychology as one of 500 stu-
      dents in the Open University Program of the University
      of Houston.

2531 al-Torki, Soraya. "Religion and Social Organization of
      Elite Families in Urban Saudi Arabia. " Unpublished
      Ph. D. dissertation, University of California, Berkeley,

1973.

2532   Toy, Barbara.   A Fool Strikes Oil: Across Saudi Arabia.
       London: J. Murray, 1957.   The author gathered much
       information about Saudi women.

2533   Traini, R.   "Arabia saudiana: associazione per l'elevazione
       della donna.   La prima donna giornalista saudiana. "
       Oriente Moderno, 43 (1963), 492-493.   About the first
       Saudi newswoman.

2534   _____.   "Arabia Saudiana: circa la libertà della donna
       nella scelta del marito. "   Oriente Moderno, (1964), 588-
       589.   How free are Saudi women to choose their hus-
       bands?

2535   _____.   "Arabia saudiana: richiamo dell'Università
       islamica di Medina all'osservaza dell'uso del velo. "
       Oriente Moderno (1962), 460-461.

SOUTH YEMEN

2536 Knox-Mawer, R. "Islamic Domestic Law in the Colony of
      Aden. " International & Comparative Law Quarterly, 5
      (1956), 511-18.

2537 Petran, Tabitha. "South Yemen Ahead on Women's Rights. "
      Middle East International, 48 (June 1975), 24-26. If
      the Republic of South Yemen does indeed apply the laws
      it is promulgating its female citizens would be the most
      liberated women in the world.

2538 Serjeant, R. B. "Recent Marriage Legislation From al-
      Mukhalta with Notes on Marriage Customs. " Bulletin
      of the School of Oriental and African Studies, 1962,
      472-498. Text of Aden Public Ordinance No. 10, 1959,
      with English translation and commentary.

2539 _____. "Two Tribal Law Cases. " Journal of the Royal
      Asiatic Society, 304 (Oct. 1951), 156-69. Text, with
      translation and notes, of legal documents concerning a
      case of elopement which occurred in the Wahidi Sultan-
      ate of the Aden hinterland.

2540 "Women in the Army. " Christian Science Monitor, Nov. 3,
      1971, p. 6, col. 3. South Yemen People's Republic
      enlists women in its army.

2541 "Yemen: Women Propose Prohibition of Foreign Wives. "
      Christian Science Monitor, May 9, 1973, p. 6,
      col. 3.

SUDAN

2542   Crowfoot, J. W. "Customs of the Rutabab. " Sudan Notes
        & Records, 1 (1918), 118-34. The life and customs of
        of an Arab tribe in the Sudan.

2543   _____. "Wedding Customs in the Northern Sudan. "
        Sudan Notes & Records, 5 (1922), 1-28.

2544   Cunnison, Ian. Beggara Arabs: Power and the Lineage in
        a Sudanese Nomad Tribe. Oxford: Clarendon Press,
        1966. Includes a description of domestic life and mar-
        riage patterns as observed between 1952 and 1955.

2545   Lampen, G. D. "The Baggara Tribes of Darfur. " Sudan
        Notes & Records, 16 (1933), 97-118. Contains some
        information on family life and marriage in Arab tribes
        of the Sudan.

2546   Zenkovsky, Sophie. "Customs of the Women of Omdurman. "
        Sudan Notes & Records, 30 (1949), 39-46. Magical
        practices of Arab women during pregnancy and child
        birth.

2547   _____. "Marriage Customs in Omdurman. " Sudan Notes
        & Records, 26 (1945), 241-55. The wedding prepara-
        tions of the Arab women of Omdurman.

2548   _____. "Zar and Tambura as Practiced by the Women of
        Omdurman. " Sudan Notes & Records, 31 (1950), 65-81.

2549 'Abd al-Nabi, Hidayah. "The First Lady Minister in Syria"
      (in Arabic). al-Ahram, Dec. 12, 1976, p. 5. About
      Dr. Najjar al-'Attar, Syrian Minister of Culture.

2550 Aissa, Samir. "The Arab Syrian Woman and the Elimina-
      tion of Illiteracy" (in Arabic). Education of the Masses,
      Jan. 1976, 113-118. The author of this article is the
      Director of the Syrian Illiteracy Program.

2551 Anderson, James N. D. "The Syrian Law of Personal
      Status." Bulletin of the School of Oriental and African
      Studies, 2 (1955), 34-49. A presentation of the law of
      September 17, 1953.

2552/3 Arab Republic of Syria. Central Bureau for Statistics.
      Highlights on the Status of Syrian Women. Research
      No. 44, 196-. Progress which has taken place in the
      various fields affecting women during the sixties.

2554 Aswad, Barbara C. "Key and Peripheral Roles of Noble
      Women in a Middle Eastern Plains Village." Anthropo-
      logical Quarterly 3, 132-152. How wealthy noble wom-
      en in a Syrian village near Hatay have tighter control
      of their property than lower class women of the same
      village.

2555 Charles, H. "Quelques Travaux de femmes chez les no-
      mades moutonniers de la région de Homs-Hama. Etude
      ethnographique et dialectale." Bulletin d'Etudes Orien-
      tales, 7-8 (1937-38), 195-213.

2556 Chatila, Khaled. Le Mariage chez les musulmans en Syrie:
      étude de sociologie. Paris: Paul Geuthner, 1934.
      The author offers an explanation for Islamic institutions
      and a justification of the veil.

2557 "Il Congresso femminile siriano di Damasco." Oriente
      Moderno, 11 (Nov. 1932), 538-39.

2558 El-Daghestani, Kazem. Etude sociologique sur la famille musulmane contemporaine en Syrie. Paris: Leroux, 1932.

2559 _____. "The Evolution of the Moslem Family." UNESCO International Social Science Bulletin, 1953, 681-91.

2560 Faris, Filiks. al-Najwa. Risalah wa-rawiyah ila nisa´ suriyah. Beirut: al-Matba'ah al-hamidiyah, 1908. An appeal to the women of Syria to work for the regeneration of themselves and their people.

2561 al-Gaby, Ghada. "The Role of the Contemporary Woman in the Spheres of Economic and Social Development" (in Arabic). English Abstract in Education of the Masses, Jan. 1976, 26-28. The author belongs to the General Women's Union of the Arab Republic of Syria.

2562 Gaulmier, J. "Notes sur les cérémonies du mariage chez les paysans de Hama." Mélanges Gaudefroy-Demombynes. Cairo: Institut Français d'Archéologie Orientale, 1935-1945, 31-40.

2563 Guys, Henri. "Moeurs des femmes musulmanes en Syrie." Revue de l'Orient, 2ème série, 1849, 36-43.

2564 al-Haffar al-Kuzbari, Salmah. 'Anbar wa-ramad. Beirut: Dar Bayrut lil-tiba'ah wa-al-nashr, 1970. Novel by a woman writer with the nationalist struggle as a background.

2565 _____. Yawmiyat halah. Damascus: Dar al-ilm lil-malayin, 1950. Diary of a young girl written in 1940-41 in which she discusses the veil and other problems.

2566 Hilmi, Majida. "The Changing Role of the Syrian Women in the Labor Force." Paper delivered at the Conference on Development in the Arab World, New York, Oct. 1-3, 1976.

2567 Ibn al-Sadat, Raghib ibn 'Abd al-Ghani. al-Qawl al-fasl al-mu´ayyad al-mansur fi sama' da'wa al-nisa´ ba'd al-dukhul bi-kull al-mu'ajjal aw-ba'dihi min al-muhur. Damascus: Rawdat al-Sham, 1315? (i.e. 1897/98?). A tract on the rights of women before the law.

2568 Jessup, Henry Harris. Syrian Home Life. New York: Dodd & Mead, 1874.

2569 al-Khuri, Colette. Ana wa-al-mada. Beirut: al-Maktab al-tijari lil-tiba'ah wa-al-tauzi' wa-al-nashr, 1962. A collection of short stories.

2570 _____. Laylah wahidah. Beirut: Dar al-Kutub, 1970.

2571 Le Guillerme, Marc. Femmes Voilées. Paris: Fasquelle,
1934. How the conflict between two cultures affects the
life of a young woman from Aleppo.

2572 Loya, Arieh. "Poetry As a Social Document: The Social
Position of the Arab Woman as Reflected in the Poetry
of Nizar Qabbani." Muslim World, 1 (1973), 39-52.
Qabbani, one of the leading contemporary Arab poets,
has often taken the defense of women's rights, and at
times caused public uproars.

2573 al-Mardudi, Abu al-'Ala´. al-Hijab. Damascus: Dar al-
fikr al-islamiyah, 1959.

2574 Mokarzel, Salloum A. "Social and Economic Trends in
Modern Syria." The Open Court, 914 (July 1932), 484-
96. Mentions the encouraging progress of female education in Syria and Lebanon.

2575 "The Muslim Women of Syria and Pakistan." Islamic Review, Oct. 1951, 38-39.

2576 Nallino, C. A. "Mancata dimostrazione femminile contro il
velo a Damasco." Oriente Moderno (1927), 493. The
women of Damascus protested against the veil, to no
effect.

2577 Qabbani, Nizar. Qasa´id. Beirut: n.p., 1956. This book
of poems includes two very famous pieces: "Hubla"
(Pregnant) and "Khubz, wa-hashish wa-qamar" (Bread,
hashish and the moon). The second poem was the ob-
ject of a heated debate at the Syrian Parliament, some
of its members demanding the condemnation of the author.

2578 Rihawi, Sedki. "L'Accession de la femme à la fonction
publique en droit syrien." Paper delivered at the
Neuvième Congrès de l'Institut International de Droit
d'Expression Française, Tunis, May 27-June 2, 1974.

2579 al-Sa'ati, Ahmad Fawzi. Kitab nuzhat al-tullab fi ta'lim
al-mar'ah wa-raf' al-hijab. Damascus: Matba'ah al-
Turqi, 1921. A treatise asking that better instruction
be given to females, but protesting against the removal
of the veil.

2580 Sakakini, Widas. "The Evolution of Syrian Women."
United Asia 1 (May-June 1949), 531-33.

2581 Sweet, Louise E. "In Reality: Some Middle Eastern Wom-
en." In Carolyn J. Matthiasson, ed. Many Sisters--

Women in Cross-Cultural Perspectives. New York:
Free Press, 1974.

2582 Syria. Da´irat al-Funun al-Sha´biyah.   Taqalid al-zawaj fi
      al-iqlim al-suri.   Damascus.   Da´irat al-Funun al-
      Sha´biyah, 1961.

2583 "Syria 1969: Divorce, One-Third of Marriages" (in Arabic).
      al-Nahar, Economic and Financial Supplement, March 1,
      1970, 14.

2584 Tresse, R.   "Manifestations féminines à Damas aux XIXème
      et XXème siècles." In Entretiens sur l'évolution des
      pays de civilisation arabe, vol. III, Paris: Hartman,
      1939; 115-126.

2585 Turjman, S.   "Syrian Women on the Way to Emancipation."
      Flash, 5 (Nov. 1971), 17-19.

2586 Vacca, Virginia.   "Il Congresso femminile siriano di Da-
      masco." Oriente Moderno, 11 (1932), 538-39.

2587 Yasin, Bu 'Ali.   al-Thaluth al-muharram.   Beirut: Dar al-
      Tali'ah, 1973. A series of essays on the family.

XVII

TUNISIA

(1) GENERAL

2588 'Abd al-Wahhab, Hasan Husni. "The Vigor of the Kairouan
Women" (in Arabic). al-Fikr, 1 (Oct. 1967), 3-11.

2589 Altuma. "Pour les femmes musulmanes en Tunisie. " Renseignements Coloniaux, 1925, 289-91.

2590 Askhalani, Hagher. "Tunisiennes, par Lucie Paul-
Margueritte. " L'Egyptienne, 149 (Nov. 1938), 24-28.

2591 Belhah, 'Izz al-Din. al-Jins al-latif. Tunis: Ittihad, 1936.
A book dedicated to the memory of feminist writer Tahar al-Haddad.

2592 Ben Amour, Aicha. "The Tunisian Woman at the Cross-
Road" (in Arabic). Thuraya, 8-9 (1946), 4-6; 10-11
(1946), 25-28.

2593 Ben Brahem, J. "Du colonialisme à la 'décadence morale':
M. Bourguiba 'sauve la Tunisie pour la seconde fois.'"
Le Monde, Aug. 14-15, 1966, 4.

2594 Ben Salah, A. "Si 25,000 femmes voulaient. " Faïza, May
21, 1961. Minister Ben Salah underlines the economic
power of women who buy for household needs.

2595 Berger, R. "Die soziale Stellung der tunesischen Frau. "
Unpublished dissertation, Freiburg University, 1964.

2596 Bernheim, Nicole. "L'Emancipation juridique et sociale de
la femme; Une Expérience aux résultats féconds. " Le
Monde Diplomatique, May 1969, 39.

2597 _____. "Les Femmes du Maghreb sur la rude voie de
l'indépendance. III: L'Expérience sans complexes de la
Tunisie. " Le Monde, Jan. 5-6, 1969, 6.

207

2598 _____ . _____ . IV: Vers le sud. " Le Monde, Jan.
7, 1969, 7. Has the emancipation of Tunisian women
reached the point of no return?

2599 Bourguiba, Habib. Combattre le libertinage. Tunis: Ministry of Public Information, 1966. Text of a speech
delivered on September 30, 1966.

2600 _____ . Les Nations ne durent qu'autant que durent leurs
valeurs morales. Tunis: Secrétariat d'Etat à l'Information, 1973. Speech given on August 13, 1973, at the
Fifth Congress of Union Nationale des Femmes de Tunisie. The President issues a warning against moral
turpitude and various excesses, he also expresses his
disapproval of large families and miniskirts.

2601 _____ . "A New Role for Women. " In Benjamin Rivlin
and Joseph R. Szyliowicz, eds. The Contemporary
Middle East, New York: Random House, 1965; 352-55.

2602 "Bourguiba avocat de la femme. " Faïza, 54 (Nov. -Dec.
1966), 8-9. The President took a personal interest in
three judicial cases and helped the women involved.

2603 "Bourguiba et la condition de la femme. " Faïza, 54 (1966),
10-11. Text of Bourguiba's speech of August 13, 1966,
in which he recommends that seducers be punished even
if the woman is of age and willing.

2604 "Bourguiba ... the President of Women Too" (in Arabic).
al-Ahram, Dec. 20, 1975, 4.

2605 Bouzid, Dorra. "Y-a-t-il une jeunesse féminine tunisienne. "
Faïza, 29 (Nov. 1962), 48-49. The author deplores the
passivity of daughters who let their parents decide their
whole life by choosing their husband. Answers to this
article appeared in Faïza, 32 (Feb. 1963), 40-41.

2606 Camilleri, Carmel. "Les Attitudes et représentations
familiales des jeunes dans un pays décolonisé en voie
de développement. " Cahiers de Tunisie, 77-78 (1972),
219-224.

2607 _____ . "Les Jeunes Gens tunisiens face au problème de
la mixité. " Confluent, 20 (April 1962), 262-73.

2608 Charfi, Mohammed. "L'Egalité entre l'homme et la femme
dans le droit de la nationalité tunisienne. " Paper delivered at the Neuvième Congrès de l'Institut International de Droit d'Expression Française, Tunis, May 27-
June 2, 1974.

2609 Chemli, 'Ali. "Our Young Girls Between Feelings and

Reason" (in Arabic). al-Shabab, 3 (March 1968), 21,
27.

2610   "Le Colloque de Lomé: la condition de la femme en Afrique. (Document de travail de la délégation tunisienne). "
Femme, Jan. -March 1965, 29-30.

2611   "Conversation with Mrs. Wasila Bourguiba: She Said That
the Tunisian Woman Has No More Problems" (in Arabic). al-Ahram, May 25, 1974, p. 5, col. 4.

2612   "Croyances et coutumes féminines au sujet des Djinns. "
IBLA, 4 (Jan. 1938), 56-63.

2613   Dammaq, Muhammad. "Woman Participates to the Building
of the Country at the Side of Man" (in Arabic). al-
Idha'ah wa-al-talfazah, 175 (July 25, 1966), 36-41.

2614   Demeerseman, A. "L'Evolution féminine dans la bourgeoisie tunisienne. " IBLA, 1 (April 1938), 3-40.

2615   _____. "L'Evolution féminine tunisienne; Ses Problèmes;
Son Programme familial, culturel et éducatif. " IBLA,
39-40 (1947), 221-236, 301-326.

2616   _____. "Le Problème tunisien. " Aperçus de Psychologie, 3 (1942).

2617   _____. "La Route féminine. " IBLA, 20 (1942), 329-46.

2618   Derouiche, Effia. "Die Frauen tunisiens. " Jahrbuch der
Deutschen Afrika Gesellschaft, 1963, 117-184.

2619   Donia. "Bourguiba, avocat de la femme, Bourguiba et la
condition féminine. " Faïza, 54 (Nov. -Dec. 1966), 8-11,
76.

2620   Donner, E. "Comment je vois les tunisiennes. " Faïza,
Jan. 1962, 32-35.

2621   "En dix ans, révolution authentique. " Femme, 5 (Feb. -
April 1966), 12-14, 19-21, 36-39.

2622   Essafi, Tahar. "Retours de flamme. " L'Egyptienne, 149
(Nov. 1938), 20-22. Article of a Tunisian lawyer about
Egyptian influence in Tunisia, considers the Egyptian
feminists as good examples for Tunisian women.

2623   La Femme tunisienne. Tunis: Documentation Tunisienne,
1960.

2624   "La Femme tunisienne fêtera demain le 16ème anniversaire
de son émancipation. " Bulletin Documentaire, 9 (Aug.

1972), 5-6.

2625 Ferida. "La Parole est aux femmes." Ferida, 1 (May
      1975), 3.   The editorial of the first issue of a new
      woman's newspaper.

2626 Gentrie, A. "L'Emancipation de la femme tunisienne."
      Notre Cambat, 24 (March-April 1968), 1-7.

2627 Ginestous, L., and P. Ginestous. "Le Vêtement féminin
      usuel à Bizerte." Cahiers de Tunisie, 7 (1959), 519-
      35.

2628 Graf de la Salle, M. "Contribution à l'étude du folklore
      tunisien: croyances et coutumes féminines relatives à
      la lune." In Mélanges William Marçais, Paris: G. P.
      Maisonneuve, 1950.

2629 Grenier, Cynthia. "Tunisia: Out From Behind the Veil."
      Ms., Aug. 1974, 88-91.

2630 "A Guest from Tunis" (in Arabic). al-Mar'ah, 7 (July 5,
      1968).   The head of the feminine broadcast visits Libya.

2631 "Habib Bourguiba et la promotion de la femme." Femme,
      April-June, 1966, 4-7.

2632 Haddad, Radhia. "Evolution de la femme tunisienne."
      Revue Française de l'Elite Europénne, 166 (July 1964),
      41-44.

2633 _____. "La Femme dans l'état et la société." L'Action,
      June 17, 1967.

2634 _____. "Woman and Society" (in Arabic). al-'Amal,
      4788 (Feb. 8, 1971), 8.

2635 Hasayun, Hasan. "The Gains of the Tunisian Woman Since
      Independence" (in Arabic). Qada' wa-tashri', 9 (Nov.
      1974), 685-94.

2636 Humani, Salwa. "The Problems of the Arab Woman." al-
      'Asfiyah, July 12, 1955, 208-319.   The text of a lec-
      ture, followed by the reaction of the audience.

2637 Ibn Mrad, Fadhilah Murirah. "The Personality of the Tunisian
      Woman" (in Arabic). al-Fikr, 1 (Oct. 1955), 2-9.

2638 Jigham, Salah. "You, the Men" (in Arabic). al-Idha'ah
      wa-al-talfazah, 314 (May 1, 1973), 18.

2639 Kirru, Abu al-Qasim Muhammad. "The Woman's Festival
      Is A Festival ... for Man" (in Arabic). al-Sha'b, 86

211   General

(Aug. 1, 1967), 40-41.

2640 al-Kitani, 'Abd al-Kamil. "Women First" (in Arabic). al-
Fikr, 5 (Feb. 1972), 64-70; 6 (March 1972), 80-86.

2641 Lelong, Michel. "Femmes tunisiennes d'aujourd'hui."
IBLA, (1959), 354-57.

2642 _____. "La Jeune Fille de demain en Tunisie: une
enquête de la revue al-Ilham." IBLA, 71 (1955), 357-
62.

2643 _____. "La Personnalité de la femme tunisienne."
IBLA, 76 (1956), 423-38.

2644 Lemanski, Witold. Moeurs Arabes (Scènes vécues). Paris:
Albin Michel, 1913. Dr. Lemanski practiced medicine
in Tunisia and was able to observe the domestic life
of his patients over many years.

2645 "The Liberation of the Tunisian Woman" (in Arabic). al-
Mar'ah, 10 (May 15, 1969), 28-29.

2646 Mabrouk, Mohieddine. "La Femme en droit public tunisien." Paper delivered at the Neuvième Congrès de
l'Institut International de Droit d'Expression Française,
Tunis, May 27-June 2, 1974.

2647 Masmuli, Muhammad. "The Feminine Ending Nun ..." (in
Arabic). al-Idha'ah wa-al-talfazah, 308 (Feb. 1, 1973),
21.

2648 Meriem Aicha. "Les Femmes musulmanes en Tunisie."
Bibliothèque Universelle et Revue Suisse, 106-108 (Oct. -
Dec. 1904), 564-72.

2649 Montéty, Henry de. Femmes de Tunisie. Paris: Mouton
& Cie., 1958. A very informative book by a long
time resident of Tunisia.

2650 Mzali, Fathia. "The Personality of the Tunisian Woman"
(in Arabic). al-Fikr, 1 (Oct. 1955), 2-9, 54-60.

2651 _____. "The Tunisian Girl" (in Arabic). al-Fikr, 1
(Oct. 1958), 2-7.

2652 Neila. "Devant la pénurie, (Questions féminines)." IBLA,
20 (1942), 408-414.

2653 _____. "Donner, c'est difficile (Questions féminines)."
IBLA, Jan. 1942, 76-85.

2654 _____. "La Femme kairouannaise." IBLA, 3 (1941),

349-58. The Kairouan woman is a very hard worker;
even wealthy women devote their time to handicrafts.

2655   "On Woman's Day" (in Arabic). al-Sha'b, 63 (Aug. 16,
1966), 6-7.

2656   "On Woman's Day" (in Arabic). al-Sha'b, 215 (Nov. 16,
1968), 47-51.

2657   Paul-Margueritte, Lucie. Tunisiennes. Paris: Denoël,
1937. Observations made by the author while she was
on a study trip funded by a "bourse de voyage du Protec-
torat."

2658   Pellegrin, Arthur. "Evolution de la femme tunisienne."
En Terre d'Islam, 1941, 231-46.

2659   _____. "Evolution de la femme tunisienne." Encyclopédie Mensuelle d'Outre-Mer, 41 (Jan. 1954), 6-10.

2660   Peretti. "La Libération de la femme est aussi la libération de l'homme." L'Action, May 10, 1967.

2661   "La Première Conquête africaine du Président: les femmes."
Faïza, 51 (1966), 9-15.

2662   Pruvost, Lucie. "Condition juridique, politique et sociale
de la femme: le neuvième congrès de l'I. D. E. F."
IBLA, 134 (1974), 349-64.

2663   "Psychologie de la femme arabe." Revue Tunisienne, 1899-
1900.

2664   Quemeneur, J. "La Femme tunisienne, évolution, clubs."
Grands Lacs, Oct. 1951.

2665   Schramm, H. "Frau und Ehe in Tunesien." Soziale
Chronik und Kommentare, 2 (1963).

2666   Sellami, M. S. "La Femme musulmane." Revue Tunisienne, 1896, 430-445.

2667   Sethom, Samira. "La Confection du costume féminin
d'Hammamet." Cahiers des Arts et Traditions Populaires, 1 (1968), 101-111.

2668   "The Share of Woman" (in Arabic). al-Idha'ah wa-al-
talfazah, 205. An evaluation of ten years of broadcasting for women.

2669   Slim, Fatma. "Lights on the Tunisian Woman" (in Arabic).
al-Shabab, Oct. 1, 1960, 38-40; Feb. 4, 1961, 34-35.

2670 Es-Snoussi, Mohammed Tahar. al-Mar'ah bayn al-qadim
      wa-al-hadith. Tunis: n. p., n. d.

2671 Sugier, C. "Les Coiffes féminines de Tunisie." Cahiers
      des Arts et Traditions Populaires, 2 (1968), 61-78.

2672 _____. "Les Jeunes Filles tunisiennes d'aujourd'hui."
      IBLA (1956), 233-39.

2673 "The Tunisian Woman" (in Arabic). al-'Arabi, 64 (March
      1964), 47-58.

2674 "The Tunisian Woman Celebrates Twenty Years of the
      Personal Status Law" (in Arabic). al-Ahram, Aug. 18,
      1976, p. 12, col. 1.

2675 "The Tunisian Woman Is More Lucky" (in Arabic). al-
      Ahram, Aug. 23, 1976, p. 12, col. 1.

2676 "Les Tunisiennes." Carthage, 3 (July-Dec. 1965), 35-39.

2677 Vabran, G. "La Femme française et la femme musulmane
      en Tunisie." Le Musée Social--Mémoires et Documents,
      1913, 41-59.

2678 Vichniac, Isabelle. "Assia, jeune fille de Tunis." B. I. T.
      Panorama, 28 (Jan. -Feb. 1968), 16-21.

2679 "Virginité et honneur." Faïza, 56 (March-April 1967), 86-
      87. The opinions of three women of the editing com-
      mittee in answer to the letter of a young reader.

2680 Washshani, 'Abd al-Salam. "The Young Woman Between
      Modernization and National Traditions" (in Arabic). al-
      Shabab, 5-6 (May-June 1968), 8-11.

2681 Willette, H. "Les Filles d'el-Djem." Le Monde Colonial
      Illustré, 83 (July 1930), 172.

2682 "The Young Girl Shows Again Her Boldness" (in Arabic).
      al-Idha'ah wa-al-talfazah, 182 (Jan. 16, 1967), 22-25.

2683 Zghal, Ahmad. "About the Personality of the Tunisian
      Woman" (in Arabic). Nadwa, 1 (1956), 50-56.

(2) ISLAM

General

2684 Abdul-Wahab, Ali. Féminisme et Islam. Tunis, 1901?
      The author wants to prove to Qasim Amin that the
      decadence of Islam is due to the ignorance of the

masses, not the condition of women. Women are the
jewels of the world, carefully kept in the shelter of the
harem.

2685 Benattar, César. L'Esprit libéral du Coran. Paris:
      Ernest Leroux, 1905.

2686 Ben Mrad, Moncef. "La Femme, l'Islam et le cinéma. "
      Charit, 2 (1973), 7-9.

2687 Bouhdiba, Abdulwahab. "La Conscience religieuse dans la
      société d'aujourd'hui. " IBLA, 114-15 (1966), 217-37.
      Text of a speech given by the head of the Sociology De-
      partment of Tunis University, in favor of Islamic judi-
      cial reforms, backing the Code of Personal Status.

2688 Foca, R. "Modernisme en Islam, l'esprit et la lettre. "
      En Terre d'Islam, 43 (Jan. 1931), 2-11. About the
      uproar caused by Tahar al-Haddad's book in Tunisian
      conservative circles.

2689 Isma'il, Muhammad al-Hajari. Mir'at al-mar'ah. Tunis:
      al-Sharikah al-tunisiyah li-funun al-rasm, 1964. An
      extremely conservative opinion on women in Islam.

2690 Lafitte, Paul. "La Femme dans l'Islam. " Revue de
      l'Islam, Jan. 1897, 165-66. Includes a review of
      Essnoussi's Epanouissement de la fleur.

2691 al-Sanusi, Muhammad. Epanouissement de la fleur ou
      étude sur la femme dans l'Islam. Tunis: Imprimerie
      Rapide, 1897. A moderate plea for female instruction
      by a high-ranking Malekite sheikh.

2692 al-Shannufi, Munsif, ed. "The Epistle of Ahmad Ibn Abi
      al-Diyaf on Woman, (Makhtut)" (in Arabic). Hawliyat
      al-Jami'ah al-Tunisiyah, 5 (1968), 49-118. The an-
      notated text of an epistle of Sheikh Abi al-Diyaf explain-
      ing the position of woman in Islam to a Christian cor-
      respondant.

2693 Tlili, Beshir. "A l'aube du mouvement de réforme à
      Tunis: un important document de Ahmad ibn Abi al-
      Diyaf sur le féminisme (1856). " Ethnies, 1972, 167-
      230. A partial translation with commentary of the
      epistle of Sheikh Abi al-Diyaf.

The Veil

2694 Bourguiba, Habib. "Droit de réponse. " Tunis Socialiste,
      Jan. 29, 1929. The arguments of Bourguiba, then a
      young Neo-Destourian leader, urging women to keep

their veil on as long as Tunisia was not independent.

2695 _____. "The Veil" (in Arabic). al-Liwa´ al-tunisi, Jan. 11, 1929.

2696 Desanti, Dominique. "No More Veils. " Atlas, 2 (Feb. 1965), 91-93.

2697 "L'Emancipation de la femme et la suppression du voile" (in Arabic). al-Hadirah, Sept. 22, 1903. Article written during the sojourn of Sheikh Muhammad 'Abduh in Tunisia.

2698 al-Haddad, al-Tahir. "The Liberation of the Tunisian Woman" (in Arabic). al-Sawab, Jan. 11, 1929. Article supporting Halibah al-Munshari who had spoken at a public meeting held by French socialists against the veil.

2699 _____. "We and the Immobilists" (in Arabic). al-Sawab, Jan. 18, 1929. Another article in favor of H. al-Munshari.

2700 Khalid, Ahmad. "Tunisian Poets in the Struggle Against the Veil and In Favor of the Emancipation of Woman" (in Arabic). al-Fikr, 6 (March 1966), 10-21.

2701 Noomane, Mohamed. "Une Soirée à l'Essor. " Tunis Socialiste, Jan. 10, 1929. Relates the intervention of Halibah al-Munshari against the veil.

(3) THE RURAL WOMAN

2702 Bardin, Pierre. La Vie d'un douar. Paris, The Hague: Mouton & Cie. , 1965.

2703 Ben Ali, A. , and A. Louis. "Zeyneb, scènes de vie sahélienne. " IBLA, 29 (1945), 75-101.

2704 Bourguiba, Habib. La Promotion de la femme rurale. Tunis: Secrétariat d'Etat à l'Information, 1974. Speech given on August 13, 1974 at the opening of the national council of Union Nationale des Femmes de Tunisie.

2705 Dornier, P. , and A. Louis. "La Politesse bédouine dans les campagnes du nord de la Tunisie: le mariage (préliminaires, les démarches, le contrat). " IBLA, 67 (1954), 251-68.

2706 _____, and _____. "La Politesse bédouine dans les campagnes du nord de la Tunisie: le mariage, la

semaine de noces." IBLA, 69 (1955), 93-126. Includes Arabic sayings on marriage with French translation.

2707   Etienne, B.   "Colloque sur la participation de la femme
       rurale au développement économique et social."
       Annuaire de l'Afrique du Nord, 1968, 831-34.

2708   "Femmes du Cap Bon." Femme, 2 (Jan.-March 1965), 7-
       9.

2709   Jouin, Jeanne.   "Le Tarf des kerkéniennes." Revue des
       Etudes Islamiques, 1948, 51-53.   Illustrated article on
       women's attire in Kerkennah Islands.

2710   Louis, A. "M. M. Sironval: La formation et la fonction
       de la monitrice rurale dans le cadre de l'école de la
       Soukra (Tunisie)." IBLA, 127 (1971), 196-98.   Review
       of a memoir written for a degree in politics and social
       science at Louvain University.

2711/2 Mzali, Fathia.   "Interview de la nouvelle présidente de
       l'Union Nationale des Femmes de Tunisie." L'Action,
       June 9, 1973.

2713   "La Participation de la femme rurale au développement
       économique et social." Rencontres et Documents, 11
       (1968).

2714   "The Rural Centers for Women" (in Arabic). al-Mar'ah,
       62 (Sept. 1967), 16-20.

2715   Shwiti, 'Ali.   "The Rural Girl" (in Arabic).   Mir'at al-
       Sahil, 2 (July 1966), 41.

2716   Simmons, John Leary, ed.   Village and Family; Essays on
       Rural Tunisia.   New Haven, Conn.: Human Relations
       Area Files, 1974.

2717   Sironval, M. M.   "La Formation et la fonction de la moni-
       trice rurale dans le cadre de l'école de la Soukra
       (Tunisie)." Mémoire de licence en Sciences Politiques
       et Sociales, Louvain University, 1970.

2718   Slim, Rafi'ah.   "Woman and Work" (in Arabic). Mir'at al-
       Sahil, 2 (July 1966), 39-40, 64.

2719   _____.   "Women's Corner" (in Arabic). Mir'at al-Sahil,
       3 (Oct. 1966), 29-30.

(4) MARRIAGE AND THE FAMILY

General

2720 Bayram, Muhammad. "Les Cérémonies du mariage en
Tunisie" (in Arabic). In Safwat al-i'tibar bi-mustawda
al-amsar wa-al-aqtar. Bulaq: n.p., 1311 A.H. (1894).

2721 Bayram, Alia. "La Naissance à Tunis dans les milieux de
la bourgeoisie traditionnelle." Cahiers des Arts et
Traditions Populaires, 4 (1971), 7-16.

2722 Belgaid-Hassine, Nourredine. "Point de vue sur la famille
tunisienne actuelle." Revue Tunisienne de Sciences
Sociales, 9-11 (1967).

2723 Ben Ali, Abd el-Jalil. "La Femme musulmane du Sahel
est-elle educatrice?" IBLA, 1 (April 1937), 7-17.

2724 Ben Belgacem, Noureddine; Kamal Eddine Bensalem; and
Abdesselam Kharouf. "Youth and Marriage" (in Arabic).
al-Shabab, 1 (Jan.-March 1971), 2-9.

2725 Ben Brahem, Josette. "La Jeune Tunisienne et le mariage."
Jeune Afrique, 120 (Feb. 4, 1963), 25-27.

2726 Ben Cheikh, A. "Tableau de notre vie familiale." IBLA,
2 (1959), 179-91.

2727 Ben Tahar, Sadok. "Woman and Family" (in Arabic).
Mir'at al-Sahil, 22 (July 1971), 30-31.

2728 Blaiech, Khadija. "Pourquoi les jeunes cadres tunisiens
hésitent entre Gabès et Venise pour leur voyage de
noces." France-Eurafrique, 211 (Nov. 1969), 14-17.

2729 Borrmans, Maurice. "Bibliographie succincte sur la
famille tunisienne." IBLA, 118-119 (1967), 279-90.

2730 _____. "Contribution à l'étude des mentalités sur la
famille: ce qu'en pensent de jeunes sahariens." Revue
de l'Occident Musulman et de la Méditerranée, 5 (1968),
15-41.

2731 Bouhdiba, Abdelwahab. "Point de vue sur la famille tunisienne actuelle." Revue Tunisienne de Sciences Sociales, 11 (Oct. 1967), 11-20.

2732 Bourguiba, Habib. "Une Priorité nationale: la réhabilita-
tion de la femme et du mariage." ESNA, 671 (1966).

2733 _____. "Une Question d'une grande gravité: l'épreuve
du sang." Faïza, 48 (1965), 8-9. Text of President

Bourguiba's speech of August 13, 1965, one of his most outspoken speeches in favor of women's rights.

2734   "Bourguiba et le marriage." <u>Revue de Presse</u>, 98 (Sept. - Oct. 1965).

2735   Bouzid, Dorra. "L'Aberrante Saison des mariages ruineux." Faïza, 60 (Oct. 1967), 10-11. Although half the population lives on less than 50 dinars a year, a wedding hall is currently rented for 500 dinars an evening.

2736   Camilleri, Carmel. "Etudes sur l'intégration familiale du jeune Tunisien cultivé." <u>Cahiers de Tunisie</u>, 33/35 (1961), 7-96.

2737   _____. "La Femme tunisienne: représentation du statut et des rôles familiaux." <u>Revue Francaise de Sociologie</u>, 3 (July-Sept. 1964), 307-324.

2738   _____. Jeunesse, famille et développement; Essai sur le changement socio-culturel dans un pays du Tiers-Monde (Tunisie). Paris: Editions du Centre National de la Recherche Scientifique, 1973.

2739   _____. "Modernity and the Family in Tunisia." <u>Journal of Marriage and Family</u>, 1967, 590-95.

2740   Cherif, S. "Le Rôle de la musulmane tunisienne dans l'inadaptation sociale de l'enfant." Bulletin d'Information. <u>Société Tunisienne de Psychologie</u>, 3 (1973), 10-14.

2741   "Croyances et coutumes féminines à propos de la première enfance." <u>IBLA</u>, 2 (1937), 36-43.

2742   Demeerseman, André. "L'Evolution de la famille tunisienne." <u>IBLA</u>, 42 (1948), 105-140.

2743   _____. La Famille tunisienne et les temps nouveaux; Essai de psychologie sociale. Tunis: Maison tunisienne de l'édition, 1972.

2744   _____. "La Famille tunisienne: rencontre de générations." <u>IBLA</u>, 118-119 (1967), 175-90.

2745   _____, and P. C. C. "Histoire vécue: les péripéties du mariage d'un vieux Kroumir." <u>IBLA</u>, 3 (1938), 29-33.

2746   Farida. "La Famille bourgeoise tunisienne: l'autorité paternelle vue par une jeune fille." <u>IBLA</u>, 1 (1939), 65-73.

2747   Hachaichi, Fatma. "La Fille-mère: problèmes démographi-

ques et juridiques. " Paper delivered at the Neuvième
Congrès de l'Institut International de Droit d'Expression
Française, Tunis, May 27-June 2, 1974. The author
practices law in Tunis.

2748   al-Haddad, al-Tahir. "Figures of Our Life at Home" (in
        Arabic). al-Sawab, Aug. 3, 1928.

2749   _____. "The Victims of Desire in Marriage" (in Arabic).
        al-Sawab, July 20, 1928. One of the very polemical
        articles of the author in which he denounces the callous
        attitude of some parents who marry their daughters
        only to suit their own interest.

2750   Hotte, Yannick. "La Femme tunisienne dans son rôle de
        mère de famille. " Culture, 2 (Winter 1970), 6-12.

2751   "Les Jeunes tunisiens et les problèmes de leur mariage. "
        Documents Nord-Africains, 556 (March 24, 1964), 1-8.

2752   Jonker, C. "Exploration anthropologique pour une étude du
        ménage familial en Kroumirie. " Cahiers des Arts et
        Traditions Populaires, 4 (1971), 55-84.

2753   Khelladi, A. "Les Questions de dot et de trousseau dans
        les mariages musulmans. " IBLA, 3-4 (1939), 319-322.

2754   Louis, A. , and M. M. Sironval. "Le Mariage traditionnel
        en milieu berbère dans le sud de la Tunisie. " Revue
        de l'Occident Musulman et de la Méditerranée, 12 (1972).

2755   Mahmoud ben Naceur. "Le Mariage chez les citadins en
        Tunisie. " IBLA, 3-4 (1939), 311-319.

2756   _____. "Notes sur le mariage musulman. " IBLA, 2
        (1939), 168-174.

2757   Mansour, Ali. "Pour se marier chez nous, il faut des
        rubis, un frigo et une villa. " Faïza, June 1961, 7.
        A young man bitterly denounces the prejudices which
        turn a prospective bride into merchandise in the hands
        of her parents and calls for the suppression of dowries.

2758   Menouillard, H. "Un Marriage dans le sud tunisien. "
        Revue Tunisienne, 9 (1902).

2759   _____. "Moeurs indigènes: comment se fait un mariage
        à Gafsa. " Revue Tunisienne, 1911, 480-87.

2760   Montéty, Henri de. Le mariage musulman en Tunisie.
        Paris and Tunis: Editions S.A.P.I. , 1941.

2761   _____. "Mutation des moeurs familiales en Tunisie. "

Etudes Sociales Nord-Africaines, 77 (1960), 18-27.

2762   al-Mukhtar ibn Mahmud, Muhammad. "The Problem of the
       High Dowry" (in Arabic). al-Majallah al-zaytuniyah, 9
       (1941), 2-5.

2763   Mzali, M. S. "Deux Usages indigènes relatifs à l'accouche-
       ment et au divorce." Revue Tunisienne, 1918, 222-25.

2764   "On se marie pour les autres." Faïza, 57 (May-June 1967),
       56-62, 90.

2765   Renon, A. "Affection maternelle." IBLA, 33 (1946), 87-
       90.

2766   _____. "Le Mariage dans le bled: le 'çedaq' ou con-
       trat." IBLA, 3 (1941), 343-48.

2767   Robert, J. "Le Mariage aux Iles Kerkennah." IBLA, 38
       (1947), 135-66. Notes on wedding ceremonies in the
       village of Remla.

2768   S. M. "Le Mariage musulman en Tunisie." IBLA, Jan.
       1942, 93-99. Review of Henri de Montety's book.

2769   Sethom, Samira. "La Tunique de mariage en Tunisie."
       Cahiers des Arts et Traditions Populaires, 3 (1969), 5-
       20.

2770   Sraïeb, Nourredine. "L'Enfant et la relation mère-enfant.
       Un example de pays musulman: la Tunisie." Les
       Carnets de l'Enfance, 10 (June 1969), 130-46.

2771   _____. "Mutations socio-économiques de la famille en
       Tunisie." Revue Algérienne des Sciences Juridiques,
       Economiques et Politiques, 53 (1974), 127-132.

2772   Sugier, C. "Les Bijoux de la mariée à Moknine." Cahiers
       des Arts et Traditions Populaires, 1 (1968), 139-156.

2773   "To Mothers" (in Arabic). al-Sha'b, 87 (Aug. 16, 1967),
       78-79.

2774   "Tunisia: Family Split." The Economist, 6494 (Feb. 10,
       1968), 25.

Family Law

2775   "L'Acte de mariage et le délit de polygamie en Tunisie."
       Die Welt des Islams, 1-2 (1959-61), 130-36.

2776   al-Annabi, Ahmed. "Le Rôle de la magistrature dans la

221   Marriage and Family

réforme de la famille (en Tunisie)." Oriente Moderno, 6-8 (July-Aug. 1971), 631-49. Translation, with notes, of a speech given in 1968.

2777 Borrmans, Maurice. "Codes de statut personnel et évolution sociale." IBLA, 103 (1963), 205-59.

2778 _____. "Le Droit de garde (hadana) et son évolution récente en Tunisie." IBLA, 118-119 (1967), 191-226.

2779 Bouzaiane, B., and A. Zghal. "La Protection sociale et les besoins sociaux des familles." Revue Tunisienne de Sciences Sociales, 28-29 (1972), 203-36.

2780 Charfi, Mohamed. "Le Droit tunisien de la famille entre l'Islam et la modernité." Revue Tunisienne de Droit, 1973, 11-38.

2781 "La Condition de la femme tunisienne à travers la législature sociale." Le Petit Matin, Oct. 29, 1963, 2. List of decrees with notes.

2782 "Edict to Limit the Dowry and the Trousseau" (in Arabic). al-Majallah al-zaytuniyah, 9 (June 1941), 1. Beylical edict setting limits of 3,000 Frs to the dowry and 20,000 Frs to the trousseau, and threatening confiscation in favor of Habous administration should these amounts be exceeded.

2783 Hasan, Zaynab. "Revolution in Personal Status" (in Arabic). al-Musawwar, July 11, 1975, 46-48. About legal reforms in Tunisia and other Muslim countries.

2784 "Le Législateur se voile la face." Ferida, 1 (May 1975), 4. The Tunisian woman is still discriminated against in child custody, mixed marriages and inheritance.

2785 Mabrouk, M. "La Femme en droit public tunisien." Revue de Presse, 186 (June-July 1974).

2786 Pritsch, E. "Das tunesische Personenstandsgesetz." Die Welt des Islams, 3-4 (1958), 188-205.

2787 Pruvost, L. "La Dot dans le Code du Statut Personnel." IBLA, 126 (1970), 265-82.

2788 _____. "L'Enfant abandonné: bilan de législation tunisienne." IBLA, 131 (1973), 141-49.

2789 _____. "Promotion de la femme et législation." IBLA, 122 (1968), 347-53.

2790   al-Sanusi, M. T.   Code du Statut Personnel annoté.   Tunis:
       S. T. A. G. , 1970.

Divorce

2791   al-'Annabi, Tayib.   "Le Divorce dans la loi et la société. "
       IBLA, 118-119 (1967), 273-78.

2792   _____.   "Divorce in Law and Society" (in Arabic).   al-
       Qada´ wa-al-Tashri', 2 (1967), 7-17.

2793   Benattar, R.   "L'Evolution récente du droit international
       privé tunisien en matière de divorce. "   Revue Critique
       de Droit International Privé, 1 (Jan. -March 1969), 17-52.

2794   Borrmans, Maurice.   "A propos de l'article 3 du Code du
       Statut Personnel: divorce et abus du droit en Tunisie. "
       IBLA, 118-119 (1967), 227-72.

2795   _____.   "Deux Etudes sur le divorce en Tunisie. "   IBLA,
       122 (1968), 255-94.

2796   Les Divorces en Tunisie, 1964, 1965, 1966.   Tunis: Sec-
       rétariat d'Etat au Plan et au Financement de Tunisie.

2797   Gaudin de Lagrange, E. de.   "Causes de divorce en Tu-
       nisie. "   Revue Algérienne des Sciences Juridiques,
       Economiques et Politiques, 4 (Dec. 1968), 1109-1115.

Mixed Marriages

2798   Ben Brahem, J.   "Un Mariage mixte de plus. "   Faïza,
       June 1961, 23-24.   Part of a lengthy polemic on mixed
       marriages.   The financial demands of Tunisian families
       are mentioned as a possible cause of marriages to
       foreign women.

2799   "Déclaration de Mme R. Haddad au journal La Presse qui
       enquêtait sur les mariages mixtes. "   Annuaire de
       l'Afrique du Nord, 1963, 899-901.   Includes the reprint
       of an article published in La Presse of January 9,
       1963, p. 3 under the title: "Marriage with Foreigners
       Is Always a Failure. "

2800   Fenniche, N.   "Attitudes des jeunes parents tunisois de 20
       à 30 ans devant le mariage mixte. "   Revue Tunisienne
       de Sciences Sociales, June 1965, 45-56.

2801   Freund, W. S.   "Le Mariage de la musulmane avec le non-
       musulman. "   Dialogue, 11 (1974), 6-7.

2802   Jay, Bernard. "Les Familles mixtes en Tunisie; Etude
        descriptive. " Unpublished Ph.D. dissertation, Faculté
        de Théologie Protestante, Strasbourg, 1963.

2803   Mabrouk, Mohieddine. "Le Mariage de la musulmane avec
        le non-musulman. " Dialogue, 7 (1974), 22-23.

2804   "Les Mariages mixtes en Tunisie. " Confluent, 35 (Nov.
        1963), 855-78.

2805   Scémama, André. De l'influence du mariage sur la na-
        tionalité tunisienne. Paris: Librairie Générale de Droit
        et de Jurisprudence, 1931.

Family Planning

2806   A. S. "La Prévention des naissances en Tunisie. " Popu-
        lation, 4 (1966), 792-95.

2807   Bchir, M. "Structure par âge et planning familial:
        l'exemple de la population de Tunis. " Revue Tunisienne
        de Sciences Sociales, 17-18 (June-Sept. 1969), 365-378.

2808   Behar, L. "Population féminine, femmes mariées en âge
        de reproduction. Taux de protection par le planning
        familial en Tunisie au 1er janvier 1974 selon le nouveau
        découpage administratif. " Bulletin, O. N. P. F. P. , 4
        (1974).

2809   Bourguiba, Habib. "Promotion de la femme et croissance
        démographique. " L'Action, Aug. 14, 1966.

2810   _____. "Woman's Promotion and Demographic Growth"
        (in Arabic). al-Mar'ah, Sept. 1966, 6-13.

2811   "Connaissance et pratique du planning familial à Tunis. "
        Revue Tunisienne de Sciences Sociales, July, 1970, 9-
        92.

2812   "Le Contrôle des naissances: Tunisie. " Revue de Presse,
        79 (1963).

2813   Daly, Amor. "Premières Expériences de planning familial
        en Tunisie. " Afrika, 39 (1966), 23-27, 81.

2814   _____. "Tunisia: The Liberation of Women and the
        Improvement of Society. " In Berelson, Bernard.
        Family Planning Programs: An International Survey.
        New York: Basic Books, 1969.

2815   Gallagher, C. "Family Planning in Tunisia. " AUFS Re-
        ports Service North African Series, 2 (1966), 1-13.

2816   Girard, A.   "Pour une observation en Tunisie des attitudes
       à l'égard du changement. " Revue Tunisienne de Sciences
       Sociales, Feb. 1966, 95-103.

2817   Girard, J.   "Le Planning familial: l'expérience tunisienne. "
       Sciences et Vie, March 1966, 52-59.

2818   Guérin, A.   "Scoubidou et sous-développement. " Temps
       Modernes, 258 (Nov. 1967), 877-90.

2819   al-Halqah al-Iqlimiyah al-Maydaniyah li-Rabt al-Thaqafah al-
       Sukkaniyah wa-Tanzim al-Usrah bi-Mahw al-Ummiyah
       al-Wazifi.   Alphabétisation fonctionnelle composante
       d'un programme de planning familial; rapport du sé-
       minaire opérationnel régional, Tunisie, Nabeul, 4-24
       septembre 1972.   Sirs al-Laiyana: UNESCO-ASFEC,
       1973.

2820   Heeren, H.   "Het Geboortebeperkingsbeleid in Tunisie. "
       International Spectator, 20 (1967), 1642-51.

2821   "J'ai adopté le scoubidou: film vécu en seize tableaux
       miracle. " Faïza, 51 (1966), 32-33.   A comic strip
       underlining the advantages of birth control.

2822   Lapham, R.   "Family Planning and Fertility in Tunisia. "
       Demography, 2 (1970), 241-53.

2823   M. H.   "Planning familial en Tunisie. " Confluent, March
       1964, 298-99.

2824   Magnin, J. G.   "Le Contrôle des naissances. " IBLA, 109
       (1965), 96-99.

2825   _____.   "La Limitation des naissances. " IBLA, 91
       (1960), 327-31.

2826   "Le Planning familial. " Progrès Social, Aug. 1964.

2827   Pompéi, S.   "La Prévention des naissances en Tunisie. "
       Population, 4 (1966), 795.

2828   Sahli, S.   "Les Contraceptrices de l'hôpital Habib Thameur:
       étude des caractéristiques socio-économiques et démo-
       graphiques. " Revue Tunisienne des Sciences Sociales,
       28-29 (1972), 237-60.

2829   Seklani, Mahmoud.   "La Famille tunisienne au seuil de la
       contraception: état actuel et transition possible. "
       Revue Tunisienne des Sciences Sociales, 4 (Oct. 1967),
       53-71.

2830   _____.   "La Prévention des naissances en Tunisie;

Planning familial et avortement. " Confluent, 50-52
(1965), 332-38.

2831 _____ ; M. Rouissi; and M. Bchir. "La Fécondité des
ménages à Tunis: résultats de trois enquêtes socio-
démographiques. " Séries Démographiques, 3 (1969).

2832 "Sur le planning familial. " Faïza, 51 (1966), 22-37.

2833 Vallin, J. "Limitation des naissances en Tunisie; efforts
et résultats. " Population, 2 (March 1971), 181-204.

2834 _____ . "Planning familial et perspectives de population
en Tunisie, 1966-1975. " Revue Tunisienne des Sciences
Sociales, Jan. 1968, 71-88.

2835 Zouari, Ali. "La Naissance à Sfax dans la société traditionnelle. " Cahiers des Arts et Traditions Populaires,
4 (1971), 17-27.

(5) EDUCATION AND SPORTS

2836 "At the Home of the Female Students" (in Arabic). al-
Sha'b, 82 (June 1, 1967), 45-49.

2837 Badday, Safia. "Le Sport féminin en Tunisie. " Faïza, 41
(1964), 30-33; 42 (1964), 24-27; 43 (1964), 24-27.

2838 Ballet, J. "Couture: (Pages rurales). " IBLA, 43-44
(1948), 373-76.

2839 _____ . "Tissu et éducation féminine. " IBLA, 40 (1947),
437-41. A plea for the revival of weaving in Tunisia,
and the availability of sewing and knitting lessons to
women.

2840 Bel Khodja, Mohamed. "La Femme arabe et l'instruction. "
Revue Tunisienne, April 1896.

2841 Ben Mustafa, Rachid. "La Femme et l'instruction. " La
Renaissance Nord-Africaine, 19--, 124-27. Translation
of his article in al-Sawab, advocating female instruction
as a religious duty.

2842 Ben Sedrine, M. "Milieu socio-familial et orientation sco-
laire; enquête dans un lycée de Tunis. " IBLA, 126
(1970), 297-304.

2843 Çadiqa. "Education et assistance. (Questions féminines.)"
IBLA, April 1942, 194-98.

2844 Cherif, Hafsia. "Woman's Education" (in Arabic). al-'Amal, May 1, 1957.

2845 Eigenschenck, Madame. "L'Ecole Louise René-Millet de Tunis." Le Monde Colonial Illustré, 84 (Aug. 1930), 198. Madame Eigenschenck speaks about the school of which she has been the head for 12 years.

2846 "Enseignement féminin en Tunisie." Revue de Presse, 101 (Jan. 1966).

2847 "L'Enseignement féminin en Tunisie." Ferida, 1 (May 1975), 34-35. Despite the official push for change, traditions are still an obstacle to female education.

2848 "Essai d'ouvroir pour fillettes ... (Expérience rurale.)" IBLA, 67 (1954), 269-72.

2849 al-Fani, Ahmad. "Mademoiselle, enseigner n'est pas un métier ingrat." Faïza, 22 (Feb. 1962), 20-23. The head of the Technical Education Division tries to convince young Tunisian women that teaching is the social vocation of woman, "all little girls play to be mummy, nurse or teacher...."

2850 al-Haddad, al-Tahir. "How to Educate the Little Girl in Order for Her to Become Wife, Then Mother" (in Arabic). al-Sawab, Aug. 17, 1928, Aug. 31, 1928, Sept. 14, 1928, Oct. 19, 1928. These articles were later incorporated in the very controversial book, Imra´tuna fi al-shari'ah wa-al-mujtama'.

2851 El-Hamamsy, Laila Shukry. "Assessment of UNICEF Assisted Projects for the Preparation and Training of Women and Girls for Community Development in Tunisia." UNICEF Document, Aug. 1969.

2852 Hergam, Ahmed. "Our Coeds in France" (in Arabic). al-Sha'b, 98 (Feb. 1, 1968), 16-22.

2853 "In America Seven Young Tunisian Women Teach and Learn" (in Arabic). al-Sha'b, 76 (March 1, 1967), 21.

2854 "L'Initiative des petites tunisiennes à l'école." IBLA, 3 (July 1941), 442-44.

2855 "L'Institutrice tunisienne." Femme, Feb. 15, 1969, 26-29, 69-72.

2856 "L'Intellectuelle tunisienne." Faïza, 39 (1964), 16.

2857 Ladislas, S. M. "Réflexions sur l'éducation féminine tunisienne." IBLA, 56 (1951), 417-32.

227 Education and Sports

2858 Liman, D. "L'Education de la femme en Tunisie: son évolution." Convergences, 2 (1969), 70-72.

2859 al-Mabruk, Munjiyah. "To Free Woman of Her Tasks to Educate Her Children." Mar'ah, 57 (Jan. 1967), 13-17.

2860 Magnin, J. "A propos de l'éducation de la fillette tunisienne: (Questions féminines.)" IBLA, July 1942, 298-313.

2861 _____. "Au service de l'enfance abandonnée. I. Les Villages d'enfants. II. Foyers d'éducation de jeunes filles." IBLA, 76 (1956), 387-414.

2862 Mzali, Fathia. "Qu'est-ce que l'intellectuelle tunisienne?" Faïza, 39 (1964), 16-17.

2863 Mzali, Mohamed. L'Education et la famille. Tunis: n.p., 1970.

2864 "Opinions on the Instruction of Women" (in Arabic). al-Hadirah, March 12, 1901. Against the concept of equality between sexes as advocated by Qasim Amin.

2865 "The Points of View of the Youth About Coeducation" (in Arabic). al-Sha'b, 79 (April 16, 1967), 48-50; 80 (May 1, 1967), 48-49.

2866 "Problems of the Female Student. Talk With a Coed from the University" (in Arabic). al-Sha'b, 106 (June 1, 1968), 18-19.

2867 Sahli, 'Abd al-'Aziz. "Sexuality and Education" (in Arabic). al-Shabab, 7 (Oct. 1967), 38-39.

2868 Thibert, Marguerite. Rapport au gouvernement de la Tunisie sur la préparation professionnelle des jeunes filles en Tunisie. Geneva: UNICEF, 1966.

2869 "The Tunisian Young Woman Faces Superior Education" (in Arabic). al-Idha'ah wa-al-talfazah, 203 (March 1, 1968), 14-18.

2870 "La Tunisienne et l'enseignement." Faïza, 21 (Jan. 1962), 18-21.

2871 Turkia, Rauni. "Adult Education for Tunisian Women." International Journal of Adult and Youth Education, 3, 120-24.

2872 Wartani, 'Abd al-Rahman al-Makki. "Youth and Coeducation" (in Arabic). al-Shabab, 9-10 (Dec. 1967), 30-31.

2873   "Women and Instruction. " al-Hadirah, Sept. 9, 1889. One
        of the main Tunisian newspapers declares in its editori-
        al that female education is fard, i. e. compulsory.

(6) LITERARY WORKS BY OR ABOUT WOMEN

2874   Abdelaziz, Souad. "Our Literature Between Quality and
        Quantity" (in Arabic). al-'Amal, Oct. 18, 1957. The
        problems of feminine literature in Tunisia: many
        poorly-written books and a few well-written ones.

2875   Azouz, Hind. Fi al-darb al-tawil. Tunis: Maison Tunisi-
        enne de l'Edition, 1969.

2876   Bechir, Zoubeida. Hanin. Tunis: Maison Tunisienne de
        l'Edition, 1968. The first book published by a female
        Tunisian poet, whose style was praised, but private life
        violently criticized.

2877   Ben Bachir, Fatima. "Un Foulard pour Sidi Amor. " Jeune
        Afrique, Dec. 20, 1961.

2878   Ben Said, Nefissa. "Les Amants de la Marsa. " Faïza,
        Dec. 1961, 20, 44-45.

2879   _____. "Le Bouquet de fleurs de thé. " Faïza, July-
        Aug. 1962, 34, 71.

2880   Bin Mami, Layla. Sawma'ah tahtariq. Tunis: n. p. , 1968.
        Nineteen short stories by a rebellious young woman who
        wants to be free and see traditions burned; hence the
        title: minaret ablaze.

2881   Borrmans, M. "Talents féminins. " IBLA, 111 (1955), 291-
        92.

2882   Boutarfa, Salah ed-Dine. "Le Voile. " IBLA, 104 (1963),
        297-321.

2883   Braham, Habib. "The Evil of the Parrot" (in Arabic). al-
        Fikr, Feb. 1964. A short story about two young people
        who cannot get married because of the social ambitions
        of the parents of the girl.

2884   Bughdir, Tawfiq. "Futilities" (in Arabic). Usbu', 4 (Jan.
        14, 1947). A short story about a May-December mar-
        riage.

2885   Butakin, Rafi'ah. "The Art of the Playwright Is Not a
        Man's Preserve" (in Arabic). al-Idha'ah wa-al-talfazah,
        290 (April 15, 1972), 23.

229 Literary Works

2886 Chtioui, Khadija. "al-Hadhba'." IBLA, 111 (1965), 311-19.

2887 Damdoune, Salem. "A Country Woman" (in Arabic). al-Fikr, 12:9, 15. The tribulations of a Bedouin woman who, left alone after the deaths of her brother and her father, has to look for work in town.

2888 Drower, Ethel Stefana (Stevens), Lady. The Veil; A Romance of Tunis. New York: F. A. Stokes Co., 1909.

2889 Ennouri, Beya. "S'il n'y avait pas eu le couffin...." IBLA, 111 (1955), 293-307.

2890 "Femme et littérature." al-Amal, Aug. 18, 1967.

2891 Fontaine, Jean. "Situation de la femme écrivain en Tunisie." Les Cahiers de Tunisie, 79-80 (1972), 285-307.

2892 _____. "Situation de la femme écrivain en Tunisie." Zeitschrift der Deutschen Morgenlandischen Gesellschaft, 2 (1974), 285-308.

2893 Géniaux, Claire, and Charles Géniaux. "Les Oiseaux s'envolent." Le Monde Colonial Illustré, 8 (May 1924), 186-88. Points out that economic necessity is prompting the Tunisian woman to go out and work.

2894 "Hind Azouz ..." (Presentation and translation by Jean Fontaine). IBLA, 131 (1973), 133-39. Bibliographical note and translation of a short story by Hind Azouz.

2895 Jabri, Salah. "Feminine Literature in Tunisia" (in Arabic). al-'Amal, Aug. 18, 1967.

2896 Lorimer, Norma. By the Waters of Carthage. New York: James Pott & Co., 1906.

2897 al-Majari, Jamilah. "Letter From Tunis: Woman and the Written Word" (in Arabic). al-Bayt, 5 (May 20, 1973), 10-11.

2898 _____. "Woman and Literature in Tunisia" (in Arabic). Sada al-mu'tamar, 3 (March 1973).

2899 "Marcelle Segal et Dorra Bouzid: les courriers du coeur européen et maghrébin." Faïza, 41 (1964). How the Tunisian journalist advises her young readers, encouraging them to study, have a career, be independent and exert their rights.

2900 Memmi, Albert. Agar. Paris: Buchet-Chastel, 1955.

2901 Memmou, Ahmed. "The Feminine Literature From the

Magazine Qisas" (in Arabic). Qisas, July 2, 1971, 53-
70; July 24, 1972, 14-47.

2902 "Najia Thameur ..." (presentation and translation by Jean
Fontaine). IBLA, 131 (1973), 125-131. Short bibliographical note and translation of a short story of Najia
Thameur who writes dramatic texts for the Tunisian
radio.

2903 Nasr, Abdelkader. "The Other Caravan" (in Arabic). al-
Idha'ah wa-al-talfazah, 268 (April 1, 1971), 16. About
women writers in Tunisia.

2904 Quwayri, 'Abd Allah. "A Wife from Masrata" (in Arabic).
Qisas, 4, 28-32. The monologue of a young Libyan
man living in Tunisia, torn between his desire to marry
his beloved or the illiterate cousin chosen by his
parents.

2905 Saydaoui, Jawad. "Le Safsari" (in Arabic). al-Fikr, 1960.
A short story about the disappearance of the veil.

2906 Shabbi, Fadhilah. Rawa'ih al-ard wa-al-ghadab. Beirut:
al-Mu'assasah al-'arabiyah lil-dirasat wa-al-nashr,
1973. A short book of poetry by a Tunisian secondary
school teacher.

2907 Skandrani, Fatma. "Une Jeune Fille est comme une fleur."
Faïza, Jan. 1962, 22-25.

2908 Slim, Fatma. Nida' al-mustaqbal. Tunis: Dar al-kutub
al-sharqiyah, 1972.

2909 Suheil, Farida. "Dalila." Faïza, Oct.-Nov. 1960, 9, 22,
47.

2910 Thamir, Najiyah. Aradna al-hayat. Tunis: Dar al-kutub
al-sharqiyah, n.d. Fourteen short stories extolling the
courage of the defenders of Bizerte.

2911 _____. al-Mar'ah wa-al-hayah. Tunis: Kitab al-ba'th,
1956.

2912 _____. Qisas wa-tamtiliyat. Tunis: Librarie Orientale,
1956.

2913 _____. Samar wa-'ibar. Tunis: Dar al-kutub al
sharqiyah, 1972.

2914 _____. "Sawt al-'anadil." al-Fikr, 9 (June 1961), 71-
74.

(7) THE WORKING WOMAN

2915   A. C. "Un Problème: le travail féminin." Le Courrier
       Financier de Tunisie, 786 (June 21, 1967), 1.

2916   al-Amri, Zohra. "La Femme et l'emploi." Faïza, 54
       (Nov. -Dec. 1966), 54-55.

2917   Attia, Halima. "Le Statut de la femme tunisienne au tra-
       vail." Revue de Presse, 191 (Jan. 1975).

2918   Belgaid-Hassine, Noureddine. "Motivation de la femme tu-
       nisienne au travail." Revue Tunisienne de Sciences So-
       ciales, 11 (Oct. 1967), 85-95.

2919   Belhassen, Souhayr. "Ah! Ce passeport qui résout tous
       les problèmes." Jeune Afrique, 773 (Oct. 31, 1975),
       52-53. Interview of a young Tunisian seamstress who
       expresses her frustrations at home and at work.

2920   Ben Salem, Lilia. "Femme au travail: le C. O. D. S. U. P. "
       Femme, 2 (Jan. -March 1965), 24-27.

2921   Bin-Mami, Layla. "The Young Woman at Work: The
       Young Woman and Public Function" (in Arabic). al-
       Shabab, 2 (Feb. 1966), 35.

2922   _____. "The Young Woman at Work: With Our Students
       in Their City" (in Arabic). al-Shabab, 1 (Jan. 1966),
       41-45, 83.

2923   "Bourguiba: What Is Important Is That Woman Work, In-
       side or Outside the House" (in Arabic). al-Ahram,
       Aug. 27, 1976, p. 7, col. 3.

2924   Camilleri, C. "Statut et rôles familiaux de la femme:
       leur représentation dans des groupes de jeunes tra-
       vailleuses tunisiennes." Revue Française de Sociologie,
       3 (July-Sept. 1964), 307-34.

2925   "L'Emploi féminin en Tunisie." Femme, 2 (Jan. -March
       1965), 20-21.

2926   La Femme tunisienne et l'emploi; colloque du 8 au 11
       novembre 1966. Tunis: Institut Ali Bach Hamba, 1967.

2927   "Femme tunisienne et travail." La Presse, March 18, 1966.

2928   Ferial. "Préparer la femme au travail." Faïza, 54 (Nov. -
       Dec. 1966), 56-57, 81.

2929   "Le Foyer ou le travail? Des tunisiennes répondent."

Jeune Afrique, 315 (Jan. 1967), 66-68. The results of an inquiry by sociologist Arlie Hoschschild.

2930 Golvin, L., and A. Louis. "Les Tisseuses de la région sfaxienne: traditions et chants." IBLA, 47 (1949), 237-62. An article which mentions many interesting customs as well as the texts of various folk songs in Arabic with French translation.

2931 Gwénolé, M. "Femme et travail." IBLA, 95-96 (1961), 301-308.

2932 Haddad, Fatma. "L'Intégration de la femme tunisienne à la vie active." Tunis: n.p., n.d.

2933 _____. "Le Travail de la femme accroît la production économique de la Tunisie." La Presse, Nov. 18, 1966, 7.

2934 Hafsia, Nazli. "La Prostitution, un des coûts de développement d'un pays sous-développé." Thèse de troisième cycle, Tours University.

2935 Harcha, Monique. "Les Travailleuses sociales en Tunisie." IBLA, 101 (1963), 55-61.

2936 Henablia, Zohra. "La Travaillite." Faïza, 40 (1964), 34-35, 42 (1964), 22-23. A woman is respected in her family only if she is financially independent through her career.

2937 Hochschild, Arlie. "Le Travail des femmes dans une Tunisie en voie de modernisation." Revue Tunisienne de Sciences Sociales, 9 (March 1967), 145-66.

2938 _____. "Women At Work At Modernizing Tunisia." Berkeley Journal of Sociology, 11 (1966), 32-53.

2939 International Labor Office. Rapport au gouvernement de la Tunisie sur la préparation professionnelle des jeunes filles et des femmes en Tunisie. Geneva, 1966.

2940 Mercury, Thérèse. "La Femme tunisienne au travail en usine, aspects psychologiques et sociologiques." Thèse de troisième cycle, Aix-en-Provence, 1969.

2941 Nassif, Hind. "The Professional Role of Women in Tunisia." Paper delivered at the Conference on Development in the Arab World, New York, Oct. 1-3, 1976.

2942 _____. "Women's Professional Roles in a Developing Culture: The Case of Tunisia." Paper delivered at the 10th Annual Meeting of the Middle East Studies

Association, Los Angeles, Nov. 10-13, 1976.

2943 "Le Point de vue du Ministre." Faïza, 53 (1966), 28-30.
Interview with Mondher Ben Ammar, State Secretary to
Social Affairs, Youth and Sports, about the professional
chances of the Tunisian women.

2944 Pruvost, Lucie. La Prostitution des mineurs en Tunisie.
Tunis: Faculté de Droit, 1973.

2945 Renon, A., and Ph. Noël. L'Embauche agricole. Tunis:
Le Bled, 1946.

2946 Rushdi, Inji. "New Experience for the Tunisian Women:
How They Managed to Become One Quarter of the Labor
Force" (in Arabic). al-Ahram, Sept. 2, 1974, p. 5,
col. 2.

2947 Thibert, Marguerite. "La Femme tunisienne et l'emploi."
Femme, 8 (1966), 12-19; Nov. 1966-Jan. 1967, 12-19.

2948 "Travail féminin face à l'opinion publique." L'Action, Nov.
19 and 26, 1967, Dec. 2, 8, and 16, 1967.

2949 "La Travaillite." Faïza, 25 (May 1962), 36-37.

2950 "The Tunisian Woman in the Theater" (in Arabic). al-
Sha'b, 115 (Nov. 16, 1968), 47-51.

(8) WOMEN'S CONGRESSES; FEMINISM AND POLITICS

2951 Attia Abul Naga, S. "L'Emancipation de la femme en Tunisie." UN Special, Feb. 1964, 9-13.

2952 Ben Amar, Aïcha. "The Tunisian Woman at the Crossroad"
(in Arabic). al-Thurayah, 8-11 (Aug.-Nov. 1946).
Text of a lecture given at the club of Sadiki College
graduates.

2953 Berque, Jacques. "Pourquoi chez la femme la crise a
éclaté maintenant et pas avant?" Faïza, 56 (March-
April 1967), 56-68, 94.

2954 Bin Mami, Layla. "The Gains of Woman Since Independence" (in Arabic). al-Shabab, 3 (March 1966), 64-67.

2955 Boulic, J. Y. "Sur le chemin de l'émancipation de la
femme: à quoi rêvent les jeunes tunisiennes?"
Croissance des Jeunes Nations, 118 (Dec. 1971), 4-7.

2956 Bourguiba, Habib. Avec des droits, la femme a aussi des obligations. Tunis: Secrétariat d'Etat à l'Information, 1968.

2957   Chemli, Monji. "Knowledge of a Misunderstood Precursor: al-Tahir al-Haddad" (in Arabic). al-Tajdid, 4 (May 15, 1961), 7.

2958   "Dix ans de promotion féminine." Femme, 6 (April-June 1966), 5-60.

2959   Essafi, Tahar. "Les Femmes et la politique en Tunisie." L'Egyptienne, 153 (March 1939), 28-30. A Tunisian lawyer and novelist mentions the first signs of female emancipation in his country.

2960   Haddad, Radhia. "L'Action de l'U. N. F. T." Confluent, 25 (Nov. 1962), 582-690.

2961   al-Haddad, al-Tahir. "About the Liberation of Woman" (in Arabic). al-Sawab, Jan. 18, 1929.

2962   _____. Imra'tuna fi al-shari'ah wa-al-mujtama'. Tunis: Imprimerie d'Art, 1930. One of the most controversial books ever published in Tunisia, a passionate plea for the rights of women.

2963   _____. "Notre femme dans la loi et dans la société." Translation and commentary by M. Mufarrij. Revue des Etudes Islamiques, 3 (1935), 201-30.

2964   Ibn 'Isa, al-Tayyib. Tahrir al-mar'ah, aw shahirat al-nisa' al-raqiyat qadiman wa-hadithan. Tunis: Matba'at al-jumhuriyah, 1962?

2965/6 Ibn Mrad, Muhammad al-Salih. al-Hidad 'ala imra'at al-haddad. Tunis: Matba'ah al-tunisiyah, 1931. Mourning of the woman of al-Haddad; or refutation of the errors, apostasy and heretical innovations included in the book Our Woman in Law and Society. A very stern condemnation of al-Haddad's book by the Malakite Sheikh al-Islam.

2967   Jammes, René. "al-Tahir al-Haddad, une victime de l'intolérance au XXème siècle." Afrique-Asie, 63 (1963), 39-43.

2968   Khalid, Ahmad. "Some Aspects of the Battle Between Traditionalists and Modernists in Tunisia" (in Arabic). al-Fikr, 1 (Oct. 1967), 31-35.

2969   Lakhdar, Salah. "Our Feminine Organization and the Promotion of Woman" (in Arabic). al-Shabab, 6 (June, 1966), 30-33.

2970   Lampiasi, I. Per le Musulmane. Tunis: J. Picard et
       Cie, 1904. Text of a speech given at the Dante Ali-
       ghieri Association on May 17, 1904.

2971   Larson, Barbara. "Tattletales and Politics, or Local Politics
       in a Tunisian Village." Paper delivered at the American
       Anthropological Association and at the 7th Middle East
       Studies Association Meeting, Milwaukee, Nov. 8-10, 1973.

2972   al-Madani, 'Umar ibn Ibrahim al-Birri. Sayf al-haqq 'ala
       man la yara al-haqq. Tunis: al-Matba'ah al-ahliyah,
       1931. A short book against al-Tahir al-Haddad.

2973   al-Madyuni, Mahmud al-Madani al-Qasibi. al-Lubab fi itbat
       al-hijab bi-al-Sunnah wa-al-Kitab. Tunis: Matba'ah
       tunisiyah, n.d. A pamphlet published in the early
       1930's against al-Tahir al-Haddad.

2974   Marzouqi, Mohamed, and Jilani Ben Hadj Yahya. al-Tahir
       al-Haddad, hayatuh, turathuh. Tunis: Bouslama, 1963.

2975   Moalla, Mansour. "Au ban de la nation." L'Action, Jan.
       9, 1956. The former president of the General Union of
       Tunisian Students speaks up in favor of vote for women.

2976   Montagne, Robert. "Une Revue féministe en langue fran-
       çaise." In his Entretiens sur l'évolution des pays de
       civilisation arabe, vol. III, Paris: Hartman, 1939; 95-
       105.

2977   Msaddi, Muhammad Qasim. "The Congress of Women" (in
       Arabic). al-Idha'ah wa-al-talfazah, 175 (July 25, 1966),
       34-35.

2978   "Municipal Councilwomen" (in Arabic). al-Mar'ah, 51 (May
       1966), 8-11.

2979   al-Nafti, Muhammad al-Shafi'i ibn Muhammad. Ruh al-
       Islam wa naqd ata' al-mulhidin. Tunis: n.p., 1931.
       Highly polemical book against al-Haddad.

2980   "Polemica sulle condizioni della donna musulmana tunisina."
       Oriente Moderno, 1 (Jan. 1931), 39-41. Mentions
       articles supporting and opposing al-Haddad.

2981   Pruvost, Lucie. "A propos du Quatrième Congrès de
       l'U. N. F. T. " IBLA, 116 (1966), 439-47.

2982   _____. "La Journée de la Femme (13 Août 1966). "
       IBLA, 118-119 (1967), 291-99.

XVIII

UNITED ARAB AMIRATES

2983 "Big Feminist Renaissance in Abu Dhabi" (in Arabic). al-Ahram, Dec. 2, 1974, p. 7, col. 1.

2984 Hasan, Zaynab. "The Wife of the President of the Amirate States Says: My Relationship with Mrs. Jihan (al-Sadat) Is Fondness and Admiration Since the October War" (in Arabic). al-Musawwar, July 18, 1975, 9-11. The wife of Sheikh Zaid bin Sultan speaks about the condition of women in the amirate.

2985 Lienhardt, Peter A. "Some Aspects of the Trucial States." In D. Hopwood, ed., The Arabian Peninsula: Society and Politics, London: Allen and Unwin, 1973; 219-29.

2986   al-Baz, Ni'mat. "Woman's Path Here Is Arduous; The
       Man Took Off His Dagger and the Woman Hung It On
       the Wall" (in Arabic). Akhir Sa'ah, 2180 (Aug. 4,
       1976), 24-25.

2987   Fayein, Claudie. A French Doctor in the Yemen. London:
       Robert Hale, 1957. At a time when Yemen was still
       a very closed country, Dr. Fayein lived there and had
       access to Yemenite harems.

2988   Gerlach, E. Aus dem Harem in die Welt-Erlebnisse unter
       den Frauen südarabiens. Leipzig: Brockhauss, 1962.
       Mr. Gerlach spent three years in Yemen.

2989   Makhlouf, Carla. "Patterns of Communication Among Wom-
       en of Sanaa." Unpublished M.A. dissertation, Ameri-
       can University of Beirut, n.d.

AUTHOR INDEX

Adham, Mahmud 560
al-Adhami, 'Abd al-Qadir 1050
Adib, Tanou 2320
Adibe, Nasrine 527
al-Afghani, Sa'id 120
'Afifi, 'Abd Allah 263-264
Aflatun, Inji 1536-1543, 1630-1635
The Afro-Arab Inter-Parliamentary Conference 561
Afro-Asian Women's Conference 562
Afza, N. 121
Ahmad, A. T. 1544
Ahmad, Anwar 520
Ahmad, M. A. D. 122
Ahmad, Najat 2007
Ahmed, Abou Zeid 1283
Ahsan, Radiyah 1636
Aissa, Samir 2550
Akel, Abderrazak el- 340
Alamuddin, Rima 1917-1918
al-Albani, Muhammad Nasir al-Din 250, 341
Albarracin de Martinez Ruiz, Joaquina 2316
Alexander, Sidney S. 494
Alfrej, R. 759
Algaiara, A. 528
Algeria, Ministère de l'Information 610
Alhilay, T. 2420
'Ali, 'Ali Muhammad 7
'Ali, Muhammad 468
'Ali, Parveen Shaukat 1636a
'Ali Imam, 'Atiyah 1545
Alia-Bsis 2450-2451
Alihé Hanoun 123
al-'Alim, 'Umar Lutfi 2008
Allag, Mme 791
Allan, George 2044
Allen, Roger 1051
Allman, James 342
Alouche, R. 1919
Altuma 2589
Aluf, Nadarah Nikulah 8
al-Alusi, Gamal Husayn 1845
al-'Alwaji, 'Abd al-Hamid 343
al-Amin, Ahmad 2376
Amin, 'Ali 1638
Amin, Amin Muhammad 1846
Amin, Lucy 1049

Amin, Qasim see Qasim Amin
Amin, Su'ad 2009
Aminah 612-614, 712, 760-761, 889-892
Amine, Rhoda Gordon 1052
'Amir, 'Abd al-'Aziz 425
'Amir, 'Ali 221
'Amir, Ibrahim 265
'Amir, Sana' 2010-2011
Amir 'Ali 124
Amiruddin, Begum Sultan Mir 125-126
'Ammar, Hamid Mustafa 1263-1264
al-'Amri, Muhammad 1351
al-'Amri, Muhammad al-Hadi 9, 127
al-'Amri, Zohra 2916
Amrouche, Fadhma Ai'th Mansour 615
Anastase Marie de Saint Elie 328
'Anbar, Muhammad 'Abd al-Rahim 1456
Anderson, J. N. D. 222, 426-429, 469-470, 1251-1253, 1847-1848, 1893, 2551
Anderson, Nels 1882
al-'Ani, Muhammad Shafiq 1849
al-'Ani, Shuja' Muslim 1850
al-Annabi, Ahmed 2776
al-'Annabi, Tayib 2791-2792
Ansari, Ghaus 10
Ansari, Makhram 128
Anshen, Ruth 114
Antonini, Paul 129
Antoun, Richard T. 334-335
Aouissi, Mechir 344, 803
'Aqil, al-Hadi 2159
al-'Aqqad, 'Abbas Mahmud 11-14, 130, 1457
Arab Republic of Egypt, Ministry of Information 1639-1641
Arafah, Bahijah 1642
Arafat, Ibtihaj 2471
'Aribi, Sadiqah 2121
'Arif, Muhammad 1643
Armand, M. L. 951
Arnaldez, R. 131
Arnaud, G. 952
Arnaud, Gabriel 15
Arnaud, Georges 996
Arnet, Mary Flounders 1644

SUBJECT INDEX

259

Fahmy, 'Azzah 1533
Family law 64, 78, 232, 340,
422-450, 452-454, 456-466,
790-800, 824, 1161, 1331-
1350, 1848-1849, 1879, 1915,
1944, 1980, 2263-2264,
2317, 2405, 2551, 2596,
2662, 2674, 2775-2790
Family life 38, 39, 198, 339-
342, 346-349, 351, 353-356,
358-364, 367, 369-374, 376,
380-381, 383-387, 390,
393-395, 398-404, 409-415,
418-419, 712, 759-760, 762-
770, 773-785, 787-789,
1042, 1052, 1297-1298, 1305-
1309, 1313, 1315-1318, 1320-
1321, 1323-1326, 1329-1330,
1905a, 2120, 2123-2124,
2126-2127, 2130, 2133, 2135,
2137-2138, 2141-2149, 2152-
2155, 2258, 2262-2264, 2266,
2274, 2286, 2289, 2291,
2301, 2378-2379, 2392, 2399,
2402, 2407-2409, 2411-2414,
2419, 2506-2508, 2544-2545,
2558-2559, 2587, 2606, 2614-
2615, 2716, 2723, 2726-2727,
2729-2731, 2736-2740, 2742-
2744, 2747, 2749, 2751-2752,
2754, 2765, 2769-2770, 2773-
2774
Farid, Fawqiyah 1568
Fawwaz, Zaynab 1494, 1953
Feminism 42, 47, 50, 92, 559-
605, 948-994, 1625-1630,
1632, 1636-1792, 1794, 1797-
1803, 1805-1824, 1870, 1887,
1900, 1929, 1953, 1956,
1965, 1972, 1996, 2002,
2218-2257, 2464-2470, 2557,
2586, 2622, 2684, 2951-
2982, 2983
Fertility and Family Planning
39, 43, 85, 330-455, 481-
498, 832-840, 1363-1391,
1871, 1874, 1899, 1999-2000,
2284, 2296, 2299, 2306,
2420-2434, 2499, 2806-2835
Fouad, Hatidjed 1597

al-Haddad, al-Tahir 2688,

2957, 2965, 2967-2968, 2972-
2973, 2974, 2979-2980

Ibn Abi al-Diyaf, Ahmad 2692-
2693
Ibn Badis, 'Abd al-Hamid 700,
705-706
Imran, Khairiyah 1562
Islam 112-120, 554a, 699-701,
703, 705-708, 1223-1249,
1903, 2101-2108, 2314, 2328,
2358, 2375, 2531, 2684-2693
Islamic law 221-249, 704, 709,
711, 1250-1260, 1893, 2013,
2308, 2493-2494, 2536

Jewelry 646, 686, 714, 2271,
2342, 2771
Khairy, Abla 1421
Literature (women in) 294, 302,
313, 543-558, 862-886, 1448-
1531, 1844, 1850, 1868, 1872,
1878, 1880-1881, 1888-1889,
1891, 1898, 1917-1918, 1923-
1927, 1938, 1951-1952, 1954,
1963, 1975, 1978, 1981,
1983, 1985, 2001, 2003,
2444-2449, 2472-2775, 2477,
2487, 2489-2492, 2495, 2514-
2515, 2520, 2564-2565, 2577,
2874-2914

Mahfuz, Naguib 1072
Marriage 24, 241, 331-332,
336-338, 341, 343-345, 350-
352, 357, 365-366, 368, 375,
377-379, 388-389, 391, 396-
397, 405-408, 410-414, 416-
417, 704, 709, 736, 803-809,
813-814, 821-822, 828, 1049,
1280, 1294, 1299-1302, 1304,
1308, 1310-1311, 1314, 1327-
1328, 1334, 1342, 1497a,
2118-2119, 2125, 2128-2129,
2131-2132, 2151, 2268,
2272, 2376-2377, 2382-2384,
2387-2388, 2400-2401, 2403,
2410, 2474, 2484, 2497,
2505, 2508, 2534, 2538,
2544-2545, 2556, 2562, 2750,